3 1389 02043 3058

613.6
Cam
7/11

34.99

D1495410

THE GUN DIGEST® BOOK OF
Personal Protection
& Home Defense

Robert K. Campbell

©2009 Robert K. Campbell

Published by

Gun Digest® Books
An imprint of F+W Media, Inc.
700 East State Street • Iola, WI 54990-0001
715-445-2214 • 888-457-2873
www.gundigestbooks.com

Our toll-free number to place an order or obtain
a free catalog is (800) 258-0929.

All rights reserved. No portion of this publication may be reproduced or transmitted in any form or by any means, electronic or mechanical, including photocopy, recording, or any information storage and retrieval system, without permission in writing from the publisher, except by a reviewer who may quote brief passages in a critical article or review to be printed in a magazine or newspaper, or electronically transmitted on radio, television, or the Internet.

Library of Congress Control Number: 2008937699

ISBN-13: 978-0-89689-938-4
ISBN-10: 0-89689-938-1

Designed by Kay Sanders & Tom Nelsen
Edited by Dan Shideler

Cover Images: Courtesey of Crimson Trace,
Streamlight and Shutterstock Images

Printed in the United States of America

Dedication

To all who have inspired me.

There are several sources of inspiration. The inspiration to live my life as a human being with a spirit is summed up in these words: *I look to the hills (heavens) from whence comes my help.*

I hope my children – Robert Alan, Matthew Henry and Bobbie Ann – come to understand this as well as I.

– Robert Campbell

Acknowedgments

Times change. My sons grew up in the pages of popular periodicals; they now have families of their own. Matthew, my tireless helper, was away at Military Intelligence School during the bulk of the work on this book. Grandson Ryan spent more time with me than with his dad during Ryan's first few months of life and this was a help for me. I had quite a few able helpers who stepped up to the plate and filled the gap with enthusiasm and vigor. These include Lee Berry, Matthew Bishop, Stacie Morrison, Caitlain and Michael Wood (JAG leads the way!) and especially Jessie McAbee.

I also must express my thanks to the industry that supported me so much, especially Black Hills Ammunition and Kimber firearms. My long-suffering editors pored over many words you will never see, all to the good. And thanks for the comments from my own favorite author, who once told me, "Bob, that is a good book!"

Contents

Dedication page 3

Acknowledgments 3

Introduction 6

Part One: The Basics of Combat Shooting 7

    Chapter 1: Continuum of Force and Use of Force 8

    Chapter 2: Safety First: Avoiding Negligent Discharge 12

    Chapter 3: Basic Knowledge: Operation of Handguns and Handgun Types 18

    Chapter 4: Choosing A Fighting Handgun – and the Basic Skills

        to Make a Good Choice 26

    Chapter 5: Specific Choices: Pistols With Promise 36

    Chapter 6: Combat Drills and the Combat Mindset 59

    Chapter 7: Malfunction Clearance Drills 80

Part Two: Advanced Drills 87

    Chapter 8: Advanced Malfunction Drills 88

    Chapter 9: Close Range Battle 94

    Chapter 10: Creating Distance 101

    Chapter 11: Firing in Urban Scenarios 107

    Chapter 12: The Knife vs. the Gun 113

    Chapter 13: Night Combat 120

    Chapter 14: Home Defense 127

Chapter 15: Cover Up 133

Chapter 16: Female Defense Drills 137

Chapter 17: Animal Defense 144

Chapter 18: Competition and Combat 150

Chapter 19: Keeping the Edge 153

Part Three: Long Guns 159

Chapter 20: The Rifle 160

Chapter 21: Handling the Rifle 169

Chapter 22: Carbine Marksmanship 175

Chapter 23: The Shotgun 180

Chapter 24: Using the Shotgun in Combat 187

Chapter 25: Quickly Getting the Long Gun Into Action 193

Part Four: Accessories And Gear To Save Your Life 197

Chapter 26: Practice Tools 198

Chapter 27: Life-saving Accessories: Holsters, Magazines and More 207

Chapter 28: Ammunition 215

Chapter 29: Protection on the Cheap 233

Chapter 30: Commonality of Weapons 246

Chapter 31: The Orthopedic Handgun 251

About the Author 255

Introduction

In today's bustling world, it is often a struggle to make time for proper training with personal defense instruments. Those who are aware of the need for personal defense realize that obtaining good tools is only part of the program. Firearms proficiency should not be an exclusive province of the well heeled or the SWAT operator. Thousands of average citizens, young and old of both sexes, go about armed with only the slightest inkling of what it is to properly use a firearm. Some regret this ignorance after suffering injury or falling into a legal pitfall.

With obligations including a family, a vocation and other concerns, few can take the time and expense to travel to a training school. Long-distance education is the norm. The only training many receive is rudimentary classroom work and qualification associated with a concealed weapons permit. Some will not receive even that level of training. Many keep a handgun in the home or business and do not carry the piece as a matter of course. Others are situationally armed, strapping the pistol on when they feel the need. Would that we all had such an early warning system!

It is easy to be overwhelmed by the amount of information available on the subject of self-defense training. While there are certain drills that are more difficult than others, the axiom KISS – Keep It Simple Stupid – is nowhere more appropriate. I don't mean to imply that my long-distance students who are reading this work are stupid – far from it. As diverse as we are, Americans share common traits. Among these traits are intelligence and courage. But trainers sometimes produce practice courses with demands that are unrealistic for the interested party. Some will excel at weapons craft and go on to attend any number of shooting schools and become expert shots. Others will learn the bare minimum they are comfortable with and hope for the best. The balance is somewhere between the extremes.

The simple truth is that thousands of Americans defend themselves every year, and do so successfully with a minimum of formal training. The weapons used are more often than not service grade firearms. The trained operator and his custom combat special less often get into the fray.

Over the years I have tested dozens of firearms. Some are good enough to ride with and have been given the nod. Others raise the question "Why would anyone choose this piece?" More than a few are triumphs of the technical over the tactical. Quite a few second-rate service firearms are still in wide use. The person serving his country at home or abroad will be issued a handgun, rifle or shotgun and must do the best he can with what he has. The man or woman behind the weapon has proven most important in endless encounters. Civilians have a much broader choice and are able to choose life-saving gear appropriate to the task at hand. In either case when the situation is bad, we go with what we know. What we know is the deciding factor in survival. But if given a choice I think most of us would choose a superior firearm and ammunition.

The knowledge contained in this book is ammunition for that choice.

What follows is a summary of over 40 years of study and knowledge gained from experimentation, constant range work, and battle with our protein-fed, ex-con criminal class. The dictum is logical: constant practice combined with proven technique works. Service-grade gear; simple, uncomplicated movement; and a fighting spirit will carry the day. Since we are primarily interested in personal defense, the majority of this book covers handguns. The handgun is a weapon of opportunity that may be carried at all times to meet an unexpected threat. The handgun will save your life and allow you to take control of a situation that might have resulted in the loss of your life.

But there have been recent incidents in America that give us pause and raise the question, is a handgun enough? On a practical scale, natural disasters such as Hurricane Katrina and manmade disasters such as the Los Angeles riots have shown that the threat of gangs and overwhelming numbers of miscreants make a long gun very attractive under certain circumstances.

A number of my chapters deal with long guns. You may not realize which firearm fits your situation best until you have read the entire book. While there are good choices in the modern world that maximize your chance of survival, this is not a wish book filled with firearms that cost many thousands of dollars. I want to show you how to best use what you have on hand, including common firearms such as the snubnosed .38 and double barrel shotgun. But you will also learn the advantages and best use of the 1911 automatic pistol and the Remington 870 shotgun. Whether you are a novice or a combat veteran, I believe you will learn something of interest.

I began writing to save lives, and this book is the logical end product of this ambition. I ask the student to meet me halfway. Read the book with an open mind, reflect on the information, and apply the tactics. Read, reflect, apply.

Be well. Be safe. Be prepared!

Part One:
The Basics of
Combat Shooting

Continuum of Force and Use of Force

Knowing when to fight is as important as knowing how to fight. A mistake in the use of force may be ruinous financially, mentally, and in terms of the quality of your life. You could be killed or crippled or end up in prison. The basic rules of combat are drummed into the head of every rookie who attends a police academy. States that issue concealed carry permits have the same information as part of their instruction. You would do well not to sleep through that part of the class.

When it comes to personal defense, no tool should be overlooked. Gordon Lightfoot designed this tactical pen for Timberline Knives. It writes very well and the rest is up to your imagination.

The continuum of force – the acceptable, progressive level of response for each display of force by an attacker – is a simple concept. Legal decisions do not allow tit for tat. Fairness must be observed. The courts have been consistent. As a ruling in my home state stressed well over a hundred years ago, "A slight blow does not allow a severe beating."

All attacks do not begin at the top of the continuum of force, i.e., with deadly force. The first component of the force continuum is verbal. The courts have held that there are no such things as fighting words. When we are threatened, we must de-escalate the situation. We can apologize for an implied slight or simply tell the party we are leaving and will offer no fight. The other party may escalate the situation with threats. You do not need to up the ante with an offer of violence. While this behavior may gall you, if you are confronted on the street, the law requires that you retreat before you injure another person.

Only when no retreat is possible may you stand and fight. A person who fights when there is another choice is crazy! There is no profit in fighting; the winner is often as battered as the loser and just as often lands in jail. If you contribute to the situation and are part of the problem, then you have created a mutual combat situation in which either side is as guilty as the other. As an example, if someone strikes you and runs away, he is the guilty party. If you chase him and engage him in a fight, then you are as guilty as he. While we may disagree with the law, the statutes are predicated on keeping the peace and avoiding bloodshed. We would do well to heed every letter of the law.

What if the assailant goes past verbal abuse? The assailant may move his garments to expose a pistol. This actually happened to an acquaintance of mine. The assailant then said, "I have fifteen for you." The pistol was a high-capacity 9mm automatic. At what point should you draw your pistol? A confrontation may become a fast draw situation quickly.

Even though I am a peace officer, my personal feelings could not be allowed to interfere with the law although I did what I could for those I felt compassion for. A fellow who is verbally attacked and gives his attacker a nasty surprise, chases his assailant down or gives a purse snatcher a good whipping may seem like our kind of fellow but legally he is in trouble. The law is very clear on these precepts. You may respond but not in kind. Reasonable and appropriate force is dictated. Let's look at some of the skills we should develop if we are serious about self defense.

The first and perhaps most important skill is verbal skill. Verbal skills can be an important defuser. I have shocked irate folks by being polite. I arrested some of them without problem after calming them down. Logic and politeness go hand and hand. The roughest con sometimes understands respect (although others respect nothing). I have saved a few knots on my head by mastering verbal skills.

The next level of force begins when you are physically assaulted. If the assailant pushes and shoves you, then opposite and equal action is allowable. You may use an appropriate level of force to push him away or keep him away from you. The redirection of force is an important open-hand skill for these situations. We need to flow like water, as Bruce Lee said, although in a much simpler form than Mr. Lee exhibited.

If there is a disparity in size, age, and gender, then the victim has more leeway in the use of force. This simply means that an elderly woman or a small person is at a disadvantage when dealing with a young muscular thug and the law recognizes this disparity. Your elderly mother is not expected to wrestle with a criminal and may move up the force continuum to the next level. As the level of force used by the assailant becomes more likely to cause serious injury or death, the response can become stronger as well.

There are also times when we are unable to access a weapon in the face of a rapid attack. We had better have a number of locks, blocks, and blows ready in our arsenal. To rely only upon the handgun is a poor plan indeed. This is a book about personal defense. Handguns are a large part of the book but using a handgun effectively is not the whole story. You must realize that the handgun is only part of the plan. The handgun is the weapon of last resort and if it is the

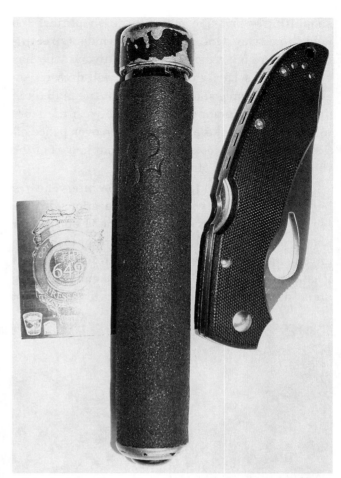

These are two equally cherished items in the author's extensive collection. The ASP retractable baton and the Spyderco folder are daily companions. There must be another level of force available besides the handgun.

only resort you are poorly prepared for the reality of street attacks. For this reason you will find a lot of advice concerning open-hand and verbal tactics in these pages. I hope it is well taken.

The late Tom Ferguson voiced the opinion that a hard right jab stopped a number of gun battles before they began. Tom, an officer of great experience, favored getting the drop on the bad guys to shooting it out with them. He was successful more often than not and lived to tell about his harrowing experiences. I wish I had known Tom better.

Another part of the law that is often misunderstood is the alter ego rule. Consider this rule carefully before you decide to be the hero and butt in where you have no business. The young man dressed like a thug chasing an elderly woman in the mall parking lot may be confronting her about shoplifting – and she may be the shoplifter! Too wild to be true? One of my correspondents recently went through this experience. Anyone who has worked mall security realizes that well-dressed, sophisticated people shoplift. Clerks at the mall often dress in a wild manner appropriate with the store in which they make a living. Undercover peace officers often do not look like cops – that is part of the role of plainclothes officers.

Before you respond to any threat or intervene in a battle you must ask yourself hard questions. Is your family accompanying you at the time? I don't know about you, but my child is more important to me than anyone I am likely to be called on to intercede for. At least one peace officer lost his child to gunfire during an off-duty gunfight. If bullets begin to fly, my first move will be to secure my family's safety. I may do that by beating a hasty retreat to a safe place or finding cover as quickly as possible. Only if my family is directly threatened will I feel obligated to respond before I have assured their safety.

I have often told my family that if we encounter a robbery in progress at a restaurant or convenience store, they should simply remain quiet and let it proceed. On the other hand, if the felons begin to search people or harass, beat or sexually abuse employees or patrons, the climate has changed. These actions would indicate a desire to kidnap, rape or murder someone. It is time for my family to hit the floor and let me take care of business. When accompanied by your family, consider first what may happen during a critical incident. Have a plan in place.

This is a lesson in the dynamics of home defense. Don't let the burst of relief upon defeating or capturing an intruder allow you to become too exuberant. This young lady is holding a handgun on the intruder and calling 911 but the taunt and foot on the back are probably too much.

The Kershaw Zero Tolerance folder is among the best designed and executed of folders and an excellent backup to the handgun.

THE ALTER EGO RULE

When you intervene in a difficulty between two or more persons, you accept all rights and liabilities of the person you are aiding. This is known as the "alter ego rule." If you happen upon a person who is an innocent victim, you may defend him or her as vigorously as they could have defended themselves if they were able. An example is a wounded police officer.

On the other hand, if the person is the aggressor, you become a party to his or her crime if you assist. If you see a man beating a woman, she may be a hugger-mugger who just stabbed him. A prostitute or her customer is not exactly the type we wish to get involved with. Kind of a nasty business all of the way around.

Is this a likely scenario? Yes it is, actually. I have seen quite a few incidents that needed deciphering. This is a sobering thought.

This book concentrates on tactics for saving your life in a worst-case scenario – but I would be remiss not to warn you of the perils involved in a mistaken action. A wrong decision is made in a second but this decision may affect your life adversely on a major scale.

One of our more accomplished writers once summed up the dictates of personal defense and the use of force. He insisted that we never shoot to kill. He stated that killing a person is irrelevant. What matters is stopping the person. When you stop this person his deeds must be so terrible that he must be stopped, and lethal force is justified in immediate action. It must not matter morally or legally if he dies as a result of being stopped.

While there are other nuances and local mores to consider, take this advice to heart. It seems like good common sense. When you strap on the handgun, you are not looking for trouble. If that is the concept behind your training you need more help than I can give. But if you are a considerate person who thinks ahead, you will realize there is great responsibility in owning and carrying a handgun. The right applies to us all, but the reality is not for everyone.

Few experienced trainers or peace officers have not witnessed an unintentional discharge. The late J. H. "Fitz" FitzGerald was a remarkable trainer who began his career during the Roaring Twenties. Fitz wrote of the many times bullets went through his clothing and of shooters who narrowly avoided shooting him dead while on the firing range. I have missed this type of excitement for the most part, but I have seen real dummies on the range. Just the same, I like to think things are better today.

An unintentional discharge is the act of firing a weapon when we do not mean for it to fire. There are many causes, but inattention to detail is the main cause. True mechanical failure is rare. Accidental discharges (ADs) happen, but by careful attention to safety rules ADs can be avoided. These rules include the truisms that "all guns are always loaded" and "never cover anything with the muzzle of the hand-

gun that you do not want to see destroyed." A third and equally important rule is "keep your finger off of the trigger until you fire." Not when you *think* you will fire, but when you actually fire. Here are the three rules:

1. All guns are always loaded.

2. Never cover anything with the muzzle you are not willing to see destroyed.

3. Keep your finger off the trigger until you fire – not when you *think* you will fire but when you actually fire.

If these rules are not followed, we will have a negligent discharge. A negligent discharge carries penalties both civil and criminal. When a handgun fires accidentally, tragedy can occur. Every precaution must be taken to avoid such tragedy.

Most accidental discharges occur when the handler is loading or unloading the weapon. Poor quality handguns and ammunition are a fatal combination. Quality handguns have positive firing pin locks, inertial firing pins with adequate strength firing pin springs, and effective manual safeties. Few will fire

This officer is moving carefully with his finger off the trigger of this Kimber pistol. This is a mark of experience.

Always keep your finger off the trigger until you are ready to fire.

out of battery (i.e., when the action is not fully closed). Ammunition quality is important. A high primer, common in poorly crafted handloads and occasionally found in substandard factory ammunition, may spark an accidental discharge. (The centerfire cartridge features a primer in a small cup in the middle of the bottom of the case head. If the primer is not flush with the case head the result is a dangerous high primer.)

Sometimes a revolver will not function at all with a high primer. An automatic pistol bolt or slide running forward to chamber a cartridge may cause a high primer to ignite, setting the cartridge off prematurely. This is called a slam-fire. Within the last month, I have suffered a slam-fire not from a poorly-constructed cartridge, but from a firing pin that was stuck forward in an old military handgun. I released the slide and BANG! I had the gun pointed in a safe direction, of course. But I was startled.

Let's look at the rules we must follow and common causes of accidental discharge.

USING THE DECOCKER

Double-action semi-auto pistols seem to cause a disproportionate number of accidental discharges, second only to those semi-autos that have no safety at all. We must develop the habit of always using the decocker to lower the hammer from full-cock position. SIG, a major manufacturer of high-quality semi-autos, warns us that manually lowering the hammer by holding the hammer and pressing the trigger can be dangerous, as the firing pin lock may not be properly engaged. The Beretta decocker works in much the same manner. The muzzle of the handgun must always be pointed in a safe direction as the hammer is lowered or during loading the handgun. Preferably, a backstop or the sandbox used by some agencies should be taken advantage of. The Safe Direction bullet stopper is quite acceptable and a good idea in every way. Simply put, be certain the finger is off the trigger when the handgun is decocked – and always use the decocker.

I carry my single-action autos cocked and locked, with the hammer to the rear and the safety on. There is little reason for me to lower the hammer on a loaded chamber. Still, for home readiness, the correct hammer position is hammer down. The way to lower a single-action hammer is to carefully press the trigger with the strong hand while the strong hand's thumb lowers the hammer. The weak side thumb is kept between the hammer and the firing pin. As soon as the hammer begins to move forward, the trigger should be released. If you do not release

If you fall with the finger on register on the trigger, the gun will probably fire.

With the finger off the trigger, your chances of an accidental discharge are much less.

the trigger, the firing pin block might not be activated and the firing pin might even be in a forward position. An alternate used by some shooters is to lower the hammer with the weak-side thumb. For shorter fingers, this works just fine. Those not willing to master the single-action manual of arms and always use diligence in loading and unloading the piece should choose another type of handgun.

UNLOADING THE AUTOLOADING PISTOL

On occasion an out-of-specification cartridge or a dirty or corroded chamber will make unloading a handgun difficult. On several documented occasions, operators unloading the handgun have suffered injury when the cartridge fired outside the chamber. In these cases, the cause seems to be the pistol's cartridge ejector or extractor coming in contact with the primer of the cartridge case. The ejector must be tall and sharp to give cases a proper kick to clear the handgun. In normal use upon firing and after the slide recoils, the cartridge case ejector gives the spent case a good shove and can give an unfired round quite a kick if the slide is racked forcibly. It does not take a lot of imagination to realize that the primer can contact the ejector with enough force to fire the case.

I recommend the following means of unloading the handgun. It is not quite as neat as the older hand-over-the-ejection-port drill, which ends up with the formerly chambered cartridge in the palm, but it is safer. To unload the pistol, remove the magazine and set it aside. Next, grasp the rear of the slide and pull it to the rear without placing the palm over the slide window. Do not use excessive force, only what is necessary to rack the slide to the rear. The cartridge will usually drop out the bottom of the magazine well. At all times keep the finger away from the trigger. Some handguns allow the safety to be in the ON position when the weapon is unloaded. This is a good idea and every safety advantage should be taken.

The older unloading drill is very neat and quite safe under normal conditions. But it must not be used if resistance is felt when clearing the chamber. In this drill the magazine is removed and placed between the fingers of the gun hand. The handgun is tilted and the weak hand racks the slide, clearing the chamber. The weak hand has been placed over the ejection port and the formerly chambered cartridge case falls into the palm of the weak side hand. Neat but not as safe as the former method.

There is a misconception among those who do not understand firearms that if the magazine is removed from an automatic pistol the piece is unloaded. Rookie law officers have died as a result of this misconception. The magazine may be removed, but a live round might remain in the chamber. A number of handguns

When lowering the hammer of a semi-auto without a decocker, let safety be your guide and maintain control at all times.

feature a magazine safety that prevents the pistol from firing if the magazine is removed, but even so this practice is not 100 percent reliable. Some pistols have been produced on special order without the magazine safety, and owners have modified many more by the removing the magazine safety. An automatic pistol should be considered loaded until the magazine is removed and the slide is locked back.

Strict adherence to safety rules will prevent most accidental discharges. There is the occasional problem pistol, but true mechanical failures are rare. Loading and unloading are fertile ground for an accidental discharge but moving with the gun in hand is also a problem area. When we are forced to draw the handgun, we will be excited, frightened, and flush with adrenaline. This can make for dangerous mistakes if we have not firmly committed proper gun handling to memory.

The single most important technique is to keep the trigger finger off the trigger until we fire. I repeat not until we *think* we may fire but until we actually fire the handgun.

There are two alternate safe finger positions, and either works well enough. The first is to keep the trigger finger straight alongside the frame of the handgun just above the trigger. The second is to adopt a crooked finger just off the trigger that can

quickly move to the trigger face. I have tested the two and find my speed equal with either. Adopt one or the other and practice diligently performing all drills safely.

A FINGER POSITION TEST

Over the years, I've developed a test for proper finger position:

Beginning with my Rock Island Armory .45, I stood facing a man-sized target at the seven yard line. I would hold the pistol in the ready position, arms extended in front of my body, facing the target. I took five passes at each drill, with three finger positions. The first position was beginning with the finger on the trigger (not recommended). The second position was with the finger alongside the frame outside the trigger guard.

Finally I tried the finger bent outside the triggerguard. The first position is not considered safe but this was a range test and we wished to measure speed. Using the Competition Electronics timer, there was no noticeable time difference between moving toward the target and firing with any of the three finger positions. There was no speed penalty in keeping the finger off the trigger but a considerable safety advantage. Even if we moved to eye level and ready, there was no speed penalty to an ACCURATE first shot.

This is a good example of the finger along the receiver for safety.

The bent finger is my favorite position as the finger can move instantly inward and onto the face of the trigger guard, but the bent finger is probably not as comfortable for long periods as when a peace officer is on the stalk. If you become involved in a struggle for the pistol, the finger alongside the frame may be broken. This happened to the author during a struggle for a flashlight when the finger was in a similar ready position. My trigger finger was bent and broken and is still scarred. I appreciate the bent finger drill but by the same token my range tests proved the straight finger is just as fast into action.

A common cause of accidental discharge that has been documented is sympathetic contraction. Muscle contraction, imbalance, interlimb reaction and other problems related to the bilaterally symmetrical construction of the nervous system may create a situation that leads to an accidental discharge. If your finger is on the trigger and you are startled, it is an even bet you will clutch the trigger.

I am aware of an accidental discharge involving a trained SWAT officer that was the result of a misstep. Standing second in line on a raid, this officer slipped as the lead man took the front door of the house down. As the second officer fell he grasped the ground for support with the weak hand and the trigger finger of his strong side hand tightened on the handgun trigger. The result was a .40-caliber bullet striking the lead officer in the back, fortunately in the plates of a protective vest.

If the weak hand clutches, mirror-image nerves on the other side of the body may clutch in reaction. The result is an accidental discharge if the trigger finger is on the trigger face. By studiously maintaining the trigger finger position – off the trigger until we fire – accidental discharges will be avoided. Those that occur will be negligent discharges.

AVOIDING ACCIDENTAL DISCHARGE WHILE HOLSTERING

It is possible to jerk the trigger even before the gun is drawn. For this reason, modern holsters cover the trigger guard. Again, the rule of keeping the finger off the trigger must be observed. The most common holster related discharge occurs not when the handgun is drawn but as it is returned to the holster. If the holster has retaining straps, the piece may become entangled in the straps and the straps can press the trigger.

This is most common with point-and-fire weapons such as the Glock and revolvers. One shooting school now prohibits Glock pistols and the inside-the-waistband holster from their classes for this reason. The Browning High Power, CZ 75, Baby Eagle and the Colt 1911 among others have positive safeties that will prevent such a discharge but a safety can't compensate for sloppy gunhandling. Another problem may occur when the pistol is holstered and the user allows his trigger finger to ride in the triggerguard. The finger will bump into the lip of the holster and pressure against the finger is translated to the trigger. This is another cause of accidental discharges. Covering garments may become entangled in a gun and holster carried concealed. Avoid these problems by carefully practicing gunhandling and holstering with a triple checked unloaded handgun. Practice until you are confident.

The proper way to holster a handgun is to angle the muzzle into the holster from the rear. The muzzle is fed underneath any safety straps and as the handgun is fed into the holster the angle is changed and the handgun is moved forward and holstered. An alternate that seems to work with some types of holsters is to angle the handgun in from the front of the holster, again clearing the holster straps.

This is the alternative crooked finger position the author prefers.

A heavier trigger action or a manual safety cannot prevent an AD. No practical trigger weight could be so heavy as to prevent an AD, and the resulting handgun would be difficult indeed to manage. Hundreds of pounds of pressure can be exerted during a struggle or when a person is startled. The answer to the problem is diligent gunhandling. The handgun action or design has little to do with safety; safety is between the ears. There is a type of pistol that seems to be involved in more accidental discharges that all other handguns put together. This is the semi-automatic pistol without a manual safety. I strongly prefer a semi-auto with a manual safety. But if we are issued a handgun with no safety, or if we simply cannot learn safety manipulation, we must go with what we know.

The single greatest shortcoming of students is unfamiliarity with the handgun. We should be completely familiar with the handgun and its features. This familiarization does not require range time and firing time. We need to understand that the trigger may be activated by means other than the shooter's deliberately pressing the trigger. With this knowledge secure in our mind, we are prepared to carry and use a handgun.

LOWERING THE HAMMER ON A REVOLVER

I have encountered two potentially dangerous situations with cocked revolver hammers within the past year. In one case, a cocked Colt Python had lain in a widow's dresser drawer for several months. She had heard a noise outside her home and armed herself and then went to investigate, cocking the hammer of the Colt as she went. She had no idea how to lower the hammer and did not wish to fire the handgun. She simply put it back in the dresser drawer.

During a visit to her home to give her a safety evaluation, she mentioned the revolver to me. When we examined the revolver, I carefully lowered the hammer and explained the advantages of double-action fire to this woman.

In a similar case a lady at home alone had cocked her revolver and investigated a noise that turned out to be a cat. She knew not to point the revolver in a dangerous direction but she too had cocked the revolver. She called her husband and he advised her to walk out on the patio and fire the revolver into soft earth. She did. While the previous cases are a good recommendation for a double-action-only revolver – that is, one whose hammer cannot be manually cocked – some practice in lowering a cocked hammer is needed.

Beginning with a cocked revolver, the grip is carefully taken on the revolver and the thumb catches the hammer and pulls the hammer to the rear slightly. The trigger finger then presses the trigger and the hammer is gently lowered. You can place the weak hand thumb between the hammer and the firing pin or cartridge if you wish. The muzzle of the revolver is pointed in a safe direction. The reason you move the hammer slightly to the rear is to ensure you have control before pressing the handgun's trigger.

The thumb should control the revolver hammer carefully before the trigger is pressed to lower the hammer.

3

Basic Knowledge: Operation of Handguns and Handgun Types

A handgun is not as complicated as many mechanical devices but deserves our full attention and respect nevertheless. Like a vehicle or a chainsaw, if handled poorly, the consequences are death and dismemberment. The most important difference in handguns is that between the revolver and the semi-auto. The distinctions in trigger action exist in either type. There are single-action, double-action and double-action-only versions of both types.

Keep in mind the revolver is operated by the shooter's trigger finger. The semi-auto is controlled but not operated by the trigger finger. The revolver is more demanding in this regard. The semi-auto loads itself after each shot is fired. The revolver requires that we operate the trigger action to index the next shot into line. There are shooters who prefer the revolver, and others who will use only the semi-automatic. Most shooters are like the author: they will use either firearm in different situations. Make no mistake, the double-action revolver is far from outdated as a personal defense handgun and remains the first choice of many experienced handgunners.

There are other types of handguns including single shots and other oddities but since this not a general interest book but rather one focusing on personal protection, we will concentrate on practical choices. Derringers are unsuited for personal defense for many reasons and have been obsolete since the introduction of quality concealed carry handguns of the "mini" or "micro" type. While some of the small handguns are difficult to use well, there is nothing more difficult to use well or that is less tactically effective than a small single-shot or double barrel derringer. They are difficult to quickly manipulate and bring into action. While chambered for serious calibers in some cases, they are very difficult to use well and even painful to fire. I suppose the original High Standard .22 Magnum Derringer has some merit at intimate range but there are better choices. With the introduction of the North American mini-revolver in .22 Magnum, the High Standard Derringer was quietly laid to rest as a viable choice.

REVOLVERS

Revolvers have a fixed barrel and a cylinder that rotates around a fixed axis, presenting each chamber in turn to the barrel as the action is manipulated. While there is a segment in the barrel called the throat that roughly equates to a chamber, the true chambers are located in the revolver's cylinder.

There are three main types of revolvers: the single-action, the double-action, and the double-action-only:

- Single-action: the hammer is cocked manually and the trigger releases the hammer to fire the gun.
- Double-action: squeezing or pressing the trigger both cocks the hammer and fires the handgun.
- Double-action only: squeezing or pressing the trigger is the only firing option. There is no single-action firing option.

In a single-action revolver, cocking the hammer moves the cylinder. (Except for mini-revolvers, single-actions are rarely used for self-defense.) In a double-action revolver, trigger action is used to move the cylinder: the hammer is moved to the rear and the cylinder comes into line with the barrel as the trigger is pressed. As you complete the trigger press, the hammer falls, firing the revolver.

This is a Ruger single-action revolver, one of the best of the breed.

A more complete description requires a look into the action of the revolver. As the shooter's finger presses the trigger, the trigger moves a part called the hand. The hand presses against a notch in the rear of the cylinder, and the cylinder rotates. The bolt stop that holds the cylinder in place drops away as the cylinder turns but locks back into place as the cylinder revolves into the firing position. The hammer is moved to the rear against spring pressure by trigger action, finally breaking out of its notch and falling forward to ignite the primer of a cartridge and fire the revolver.

Revolvers usually don't have manual safeties like those found on semi-autos. There are, however, several means of allowing the hammer to rest safely on a live primer. The transfer bar system is universal in modern revolvers. This bar, which is located between the hammer and the firing pin, stays out of the way until the trigger is deliberately pressed. As the hammer moves into the cocked position, the transfer bar rises into position. The hammer falls on the safety bar, which then falls on the firing pin. In other words, the hammer never directly touches the firing pin. If the trigger is not held fully to the rear, the transfer bar drops out of the way, thus preventing the hammer from contacting the firing pin. Unless there is something terribly wrong with the revolver, it cannot be fired if the trigger is not held to the rear, thanks to the transfer bar.

Timing is important in a revolver. As the firing action begins the bolt stop drops away to allow the cylinder to turn but then returns to position and locks the revolver cylinder in place as the handgun is fired. The trigger acts on the hammer to press the hammer fully to the rear. The hammer trips and drops and fires the revolver. The trigger is released and a reset spring drives it forward. You are ready to fire again. If the cartridge has not fired, you can simply press the trigger to repeat the process and hopefully have better luck with the next cartridge.

As stated above, practically all defensive revolvers are double-action types. The term double-action simply means that the trigger both cocks and fires the revolver. Most double-action revolvers have a single-action option. In single-action fire the hammer is drawn fully to the rear until it clicks and sets in the single-action hammer notch. The hammer is in a "cocked" position.

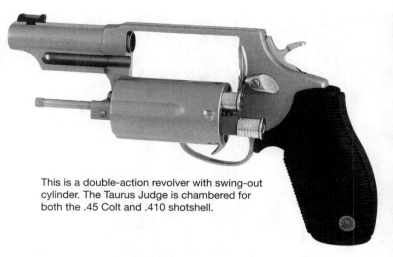

This is a double-action revolver with swing-out cylinder. The Taurus Judge is chambered for both the .45 Colt and .410 shotshell.

Other revolvers, most notably those with concealed hammers, are double-action-only. This means that a long press of the trigger is the only way to fire the revolver. There is no way to manually cock the hammer; there is no single-action notch.

The double-action trigger press should always be used when practicing with a combat revolver. I will admit that there is some merit in the single-action option in a four-inch barrel service weapon as good, accurate fire can be maintained well past fifty yards. This is substitute rifle fire. But for most of us, most of the time the revolver should be fired double-action-only. A smooth double-action revolver trigger can require twelve lbs. or so of force to operate. A single-action trigger will usually break at four to six lbs. in factory revolvers.

Double-action revolvers feature a swing-out cylinder. A cylinder catch is pressed to the rear (in the case of the Colt) or forward (in the case of most other makes). When the cylinder is released and pressed out of battery, the revolver can be loaded by pressing cartridges into the chamber one round at a time. To unload the revolver, an ejection rod is attached to the cylinder pin that ejects all cartridges simultaneously.

There are loading aids called speed loaders that help in quickly replenishing a revolver. These devices hold a cylinderful of cartridges. To use a speed loader, the device is moved to the empty cylinder and the bullets are guided into the charge holes simultaneously. A knob is then rotated to release the cartridges. Some speed loaders rely on pressure only to hold and release the cartridges.

A single-action revolver features a solid frame and gate loading mechanism. It is ponderously slow to

These are two good revolvers from Taurus. The double-action revolver is immensely popular and remains a good choice for personal defense.

At this point, for what it is worth, I have to admit that despite my best advice to the contrary the single-action revolver is far from dead in personal defense. I personally know two men, one in his 80s, who carry the single-action on a more or less regular basis. Neither is limited in handgun choice. I also personally know a trial lawyer who appreciates a good handgun but despises certain polymer frame pistols without a safety. His house gun is a Colt Single-action Army in .45 Colt. He is not a recreational shooter. He makes a good argument for the single-action revolver. He knows at a glance if the revolver is safe. It is safe when the hammer is down. When the Colt is loaded, he can see the cartridge rims. He feels that the need to cock the handgun is a deliberate action that he will not undertake lightly. He also points out correctly that a 4-3/4-inch barreled .45 Colt is lighter than any four-inch-barreled double-action big bore revolver. The 4-3/4 .45 handles as quickly as a four-inch .38 double-action.

I have used the single-action United States Firearms Rodeo in .45 Colt extensively. It is very accurate and fires a fight-stopping cartridge. I sometimes pack it in the boonies when two-legged bad guys are rare but animals aren't. It is always at rest and safe with the hammer down. But most shooters have enough problems without using a single-action revolver for personal defense. Just try to run a combat course and see how often you fumble cocking the hammer under stress. To each his own, but the novice needs to begin with a double-action revolver if a revolver is his or her choice in the first place.

While on the subject of revolver firepower and the single-action, let's look at cylinder capacity. Revolver cylinder capacity ranges from five to ten rounds, depending on the caliber. Four shot "cloverleaf" revolvers have been manufactured and monstrosities rivaling the capacity of a semi-auto have been produced in the past for one reason or another. But five and six cartridges seems right for centerfire revolvers and nine rounds is perfectly workable with rimfire calibers. A few double-action revolvers have been produced with cowboy-type loading in which the cylinder is loaded by a gate. The single-action is reloaded by opening a gate on the side of the frame and laboriously ejecting one cartridge at a time by using a hand operated ejector rod. Then you thumb the cartridges home and hopefully begin again.

load, unload, and reload. I enjoy single-action revolvers for nostalgia but not for defense. The single-action requires the hammer to be cocked for each shot. This means breaking the firing grip as thumb travel to the hammer is required. This is slow as molasses on a pine cone. I am certain that some very good hands would be deadly adversaries if armed with a single-action revolver but the single-action is not for most of us and even those who use the single-action well would be better served with another handgun. An exception is the North American Arms mini-revolver, a special purpose weapon that fits neatly in the palm of the hand. In its limited niche as a last-ditch hideout gun, this revolver has no peer. It has more real power and far more reliability than any .25 automatic.

For the lad or lass who is a good hand at cowboy action shooting, the single-action revolver might be kept at home, ready, out of familiarity. The SAA is a charming piece, and it's important historically. But even single-action fans have to admit the piece isn't likely to be reloaded quickly. I recall Colonel Jeff Cooper's words in this regard. Cooper actually went to war in the Pacific with a Colt Single-action Army .45. So did General Wainright, General McArthur and possibly a few others. Patton took his to Europe. Both Patton and McArthur had used their .45s to good effect in Mexico. When Patton ran out of bullets during a battle with Mexican bandits he did not solve the problem for the next time by using a .45 automatic – he started carrying two revolvers! We give George S. Patton a salute concerning his love of revolvers. They did not let him down. But Colonel Cooper remarked that trying to reload that relic (the Single-action Army) one round at a time in the dark in a foxhole quickly convinced him the US Government knew more about combat handguns than he did!

Trigger-cocking or double-action revolvers were introduced soon after single-action revolvers and re-main the superior type. The double-action requires manipulatory skill but can perform surprisingly well. The long press of the double-action trigger can be quite smooth, giving a rolling let-off that many find quite controllable. Some who tend to clutch a light single-action automatic's trigger will thrive with the double-action revolver. The swing-out cylinder of the double-action revolver allows reasonably rapid reloading. You can instantly check to see if the revolver is loaded and the act of opening the cylinder makes the revolver safe.

Overall, the double-action revolver is a good choice for personal defense. Double-action-only revolvers became popular in police work just before the replacement of revolvers by automatics in police holsters. Only a long press of the trigger can fire DAO revolvers. The hammer cannot be cocked for a single-action press. Many police agencies converted their revolvers to double-action-only after a spate of incidents in which accidental discharges of cocked handguns maimed or killed suspects. Some of these suspects were innocent of wrongdoing.

The Taurus PT1911 is a good example of a quality 1911. Note the cocked and locked hammer and the advantage of the grip safety, features that set the 1911 apart from all others.

SEMI-AUTOMATIC PISTOLS

First, let's talk definitions. A semi-automatic handun, or semi-auto, is one that automatically loads itself after the first cartridge is fired and automatically ejects empty cartridges as they are fired. Semi-autos are sometimes called "autoloaders," which is an accurate term, or "automatics," which isn't. Properly speaking, an automatic is a gun that keeps firing as long as its trigger is held back or until it runs out of ammunition – a machinegun, in other words.

There are variations upon the autoloader, but all have common traits. The energy of the cartridge is used to operate the action. The pistol fires and the slide or bolt recoils to the rear. The extractor pulls the spent case from the chamber and the ejector gives the cartridge case a kick to eject it from the slide window. As the empty case is ejected, another cartridge is stripped from the magazine and fed into the chamber by the forward motion of the slide. The pistol is ready to fire again.

While the above description is simplistic, the operation of a autoloader is blindingly swift. Most self-loaders feed from a detachable magazine but some have used integral magazines. There are two types or methods of semi-auto operation in common use, the blow-back and the locked breech. Others, such as gas-retarded blowback actions, are less common but sometimes encountered.

The blowback design is simplicity itself but is suited only for relatively weak calibers. In the blowback, the barrel is fixed in position on the frame and the slide recoils to the rear on firing while the barrel remains stationary. The recoil spring is compressed as the slide recoils and the spring brings the slide back into battery after the spent case is ejected. The majority of .32 and .380 caliber pistols are blowback designs, as are .22s.

To contain the force of more powerful cartridges, the locked breech was developed. Handguns chambered for 9mm Luger and larger cartridges almost always are locked breech types. Other than the requirement to contain the pressure of the cartridge, locked breech designs mitigate recoil to an extent. In the locked breech design, the barrel and slide are locked together in recoil. When the locked unit reaches the end of its recoil, the bullet has exited the barrel and pressure abates quickly. At this point the slide continues to the rear, and the spent case is drawn from the chamber by an extractor and the ejector gives the

cartridge a kick and the case flies free. The slide now moves forward and the loading block on the bottom of the slide strips a cartridge from the magazine and presents it to the chamber. The locked breech design requires that the barrel tilt in recoil as it travels to the rear of the pistol. This is handled by a swinging link in the 1911 pistol and by angled camming surfaces in other pistols. The Beretta 92 uses the Mauser/Walther oscillating wedge-type lockup.

While these operating principles govern all automatic pistols, there are wider variations in types of trigger action. Just like revolvers, semi-autos may be single-action, double-action, or double-action-only. Regardless of trigger type, all semi-autos must have a live cartridge in the chamber before they can be fired. This is usually accomplished by drawing the slide fully to the rear and then releasing it (an operation known as "racking the slide").

In a single-action semi-auto, the trigger releases the hammer or striker to fire the handgun. When the slide recoils, the hammer or striker is cocked again – and the trigger is reset – and the pistol is ready to fire again. Single-action pistols may be kept at ready by cocking the hammer and then placing the pistol on safe.

Some shooters, however, are uncomfortable with carrying a cocked handgun no matter the safety devices inherent in the action. The double-action semi-auto mechanism was developed for these individuals. The double-action semi-auto is both cocked and fired by a single long press of the trigger. A draw bar transfers force from the trigger to the hammer. Pressure on the draw bar from the trigger cocks the hammer and releases it, firing the pistol. After the pistol fires, the slide recoils and cocks the hammer for subsequent firing. So, in effect, the double-action semi-auto is a double-action pistol only for the first shot. After the first shot, the pistol fires in the single-action mode.

Double-action pistols usually feature a decocker that lowers the hammer safely without manipulation of the trigger by hand. Some, called selective double-action pistols, must have the hammer lowered by hand. They have a slide lock safety as a single-action pistol does but feature a double-action first shot trigger. When engaged in tactical movement a selective double-action may be placed on safe after the first shot is fired and then it is in the cocked and locked mode. A double-action pistol of the conventional type would have to be decocked during movement to assure safety.

There are those who are uncomfortable with the single-action trigger press in any form. Double-action-only (DAO) pistols were developed to calm these fears. The double-action-only pistol features a single long press of the trigger. After the pistol is fired, the hammer rides down with the slide and another long press of the trigger is required to fire the pistol. The double-action-only has become popular in police work. It offers an ease of training and a simple manual of arms, but it is more difficult to produce good results in rapid fire with this type of trigger action. Precise fire is challenging at longer ranges. Many consider the double-action-only pistol a triumph of the technical over the tactical.

The Glock safe action is sometimes termed a double-action-only. Others feel the Glock is more of a single-action without a safety. The Glock striker is partially prepped by the slide action as the slide is racked. The striker is partially cocked, in other words. When the Glock trigger is pressed to the rear, the striker is brought fully to the rear and finally breaks against spring pressure, running forward and firing the pistol. While classed as a double-action-only by many authorities, the Glock is definitely a different breed. The author finds the pistol a double-action since the trigger both cocks and fires the pistol.

What follows is the manual of arms for each type of handgun. In simple terms, the manual of arms is the action required to make the handgun ready for use, for safe carry, and to fire the handgun. Carefully consider your level of dedication and ability and choose the handgun that suits your ability and desire to train.

The Glock pistol is controversial, partly because of its lack of a manual safety. While opinions differ, the Glock is officially classified as a double-action-only.

Single-Action Revolver

Load by placing the hammer at half cock and opening the loading gate and inserting cartridges one by one as you turn the cylinder. Modern Ruger revolvers are left hammer-down during this operation. I adhere to the "five beans under the wheel" rule. Traditional single-action revolvers are not safe to carry fully loaded with six rounds. Load one cartridge, skip one chamber, load four cartridges, and then cock and lower the hammer. The hammer will be on an empty chamber. To unload, open the loading gate, align the spent case with the ejector, and manually eject each case one by one. The manual of arms is simple:

Holster.

Draw.

Cock hammer.

Fire.

Double-action and Double-action-only Revolver

Double-action revolvers are loaded by opening the swing-out cylinder by depressing the cylinder latch and loading each chamber individually or by using a speed loader. The cylinder is returned to battery after the revolver is loaded. To unload, swing the cylinder out and press the ejector rod. After that:

Load.

Holster.

Draw.

Fire.

Semi-automatics

Single-action Semi-auto

The single-action auto can be carried chamber empty, hammer down on a live round, or cocked with the safety on. For the purposes of this illustration we consider a single-action properly carried cocked and locked, safety on. To load, lock the slide to the rear and insert a loaded magazine. Press the slide lock or pull the rear of the slide and release to load the automatic. Then:

Load.

Place safety on.

Holster.

Draw.

Move Safety Off.

Fire.

This is a single-action 1911 automatic customized by Hilton Yam, a master pistolsmith.

Double-action Semi-auto

Double-action automatic pistols are always carried hammer down. The pistol is loaded, decocked, and holstered. Then:

Load.

Decock.

Holster.

Draw.

(If the pistol is carried with the safety on, the safety can be disengaged at this point.)

Fire.

Double-action-only Semi-auto

Double-action only pistols are the simplest of automatics. Load and fire, point and shoot.

Load.

Holster.

Draw.

Fire.

The SIG pistol (top) is a double-action first shot pistol with a frame-mounted decocker. This is a very popular type. The Kel-Tec (bottom) is a double-action-only pistol, perhaps a better choice for action type in a hideout pistol.

WHICH TYPE OF HANDGUN IS BEST FOR YOU?

If simplicity means something to you and you are primarily interested in personal defense at moderate range, the double-action-only handguns have much to recommend. If you wish to be all you can be, the single-action auto is appealing. Each requires a commitment to gunhandling and training.

You have to ask yourself if you can deal with the operation of either type, and which is appropriate to your mechanical skill level. The double-action auto pistol requires coordination; the double-action-only requires concentration. If you are comfortable with applying heavier trigger force with every shot, and prefer the same trigger press for each shot, then the double-action revolver or double-action-only auto will make a viable choice for you. The single-action auto is my preferred handgun by a margin, but I realize I am required to put more time and effort into this handgun in training. I carry DAO pistols in deep concealment.

The rewards of the single-action pistol are many, including speed and accuracy. There are those who are frightened by a single-action auto. The revolver is a good choice for these individuals. When you consider the number of times a revolver has saved the lives of good men and women, the revolver can hardly be considered an also-ran. I recommend a double-action revolver as the beginner's handgun but by the same token many experienced individuals carry the double-action revolver by choice. Learn the manual of arms of your chosen handgun and learn it well. It may save your life.

The Taurus 24/7 is not only reliable; it is light enough and features a positive manual safety.

4

Choosing a Fighting Handgun – and the Basic Skills to Make a Good Choice

Choosing the handgun is the first decision you will make. Then you will train to master it. If you have obtained a handgun that is not compatible with your lifestyle, by all means give it an honest try but choose another handgun if things don't work out. The 1911 is not for everyone and neither is a Magnum revolver. Many trainers assume that everyone will be using a high-quality semi-automatic and wrap their course of fire and training material around that premise. The man or woman using a snubnosed .38 for personal defense may find little of value in that course. I am often associated with the 1911 but I am not blind to change. I own an Armalite AR-24 in 9mm Luger that is a well-made and accurate handgun. If I had run across the CZ 75 before the 1911, I might have been led down a different path, but I adhere to my 1911 while owning several good CZ 75 pistols. I sometimes carry the Smith and Wesson Model 21 .44 Special revolver in the boondocks. The point is, I can no more choose your handgun for you than choose your spouse. But I can point out the differences and the way each operates.

You should have a mission statement before choosing a handgun. You must identify likely threats. In all likelihood you are arming yourself because of a threat or recent events that have struck too close to home. The first thing to be considered is your personal scenario. Do you work on a ranch and have a need to drop a wild steer if need be? Do you run a jewelry shop and fear a takeover robbery? Is your primary concern a mugger? Do you fear the Goth in the long coat with an automatic rifle bursting into the school at which you teach? In the first situation, a Magnum revolver would be indicated. In the second, several high capacity semi-autos on the person and stashed around the premises would be a good choice. If you face our protein-fed ex-con criminal class on a daily basis, then the .45 auto is a top choice.

The female who fears an attack at intimate range may prefer a snubnosed revolver. The snubbie can be

This young woman is testing the feel and grip shape of different handguns. One fits well; the other is a bit large for her hand.

pressed against an adversary's body and fired repeatably with no danger of jamming. But if history shows that shootings are likely to occur at longer ranges when they involve those in your personal situation, the snubnosd .38 is not the best choice.

As you can see, what is required to make an intelligent decision is to carefully consider your situation and your needs. It is poor planning indeed to choose a handgun based on looks or other's recommendations and then attempt to make it fit every need. The mission must be understood first! As an example, I admire the Kimber Target Model very much. It is a fine handgun on every count. I would have loved to have had that handgun on my duty belt when I was a peace officer. This pistol outperforms my old service Colt in every way. But to purchase this handgun and expect to be able to carry it concealed in every situation or to expect the pistol to be used efficiently by a less interested spouse is a flight of fantasy. By the same token, if thugs overrun an inner city pharmacy and the pharmacist is carrying a snubnosed .38 because it is light and handy, he may be seriously outgunned. A female assault victim who places her light .380 against an opponent's body and finds that the disconnector prevents the pistol from firing when pressure on the muzzle forces the slide to the rear – or finds that the pistol jams after one ineffectual shot – is in deep trouble.

It is true that there are fine general-purpose handguns available that can handle a number of chores well. The Kimber Pro Carry is a terrific pistol, concealable and reliable. I would be far from helpless defending myself against a large animal and the Pro Carry holds eight powerful cartridges. The CZ 75B is relatively compact and is chambered in the powerful .40 Smith and Wesson cartridge. These are true general-purpose handguns well-suited to a wide range of duty. If deep concealment is part of the agenda, then compromises must be made.

It is unfortunate that much of what is taught in shooting schools and in books is appropriate only for peace officers or the well-heeled who arm themselves with the best 1911 or German steel and practice ruthlessly in the implementation of the best tactics. The fellow carrying his Kel-Tec 9mm in a belly band holster may be the more common denominator but few will address his needs. I am certain if you purchased this book you are intelligent and interested in personal defense. You realize that standing on the line drawing from a quick draw range holster has little application to personal defense. A 1,000-round combat course at a recommended school may sharpen your skills – but are these the skills you truly need?

Will you attend class with a special range pistol or with your chosen concealed carry pistol? Quite a

The Springfield XD features a grip safety that sets it apart from other polymer frame handguns. As a bonus, the grip fits most hands well.

few concealed carry handguns become uncomfortable in extended firing.

I am able to fire a steel-frame 1911 comfortably for hundreds of rounds in practice and even enjoy the challenge of performing as well as possible. I am able to do good work with my Kel-Tec PF9 ultra compact pistol for the first few magazines. After that, the strain of maintaining a Gorilla Grip more so than recoil begins to tell on me. But if the Kel-Tec fills the bill for your personal scenario, you must pony up and do the practice work.

I believe that we need to practice drawing the pistol and making a telling hit or two as quickly as possible. We will practice for worst-case scenarios but we may easily overstretch the capability of a handgun by playing the great "what if" and not concentrating on "what will." Consider your likely threat. Too often the hardware is chosen before a mission statement is fully understood. If your likely place of attack is inside your shop, you need only practice at a distance no wider or deeper than this location. But you need

These two shooters are staging a shootout between competing types. This is a good idea for those who are considering an important investment.

to be certain your handgun is perfectly sighted in for this distance. You must be able to consistently hit small targets at moderate range. If your adversary has taken cover and presents only an exposed elbow or ankle, then that is your target. That big, friendly B27 "bad guy" silhouette target isn't always an accurate depiction of the likely target. If a takeover robbery is a real and present danger, then you should practice quickly firing at several targets placed a few feet apart. A high capacity pistol is a good choice for such a situation. The ability to quickly place one or two rounds into a threat and proceed to the next target is a skill that should be practiced and practiced often.

If a home invasion is the likely threat, then you need to be able to connect quickly at moderate distances, after positively identifying the target. A young lady sleeping with a .38 under her pillow has more leeway in marksmanship than the peace officer who may be called upon to make a shot at longer distances.

When we are making a choice of handguns and especially when we are working up our personal practice regimen, sobering thoughts arise. There are handguns I enjoy firing; some of them are pretty old and others fascinating. A few seem capable enough on the range. But I would not deploy them in a defensive situation by choice. By the same token, I enjoy participating in shooting events of all types but I do not confuse these events with reality-based training. I concentrate upon skill building exercises consistent with the likely difficulty I will face.

That being said, there are skills we must have or no advanced practice will be beneficial. The basic skills are defined below. Study and understand each and implement them in your practice regimen. If you are aware of the demands of these skills, you will be way ahead in choosing a combat handgun.

THE FIRING GRIP

The hand should grasp the handgun firmly. The ideal grip is found when you squeeze the handle until your hand trembles then back off a bit. The grip should be firm but relaxed to allow proper motor movement. The fit of the handgun should allow the trigger finger to comfortably reach the trigger face and to properly control the trigger. A too-large handgun will be difficult to control. Few of us can manage a Glock Model 21 .45 well and quite a few shooters have problems with the Beretta 92. Large-frame .44 and .45 caliber revolvers are beyond most of us to quickly present from a holster and deploy effectively. If the pistol does not fit your hand well, it will not improve in fit with firing! Your hand will not conform.

The two-hand grip I have come to use depends on more force from the support hand, making for greater flexibility in the strong hand. I practice the competitor's grip, with about 60 percent of the muscle force used in controlling the pistol coming from my non-dominant hand. It works for me; for others, it is at least worth an experiment. But in order to make use of these grip styles, the handgun's handle must be comfortable in your hand. Consider the size and angle of the handgun grip first.

TRIGGER PRESS

This is the single most difficult element of marksmanship for most shooters to master. The trigger must be pressed firmly to the rear without any deviation from the path. To mash the trigger to one side or the other will cause a missed shot.

If the trigger feels heavy and rough in the gun shop, you will have a difficult time mastering the handgun. The trigger press must be rhythmic. You must have a certain cadence with the trigger – fire, reset, fire – with equal intervals between firing and the reset. You may be off a little on sight alignment at close range and make a hit, but if you jerk the trigger you will miss. If the trigger action of the handgun is hard, rough or inconsistent your practice time will be wasted. Dry fire practice is essential and must be done in a safe and controlled manner.

SIGHT ALIGNMENT

This is the alignment of the sights in perfect relation to the target. The front post should be squared in the rear notch with equal amounts of light on each side and the front post even with the top of the rear sight wings. If the sights are too small for rapid acquisition of the sight picture or your eyesight does not allow proper focus on the sights, then the particular handgun is not for you. Know what sight alignment is first, then choose a handgun with good sights.

The sight picture of this Taurus 1911 is practically ideal for all-around use.

SIGHT PICTURE

This is the superimposition of the sights on the target. The sights can be sighted to strike to the point of aim with care and adjustment. The *dead-on hold* means the bullet will strike the area the front post covers. The *six o'clock hold* means the bullet will strike just above the front post. Most of us prefer a front post that is small enough to allow a 2-1-2 sight picture. This simply means a good sight picture in which the post is smaller than the sides of the rear sight. A 2-2-2 sight picture as found on the blocky Glock sight is not the best for good shooting past conversational distance. Consider the sights on your chosen handgun.

FOLLOW-THROUGH

Follow-through means holding the weapon firmly after the shot is fired. Since the handgun recoils while the bullet is still in the barrel, follow-through is an important part of the overall picture. Grasp the handgun firmly at all times, keeping the sight pic-

The SIG P220 target model is a fine handgun on all counts but a bit large for efficient concealed carry. For home defense this is a good handgun.

This shooter is working out with the Kimber 1911. He has the finest equipment and will probably excel with regular practice.

ture steady as possible as the weapon recoils. Follow-through is very important and allows rapid controlled fire, regardless of the type of handgun.

Much is said concerning a handgun's controllability. What sets the cadence of fire? It's not how quickly you can press the trigger. I am pretty certain a monkey could be trained to press the trigger quickly. Cadence of fire is determined by how quickly you are able to bring the sights back into line with the target and press the trigger. That is control. If you fire before the front sight is back in the rear notch you will get a high hit or a complete miss. How quickly you can fire accurately is what is important.

With these basic skills in mind, you are ready to choose a handgun. You have not yet mastered these skills but you know a little about the skills you need and the requirements the handgun must meet. I recommend you fire a few handguns before choosing one. A well-stocked range with rental handguns is ideal for this purpose. There you will find handguns with poor sights and others with excellent sights.

There are other considerations, too. Some handguns have grip frames that are not suited to your hand size and finger length. Others force a long reach on the trigger finger. The goal is to find a handgun that fits you hand perfectly from the start. Of course it's possible to adjust your grip to fit nearly any handgun, but why bother? Why not choose a handgun that fits you? Choose well from the beginning or your practice may be wasted.

Once you have learned to operate the handgun safely and have begun producing hits with it, you

will progress to combat shooting or speed shooting. The beginning drills build proficiency. Some of the drills discussed in this book may save your life.

The handgun can be a general-purpose instrument or tailored to a specific demand. Interestingly the largest and smallest handguns are the most specialized. I have not examined every type of handgun in the world but I have experience with the general types and the popular models. There are considerable arguments to be made for the double-action pistol, the single-action and the double-action-only auto. For some reason, these arguments often turn emotional and egos intrude. This is unfortunate as the true efficiency of a handgun is obscured by such mental hazards. The question we must ask is which handgun gives us the greatest chance of surviving a lethal encounter with a theoretical mastery of the piece but with the skill level we possess.

This question must be answered. Some of us would fumble the single-action semi-auto and not perform at our best. Others would be very uncomfortable with the light action of the Glock. Practically any interested shooter with a minimum of instruction can use a number of handguns.

Next, we must ask what we expect the handgun to achieve. I find that many individuals purchase a handgun based on looks, caliber or brand without positively identifying the mission they wish to accomplish. It's like purchasing a perfectly good drag racer when what you really need is a half-ton truck.

The handgun is a weapon of opportunity. It is worn to answer unexpected threats. We must have a realistic ability to meet and deal with these threats. The weapon must have a comfortable grip that fits the hand well. As my friend Frank McCallops has stated, handfit is everything. If a pistol does not fit his hand he doesn't take long to place it back in the case. Another friend states that the brand of gun doesn't matter as much as how well he shoots it. They are on the right track. The grip, controls and even the cocking serrations on the slide must be well designed and appropriate for the hand size of the shooter.

Also, the handgun must be fast into action. That means you should be able to quickly access the weapon and get it onto the target. Some of the large, heavy handguns are quite usable on the range but too large for anything but deliberate presentation from the holster. The piece should be relatively compact and free of sharp edges. It must be as reliable as possible – or, as Colonel Jeff Cooper stated, "as reliable as a machine can be."

The sum of all these requirements should produce a handgun that is easy to use quickly and efficiently.

ACCURACY

The pistol must be accurate enough for the mission at hand. I have on hand several handguns capable of grouping five shots into one inch at 25 yards. This is extraordinary for a handgun, and something appreciated as I am a sport shooter and gun crank. This is an expensive level of accuracy. Realistically, four inches is acceptable and even five inches at a long 75 feet will save your life.

One of my correspondents once made his living jumping out of airplanes. He maintains that a quick six-inch group at seven yards will save your life. Accuracy is relative to the environment but if the expected combat zone is a small shop or business, target grade accuracy is unimportant. At seven yards few handguns will fail to place five shots into a single ragged hole.

Below is an accuracy comparison for general illustration.

As you can see, the difference in the most accurate handguns and compact defense handguns is slight at conversational range. How the pistol is used will count for the most. Full size handguns are easier to handle and my results are from deliberate shooting. They are accurate depictions of the accuracy potential of each handgun.

WOUNDING POTENTIAL

The next consideration is wound potential. The handgun must be capable of producing sufficient wound potential to stop an aggressor with one or two well-placed hits. This means a big-bore pistol or a medium-bore with high velocity ammunition. There is

Accuracy chart and comparison of several handguns

(Group measured in inches; five shots fired off a solid bench rest)

Handgun	Ammunition	7 yard group	25 yard group
Kel Tec 9mm	Winchester 115 grain ball	2.1	8.0
Browning Practical	Winchester 115 grain ball	.5	2.0
FM Detective	9mm Fiocchi 123 grain ball	1.0	3.5
Daewoo DH 51	9mm Fiocchi 123 grain ball	.9	4.25
Smith and Wesson Combat Magnum	.357 Winchester 145 grain Silvertip	.5	1.5
Rock Island Armory 1911 .45	Black Hills 230 gr. RNL	.8	4.5
High Standard G Man .45	Black Hills 230 gr. JHP	.7	1.25
SIG P229 .40	Black Hills 155 gr. JHP	.8	2.0
Armalite AR-24	9mm Cor Bon DPX	.5	1.9

some controversy here but I do not think that it exists among experienced veterans. When a peace officer who has worked Area Six in Chicago or Fort Apache in the Bronx speaks, he speaks with authority. While he has seen many gunshot victims, he may not have seen the bullets impact. He may have arrived just after the fact. But often enough the victim or perpetrator is running around and getting into mischief with a small bore bullet or two in his body. The 9mm and .38 are little enough for personal defense. These cartridges have given poor results in any number of critical incidents. The .40 Smith and Wesson has given peace officers a cartridge that is not perfect but that offers performance far outclassing the mediocre small bores that were once universal.

Calibers beginning with "4" are effective but the .45 ACP is the most practical. A properly designed .45 semi-automatic is light and handy enough for concealed carry. Big-bore revolvers are heavy, difficult to conceal, and often generate heavy recoil. But for the man or woman who prefers the revolver there are good large bore designs. As for the semi-automatic there is little question as to the effectiveness of the .45 ACP cartridge. Yes, there have been conflicting studies of handgun cartridge effectiveness. Only repeatable and verifiable experiments and laboratory testing gives us a true idea concerning wound potential. The stopping power studies, with the possible exception of the Police Marksman's Association compilation, are flawed.

The large bores offer more wound potential. Handgun calibers beginning with the .40 caliber let out more blood and let more air into a wound. The body does not react to energy dump or any other fallacious event. The body is a closed pressurized system. Blood loss and actual damage are the only means we have of stopping a human adversary. This fact has been established so many times it seems ludicrous to continue to expound on the conclusions of many respected researchers, beginning with Colonel Thompson and Dr. LaGarde. But it is necessary to clear the air.

Not long ago, a self-proclaimed expert claimed that load selection was more important than marksmanship because we could choose the load but not the place it was delivered. This went against the tenets of marksmanship I have learned and attempted to teach for over twenty years. It is reckless, and I hope that the reader sees through this nonsense immediately. The greatest single way to improve the performance of a weak cartridge is marksmanship. Whatever caliber you choose, be certain to choose a cartridge with adequate penetration. Once you have penetration, marksmanship can carry the day.

So far we realize we need a reliable handgun with adequate wound potential. When looking at the handgun and its operating requirements, there are some who will prefer a double-action pistol to the single-action. That's fine, but the true goal must be kept in perspective. The goal is to incapacitate the adversary. Few who haven't been there realize how quickly a gunfight can occur. It begins and ends in an instant. Whichever handgun type you prefer, the problem will be the same.

The handgun must handle the problem that exists, not an artificial problem on the range. As such, we must have a handgun that supports the shooter's skill level. When we draw and address the front sight and press the trigger, we wish to do so in a minimal amount of time. The single-action auto, properly carried cocked and locked, is the best choice for this mission. There is no fumbling with words on that one; the 1911 style auto is regarded as the fastest handgun to an accurate first shot of any automatic pistol. For some hand sizes, the Browning High Power may be even faster to an accurate first shot. But there is a deficit in power that must be addressed if we use the 9mm High Power.

A RECOMMENDED EVALUATION METHOD

In order to rate the prospective handguns, I have devised a short course that will tell the tale in combat handguns. This course fairly evaluates and compares handguns. There would be little point in my firing my personal handguns on a course I designed and then comparing competing handgun types. It is obvious the handguns I have the most experience with would shine while types that do not suit my mindset and physical ability would suffer. The value is for an independent shooter to compare and rate handguns that he or she may adopt. The course is variable as to the exact specifications. I like to think I am a fair man and this course took some time and effort to develop, and in the end it is a great tool in evaluating an individual's performance with a handgun.

Of course there are other considerations, too. Running the course with a long slide Glock, you may ace the course but you wouldn't carry that piece concealed. The course has run from fifty to three hundred rounds within the variations. Each part of the drill focuses on handgun performance in a variety of situations. I feel that this is a good course of fire to determine the best handgun for the task at hand. When you have fired and counted your X ring hits, it will be obvious which handgun truly is the best choice for your shooting style, hand size and personal temperament. You may honestly prefer the double-action-only and do quite well with the type at moderate range, but a combination of short and longer range shooting is a better indicator of the combat ability of a handgun.

Here is a sample course. The number of shots for each drill is indicated.

Sample Shooting Evaluation

One hand shoulder point, 7 yards, 5 rounds, repeat again for ten rounds.

One hand shoulder point, weak hand, 7 yards, 5 rounds, repeat for 10 rounds.

Two hand point, 7 yards, 5 rounds, repeat for 10 rounds.

Double taps, 7 yards, fire 2 shots five times.

Controlled pair, 10 shots, fire 2 shots five times.

Two hand rapid fire, 10 yards, 5 shots repeat for 10 rounds.

Two hand weaver stance, 10 yards, 5 shots, repeat for 10 rounds.

Two hand barricade, 15 yards, 5 shots, repeat for 10 rounds.

Off hand, 15 yards, 5 shots, repeat for 10 rounds.

Barricade, 25 yards, 5 shots, repeat for 10 rounds.

This 100-round course of fire will offer an excellent comparison between handguns. Be scrupulous and record your score, comparing several handguns. You may be able to rent handguns from a well equipped shooting range such as Rex's in Hendersonville, North Carolina. You can cut the ammunition expended in half for a fifty round course for economy and perhaps get the same general idea, but a fifty round course will not tell as much as a hundred round course. Perhaps the hundred round course would be the graduation exercise as you narrow your choice. You may arrive at the same conclusions I have. You may find yourself completely uncomfortable with the 1911 and gravitate to a double action only handgun.

The Heckler & Koch P7 9mm features a squeeze cocker that takes some acclimation. For those willing to master it, this is an excellent defensive handgun.

On the other hand the single action 1911 and the Browning High Power are the easiest handguns to use well for the author by a considerable margin. They set low in the hand as a result of a low bore axis. (Bore axis is the height of the center line of the bore above the hand.) This low axis gives the handgun little leverage to recoil against. The pistol is maintained in the same position shot after shot. There are handguns that are comparable, such as the CZ 75, but the 1911 and the High Power are at the top of the heap.

Quite a few shooters are able to perform well with the Heckler & Koch P7, but the price and limited availability of the P7 are considerable disadvantages. If you choose a double-action or double-action-only pistol, the question you have to ask is this: "Am I willing to sacrifice combat ability for a perceived advantage in handling?" Weigh the balance. Glock shooters often do very well and many who prefer the Austrian pistol feel that the mental attitude is more important than the hardware. They will be difficult to tangle with in a real fight.

The single-action trigger I like so much in the 1911 can be a drawback to others. There are shooters who clutch the single-action trigger and who cannot become accustomed to cocked-and-locked carry. I have seen these shooters excel with the SIG pistol. The SIG features a butter-smooth double-action first shot trigger press and a grip that sits well in the hand. Among modern semi-automatic pistols the Glock is among a very few that does not place the technical over the tactical. While I prefer a handgun with a safety, the Glock cannot be faulted on its shooting characteristics. Trigger reset is fast, the bore axis is low, and the pistol is usually reliable.

BIG-BORE OR SMALL?

There has been an ill-considered trend toward small-bores in some circles, with a focus on ammunition that is designed to maximize the small bore in order to give the shooter a level playing field. For example, the 9mm Luger needs top-quality expanding ammunition for best performance. I prefer the large bore, the .45 ACP, and find the .40 acceptable. I also sometimes deploy the powerful and accurate 10mm automatic cartridge.

I admit I own several quality 9mm pistols. I like the light weight and the ability to use the pistol quickly and well, so I suppose I too am guilty of the siren song of the lightweight pistol. With well-designed ammunition the 9mm should be adequate for the task at hand. With 115-grain JHP bullets traveling at 1,300 fps, the 9mm can deliver good performance. The Cor-Bon 115-grain JHP breaks over 1350 fps from my five-inch-barreled FM High Power. The Black Hills 115-grain JHP +P offers exceptional performance. Either of these, or the Winchester 127-grain SXT +P+, will maximize the 9mm Luger cartridge. Just the same, the .45 ACP is more effective with good loads and is acceptable with non-expanding ammunition.

Standard 230-grain, full-metal-jacketed, ball ammunition in .45 ACP caliber is a good to outstanding stopper, with excellent feed reliability. The same cannot be said for 9mm ball. The Police Marksman's Association study found 9mm ball ammunition effective in stopping a felon with a single shot to the chest about one time in four. There is a lesson here. If the hollowpoint of a modern bullet becomes plugged or closes on striking bone, expansion will not occur. The round becomes hardball. The question is, do we wish to make a hit with 9mm or .45 caliber hardball? I think the answer is obvious. The .45 ACP is the first choice, the .40 acceptable and 9mm pistols acceptable only with the fastest and best designed of hollowpoint bullets.

The Kimber Custom II is an affordable 1911 that is among the best of the breed.

REVOLVERS AND FIRST SHOT HITS

A handful of revolvers have developed a reputation for a high first shot hit probability. The revolver is as strong on first shot hitting as the modern double-action and double-action-only automatics. A fast first shot is the type of fighting that saves the day. The revolver will not run a combat course with a semi-auto but then we don't run fifty rounds in a gunfight either. A revolver will allow a practiced shooter to get the handgun on target, put a big post front sight on the target, and get a sure hit. The easy, smooth rolling action of a well-tuned revolver is controllable in rapid fire, allowing a good shooter to make hits under stress. Most shooters are far less likely to clutch or jerk a double-action trigger. The revolver is far from dead, and is still saving the lives of good guys and gals on a daily basis.

As I write this, I have just finished speaking with a friend who was accosted by an armed thug in Charleston, SC. This assault took place as my friend was making a night deposit at a bank. This is something that I don't recommend, but businessmen must occasionally make night deposits. The thug drew down on this man and demanded his money bag. A passing vehicle momentarily distracted the thug as he held a handgun on this businessman. My friend drew a Charter Arms .44 Special and fired a single shot, solving the problem.

I have also corresponded with an experienced trainer who was running a concealed carry class in my state. Like many of us, he has adopted the 1911 .45 semi-automatic as his primary carry gun. But this man has plenty of time in service with the 1911. He told me, "Bob, some people have no business with an automatic pistol."

THREAT VALUE

A final criteria that is worthy of consideration is threat value. The handgun should LOOK like a handgun. Some pistols don't look very real. While they are real and will work as designed, they have a deficit in threat level. Several old time cops told me that a nickel-plated pistol looks larger under streetlights. While deterrence is not something that can be qualified, it is obvious that the majority of defense situations are solved by the presence of a gun and not by firing the gun. The National Rifle Association has proven this in years of research.

When choosing a handgun, the question is always reliability first, and then combat ability. With these criteria you cannot go wrong.

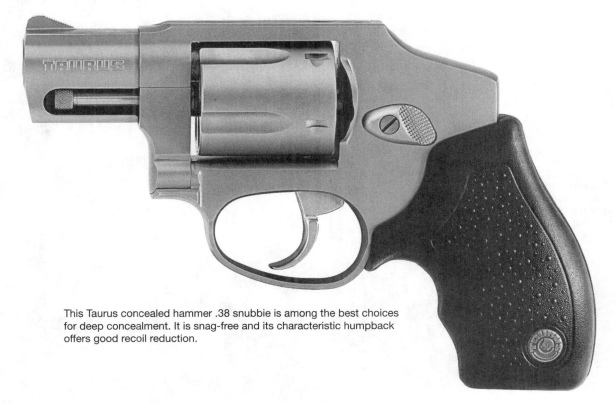

This Taurus concealed hammer .38 snubbie is among the best choices for deep concealment. It is snag-free and its characteristic humpback offers good recoil reduction.

5

Specific Choices: Pistols with Promise

In the next few pages we will look at several of the best choices for personal defense. These include the handguns that I feel are the best possible choices, and others that may work for a specific mission or for a person who for some reason or another prefers a certain type of handgun. Whatever our choices, I have confirmed that these handguns are reliable and accurate enough for personal defense use. I am not going to make a blanket referral for service-type handguns but it is important to understand that the service pistols originally designed for military service are the most reliable. These include the 1911, the High Power, the CZ 75, the Beretta, the Heckler & Koch and the Glock.

Concealed carry is an important consideration. It is good to keep in mind there are several sizes of handguns. These are loosely referred to as the pocket pistol, belt pistol and holster pistol. The pocket pistol is a lightweight. The belt pistol is a medium-size handgun well-suited for personal defense. The holster pistols are police service guns. These are simplistic terms but good enough for now.

Now, let's look at some of the best handguns on the planet.

SEMI-AUTOS

The Browning High Power

The Browning High Power was the original 9mm high-capacity pistol. With thirteen rounds in the magazine, the High Power has a comforting reserve. Although the High Power was introduced in 1935, we must remember that today's modern High Power is a different handgun, with better sights and better made of better material.

For many years, the Browning 9mm was THE elite pistol. Agencies such as the New Jersey State Police fugitive squad, the FBI's Hostage Rescue

The Browning High Power offers an excellent balance between power and controllability.

Team, and the British anti-terror SAS used the High Power. While the High Power is not in service with these agencies at the present time, it served well. In its time, it was used by the military services of over one hundred nations. The High Power has seen use in Iraq with favorable reports.

To say the High Power is the most proven and widely used military handgun of all time is an understatement. The double column controlled feed magazine has proven reliable in action for over seventy years. There is a caution to load only twelve rounds in the magazine for best feed reliability, but this practice may be outdated. My High Power magazines have proven reliable with the full load of thirteen rounds and some of them date to the 1960s.

The High Power is blessed with a grip that fits most hands well. The pistol is not overlarge for use by average hands, in contrast to many fat grip double-action pistols. The single-action trigger press of the High Power is straight to the rear, and while sometimes heavy it can be tuned well. The High Power features a magazine disconnect that prevents the pistol from firing if the magazine is removed. This disconnect does not allow the magazine to fall free; the magazine must be pulled free. This is a greater drawback in some eyes than in others. The intention was to make for safe handling and to prevent the magazine from falling free and becoming lost. The original prospective buyer of the pistol, the French, may have been anal retentive in this regard. Just the same, an experienced pistolsmith may produce a good trigger action and a pistol that drops the magazine free while retaining the magazine disconnect. Notably the Browning Practical Model, the best of the Browning-made High Power pistols, features a spring-loaded magazine that absolutely dives from the magazine well!

Don Williams of the Action Works produced a top flight custom High Power for me. The magazines drop free and the magazine disconnect is retained. In standard High Power pistols, the disconnect does not give the option of using the pistol as a single shot or firing the round in the chamber as you reload. The theoretical problem of addressing a threat as you reload is often discussed, and it is a possible scenario. The trigger action and the magazine's failing to drop free are also issues. However, another issue is removing a "safety device" from the pistol. There are those who feel that the removal of any safety device from a handgun is tantamount to reckless handling. Few if any gunsmiths would remove the magazine disconnect for you. As an individual, you may remove the disconnect if desired. As for myself, my High Powers retain the magazine disconnect. To each his own.

The trigger action varies on older High Powers, but recent FM High Powers from Argentina, my present first choice among all High Power variants, run smooth at four to five lbs. trigger pull. The hammer of early High Powers was notorious for hammer bite. Today we have hammers that are far friendlier. This depends on hand size and the hammer design, but the hammer can be changed to a more friendly type or simply ground and polished. The High Power once had a reputation for failure to feed hollowpoint bullets. I have never experienced this problem, and I have used a number of High Powers of all series. My 1961 High Power feeds all modern designs. At any rate, the Argentine FM feeds anything I care to stuff in the magazine. Modern JHP bullets are of a better design, feedwise, than some available in the past.

The best of the Browning High Powers is the Browning Practical Model. The sights are excellent and the Practical Model nearly always sports a very nice four- to five-lb. trigger. The Practical is serrated in the right areas and is delivered with hand-filling Pachmayr grips.

What makes the High Power a good combat and concealed carry pistol? Although it is a full-size 9mm high capacity pistol with enough weight to make for excellent control, it is thin and flat. No other service pistol is as thin as the High Power. The Glock and the SIG are downright fat in comparison. The pistol fits most hands well, and its trigger is easier to control than most. A low bore axis allows the High Power to set low in the hand, resulting in little muzzle flip. There is no leverage for the handgun to rise. In rapid loading drills, the high capacity magazine tapers to the magazine well, making for quick and sure reloads.

In short, the High Power has many good design features and no bad ones. It is well proportioned for the 9mm Luger cartridge. After all, why choose a 9mm that is fatter than the 1911 .45? The magazine disconnect is a laudable feature in some eyes and a problem to others, but most of us ignore it. The only problem with the High Power is the same defect shared with every small-bore pistol. The 9mm Luger cartridge is not my first choice for personal defense but with select loads it can be effective.

The early Browning High Power pistols used small safeties that were difficult to manipulate. Still, it can be done with practice. Modern pistols feature among the best-designed ambidextrous safeties found on any handgun. A Cylinder and Slide Shop safety can be retrofitted to older handguns. The High Power is the easiest handgun to shoot well of any discussed in these pages. It is light, kicks little, accurate, slim, and fast in action. It is fashionable to note that the 1911 .45 is the fastest handgun of all to an accurate first shot hit, but the High Power will give the 1911 a run for the money and in some cases beat the 1911. (The 1911 remains the fastest big bore.) An experienced operator can make the High Power do wonders.

Final recommendation: The High Power Practical is an excellent all-around handgun. The Argentine-produced FM High Powers have proven to be fine performers in every regard. However, the European produced FEG, a High Power clone, while usually made of good material, is often very rough internally with a heavy trigger action that is difficult to tune. I would avoid the FEG except for recreational shooting.

The 1911 .45 Auto

The 1911 is the ne plus ultra of combat pistols, the standard by which all others are judged. At one time it was the only big bore semi-auto pistol. The 1911 incorporates a single-action semi-automatic action with the best fight-stopping cartridge we are likely to produce. The 1911 is not for everyone, but the man or woman who is willing to learn the manual of arms of the 1911, and practice often enough to control the pistol's recoil, is as well armed as we can be with a handgun. The 1911 has many good design features, so good that modern designers have attempted to incorporate these features into their own handguns. The Beretta Vertac, as an example, has a grip modeled after the 1911's. The H&K USP has several features that are 1911-like.

The 1911 features a grip that fits most hands well. This handle holds a seven-round magazine.

(Modern production may feature a modified eight-round magazine.) The grip allows those with average-size hands and fingers to control the trigger. A straight to the rear trigger compression is quickly learned. Understand this: the cut-rate, roughly-finished 1911s do not adequately represent the 1911 tribe. Military Colt 1911s were very good pistols, and would serve today if in good condition, but the small sights of these pistols were a limiting factor. Today, we have first-class 1911 pistols that give good results and are made of good material.

The Kimber Custom II and the Springfield Loaded Model are arguably as good at it gets in the 1911. These handguns are not inexpensive, but are masterpieces of the gunmaker's art. The Rock Island Armory 1911 is a surprising piece, affordable but reliable and well made. It will require a set of high-visibility sights to be all it can be, but it is capable of defending your life in true 1911 fashion as issued. The Springfield GI pistol is a good choice for those favoring the GI type. The Springfield Mil

These two aluminum-frame 1911s are among the author's favorite carry guns. The Springfield LW Loaded Model (top) is a fine shooter. The Smith and Wesson SW1911 has accompanied the author from Washington to California, Arizona to Texas, New Orleans, and many other places, giving a great feeling of confidence.

Spec is a reasonably priced handgun that features good sights and a scalloped ejection port. The Mil Spec is among the better buys and a proven pistol that gives excellent service. When the time came to purchase a good all-around 1911 for my son, the Springfield 1911 was my choice.

Advantages of the 1911

The 1911 features a low bore axis. This simply means the center of the bore sets closer to the hand than is the case with most handguns. This limits muzzle flip, as there is little leverage for the pistol to rise in recoil. The 1911 chambers a powerful cartridge but the essential design elements make for a package that aids in controllability. The accuracy of the type can vary considerably. I don't think it is unusual for wartime pistols in excellent condition to place five rounds of .45 ACP service ammunition in five inches at 25 yards, although some do much better. A well-worn example will do worse. The Rock Island Armory guns are modern equivalents of the GI .45 and will do less than five inches on average. My High Standard G Man, a top-end pistol, will group quality ammunition into an inch or a little less under perfect conditions. But the barrel bushing is tight and tools are required for disassembly. The barrel is a match grade type that is well-fitted to the slide.

Roughly, three Rock Island pistols may be had for the price of one G Man. The point is that the 1911 is usually a good pistol as issued but the more highly developed handguns are extraordinary pistols and you pay for this performance. It is often said that the older handguns rattled when shaken, as they were made loose enough for good reliability. (A too-tightly fitted pistol can jam under battlefield conditions, where dirt and debris are all too willing to bind up its action.) As long as the locking lugs and the barrel bushing are reasonably tight, the pistol can give good accuracy despite these accommodating tolerances.

The question of feeding hollowpoint ammunition is sometimes raised with older handguns. If the magazine well is properly centered in the handgun, with the proper travel from magazine to feed ramp, even older 1911s feed well. Modern pistols are much better in this regard. The Wilson Combat magazine has raised the bar considerably in quality magazines.

Old style magazines simply bumped round nose 230-grain ball ammunition off the feed ramp and into the chamber. This worked fine with ball ammunition but less so with other styles. Wilson Combat magazines have a higher feed angle, feeding the bullet directly into the chamber. Often the use of Wilson Combat magazines alone will allow the use of practically any bullet style. If your 1911 will not feed a certain loading, do not use that loading and choose a feed-reliable alternative. The cartridge should be made to fire in the pistol – the pistol should not be modified to match the cartridge!

The 1911's main advantage is that the pistol can be carried cocked and locked and be instantly ready for action. The hammer is fully cocked and the safety is on. When the pistol is drawn, the safety is taken off and we are ready to fire. This allows for brilliantly fast shooting and a high probability of a hit with the first shot. This type of carry scares some people and they will not deploy the pistol. Worse, administrators, both police and military, do not wish their young charges to carry a handgun in this manner. The 1911 is perfectly safe to carry cocked and locked but if for some reason the pistol cannot be carried cocked and locked, the advantages of the model are eliminated.

In addition to the slide lock safety, 1911s feature a grip safety. This safety will not allow the pistol to fire unless completely depressed. If the shooter loses control of the pistol and drops it, the grip safety locks the trigger. The slide lock safety can be instantly pressed into the safe position. Some but not all modern 1911s feature a positive firing pin block or drop safety that locks the firing pin until

The SIG Granite Series Rail 1911 is a first-class .45 with exceptional fit and finish.

the trigger is pressed completely to the rear. This array of safeties makes the 1911 a safe handgun, although true safety is between the shooter's ears. None of the 1911's safeties hinders speed. There is nothing to prevent the handgun from making a fast first-shot strike. Despite the power of its cartridge the 1911 is controllable in rapid fire; it exhibits little muzzle flip for the caliber and the trigger resets quickly. The 1911 is simply a first-class fighting pistol. Just the same, the 1911 demands diligence in handling. The pistol must be handled correctly, and for best results the handgunner should practice on no less than a bi-weekly basis.

The 1911 is the standard by which all other handguns are measured and will remain so for many years to come. It is sometimes criticized as an old design, but the modern 1911 bears little resemblance to the earliest models. The average shooter would find little in my Smith and Wesson SW 1911 to harken to the 1911 service pistols used in Mexico in 1916 but we know that modern pistols are based on the original. Before condemning the 1911 out of hand, give a good example a thorough test fire. I did so nearly forty years ago. I am still impressed with the 1911.

Evaluating the 1911

When you're choosing a 1911 pistol, the cost is weighed against the accessories or must-have features of the pistol. Reliability is not debatable. I agree with many shooters that the Kimber line offers an excellent value. Kimber's introduction of affordable handguns with top-end features nearly put the industry into a panic. Competition from Kimber is directly responsible for the Springfield Loaded Model and Colt XSE, at least in my opinion. There are no low end Kimber pistols with poor sights. All are equally reliable and have good features. To obtain a 1911 with considerably better performance means that we have to go the custom route or jump to a pistol that is truly a high production custom item such as the Wilson Combat Close Quarters Battle Pistol. The Wilson Combat pistol is a very good and reliable handgun that uses excellent parts. Other high end pistols are sometimes too tight for best reliability and have proven finicky.

Smith and Wesson 1911 Pistols

The Smith and Wesson 1911 was eagerly awaited. It was almost as if we were putting a Chevrolet Corvette engine in a Ford Mustang. The SW1911 represents an excellent confluence of design. The 1911 profile and operation is maintained and the internal parts are first-class. Smith and Wesson chose to obtain custom quality safety and internal parts from proven vendors.

Novak sights are standard equipment on a high-end Smith and Wesson. But Smith and Wesson's experience with stainless steel double-action pistols also shows. The front strap (i.e., the front part of the grip frame around which the fingers curl) is striated rather than checkered. This works just fine. Smith and Wesson also chose to go with an external extractor on the Smith and Wesson SW1911. I have used the internal extractor for years with fine results on the 1911 but occasionally I have replaced an extractor. When building a top-end pistol I use a Wilson Combat Bulletproof extractor. My Caspian custom pistol uses the Wilson Combat-designed external extractor. While 1911 purists may feel the 1911 extractor is just fine, we have to reflect how rarely, if ever, we have seen a Smith and Wesson external extractor need replacement. Police departments have used thousands of Smith and Wesson 5906, 4006 and 4506 pistols with no complaints. We must take the external extractor at face value.

The Smith and Wesson SW1911 line includes a special lightweight frame version designated the SW1911 PD. An aluminum frame is alloyed with a certain amount of scandium. I would have preferred a ramped barrel be included in the SW1911 PD but the pistol performs well. It is the best Commander-type (i.e., compact) pistol I have ever handled and used. I cannot give a higher recommendation.

Springfield Loaded Model Lightweight

The problem with lightweight frames is not longevity. Aluminum frames last longer than the shooter in most cases. But aluminum frames are subject to gouging and incipient wear. If a gunsmith attempts a throating polish of the feed ramp on an aluminum frame pistol and breaks through the anodizing, the pistol will wear more quickly. Blunt nose hollowpoint bullets and even lead semi-wadcutters will gouge the aluminum feed ramp. In time the ramp will be gouged out of shape and cannot be reworked. You will need to either replace the frame or obtain and fit an Evolution Gun Works steel feed ramp insert.

It is true that aluminum frame handguns have survived thousands of rounds in service but equally true that many have experienced serious feed ramp troubles. The best cure for aluminum frame feed ramp problems is to fit a ramped barrel. A ramped barrel is a 1911 barrel that features a one piece-feed ramp resembling the Browning High Power design. This barrel replaces the two-piece feed ramp of standard 1911 pistols and requires frame modification. A custom ramped barrel from Bar-Sto precision is a great addition to an original Colt Commander. If I chose to carry and use an original Commander, I would either load hardball or Cor Bon's PowRBall to prevent feed ramp wear.

Based on the 1911, the Springfield Lightweight Loaded Model uses a factory ramped barrel. This is a good setup. The ramped barrel was originally developed to give competition shooters an advantage not only in feed reliability but in safety as the ramped barrel's design more fully encloses the cartridge case head. A ramped barrel is practically a requisite for an aluminum frame 1911. The Springfield Lightweight Loaded Model is a full-length Government Model with five-inch barrel but features an aluminum frame. This makes for a light packing pistol but one that features the full-length sight radius when called into use.

The Lightweight Loaded Model has many good features including a beavertail grip safety and ambidextrous safety. The Loaded Model features Novak Sights. My example also features tritium inserts. Overall, the Lightweight Loaded Model is a first-class fighting handgun. The shooter must strive to learn to control recoil, but when all is said and done the pistol is well worth mastering.

SIG GSR

SIG introduced their 1911, the GSR, to great expectations. The pistol is four-square American, not European, in execution. The slide has been modified slightly to more closely resemble other SIG products, but this a semi-custom 1911 that is basically a custom shop item. SIG wisely chose to obtain Caspian slides and frames and carefully choose the best components for the trigger and internal parts. Novak sights were chosen for the obvious reasons. The pistol is delivered with a light rail.

GSR stands for Granite (a tribute to the home of SIG USA: New Hampshire, the Granite State) Series Rail. The rail offers the mounting of numerous devices including the Surefire X300 light. The SIG maintains an excellent balance and unlike several other "parts gun" 1911 pistols offered by well known manufacturers, the GSR has proven to be reliable, accurate, and effective. My personal example has proven to be an extraordinary handgun in all regards, but then a quality 1911 can be pretty special. After a few months of evaluation including a trouble-free run of 1,000 rounds of Mastercast 230-grain JHP ammunition without a single hiccup – and no cleaning – the GSR is an outstanding addition to my battery. The performance of the GSR is in line with any number of custom handguns I have tested.

Colt Defender

Colt is still a force in the market – if not in numbers, then in legend. The Colt Defender is among the neatest lightweight 1911 pistols ever produced. While it is true that there is a certain attraction to any handgun with the little Colt pony on the slide, the Defender performs well. You cannot expect a lightweight Officer's Model pistol to shoot with the Government Model and the Defender will not punch small groups at 25 yards. But just the same it is surprisingly accurate.

The pistol is supplied with generously proportioned Hogue grips that aid in control. The sights are good and the controls are crisp and positive. I would have liked a lighter trigger but then light triggers are contraindicated these days on light defensive pistols. The Defender's trigger compression is a smooth seven pounds, usable and offering a degree of discretion. It is not a heavy lawyer-inspired trigger but reasonable for use on the Defender.

During my testfire, the pistol showed a tendency to fire low and I feared I was anticipating the shot. But then my young friend Lee Berry experienced low shots during the trials with the Defender as well. The pistol feeds anything you care to stuff into it and quality magazines are available from Metalform. My example is loaded with Winchester's SXT. The Defender is a good choice for concealed carry for the 1911 fan.

The Alternatives

The CZ 75

Over the years, I have met many handgunners who simply did not like the 1911 or the High Power. For one reason or the other they didn't trust cocked-and-locked carry or did not like the age of the design. Yet, when drifting toward the various oversize 9mms with thick butts and a safety/decocker that is difficult to access with the shooting hand, they are unnecessarily limiting themselves. Another alternative exists, one that allows these men and women to be well armed with a handgun that does not limit the shooter. It's a pistol that is so good that Colonel Jeff Cooper found it "an embarrassment that it was not made in the United States." What is this pistol? It's the CZ 75.

The CZ design team did a great job with the CZ 75. This pistol is loosely based upon the Browning High Power but we must give our Czechoslovakian friends credit for producing an outstanding handgun with a confluence of proven design and original features. The CZ 75 features a grip slightly larger than that of the High Power but holding two more rounds in a double-column magazine. The CZ features a double-action mechanism that is simple and quite smooth in operation. The CZ also features a frame-mounted safety that is easily accessed by the shooting hand. (Frame-mounted safeties are accessible. Slide-mounted safeties can be a problem.)

Most CZ types do not have an on-safe position for double-action carry. The safety may be pressed on only when the hammer is cocked. So, the CZ 75 is a selective double-action. The pistol may be carried either hammer-down, ready for a double-action first shot, or cocked and locked in the single-action mode. Even those who prefer a double-action first shot pistol will recognize that when moving, it is more desirable to thumb the safety on than to decock the hammer.

The CZ is the obvious first choice as an alternative to the Browning High Power. It offers double-action in a comfortable frame. The pistol is reliable and accurate. I once fired a four-inch 50- yard group from a solid rest, back against the concrete wall of

The Czech CZ 75B is among the better Europeans, a steel-frame .40 with good features.

the range house, pistol braced on my knees, with the CZ 75 and Black Hills 124-grain ammunition during a police qualification. The pistols feed reliably and exhibit high overall quality in manufacture.

Another advantage of the CZ 75 is its reversed slide rail arrangement. The slide of the CZ rides inside the frame. This is a theoretical aid in accuracy and a real aid in lowering the bore axis of this pistol to dimensions comparable to those of single-action designs. The CZ is a fine pistol but has several drawbacks that are related to its halfway position as a selective double-action pistol. These do not bother me; I see the CZ as a double-action pistol I can live with. But for a double-action pistol, the lack of a decocker has posed a problem for CZ shooters. To lower the hammer, the trigger is pressed as the hammer is carefully lowered with the thumb. In a true single-action you can proceed with never lowering the hammer if the pistol is always carried cocked and locked. But with a double-action first shot pistol, after the pistol is loaded the hammer must always be decocked. Manually lowering the hammer is considered hazardous. The Walther P-38 pistol introduced a decocking system to the double-action first shot pistol and many double-action pistols introduced since have included some variation of the Walther type. The Magnum Research Baby Eagle solves this problem with a slide-mounted decocker. There are modern CZ variants with a frame-mounted decocker, which solves a lot of problems.

I respect the CZ 75 very much. It is a fine pistol. It is limited by its 9mm cartridge, but no more than the High Power. The CZ 75 may be more robust and have greater longevity than the High Power. Various military tests seem to bear this advantage out.

The author has great confidence in the Baby Desert Eagle. It is among the best of the CZ types and therefore among the finest handguns in the world.

Other CZ Pistols

There are other versions of the CZ I would be remiss not to mention. One of these is the CZ 75B compact. This is a first-class pistol in every regard. There are versions of the compact available in both steel and aluminum frame and with the conventional safety and a frame mounted decocker. In common with the full-size CZ 75 the slide rides low in the frame due to the unconventional slide rail arrangement, resulting in an extraordinarily low bore axis for a double-action handgun. In this version the compact actually handles better than the full-size version, in common with the Baby Eagle's short barrel variants. Those of us who are comfortable with the original system will find the CZ Compact an excellent choice. I still regard the Baby Eagle as the best choice for most shooters, and probably the best double-action pistol I have handled, but there are no flies on the CZ 75 B Compact. Best of all, my version is in a caliber that begins with "4" – the .40 Smith and Wesson. The CZ 75 is an excellent .40 caliber pistol, of sufficient size and weight to effectively control recoil. It's a great all-around performer.

There have been .40 and .45 caliber versions of the CZ introduced by the maker and by those who clone the pistol. Most were overly large and bulky.

But then, enter the Baby Eagle.

The Baby Eagle

The Baby Desert Eagle, or Baby Eagle as its adherents affectionately call it, is a CZ-based design from Israel. (The importer, Magnum Research, also imports the awesome Desert Eagle .44 Magnum automatic pistol. Hence the marketing term Baby Desert Eagle.) The pistol has also been known as the Jericho and the Uzi pistol. Reportedly, the parts are produced by Tangfoglio in Italy and the pistol is finished in Israel. Regardless, the Baby Eagle is a world-class handgun in all regards.

After some study, I find the Baby Eagle a better alternative to the single-action pistol for most shooters than any other double-action pistol. If you do not wish to carry a cocked and locked pistol, you will probably not be comfortable with manually lowering the hammer. Manually lowering the hammer is more of an issue with a double-action first shot pistol than with a single-action pistol. The Baby

Eagle features a slide-mounted safety that is also a decocker. The pistol may be carried on safe or off safe. Considering the differences in speed between frame- and slide-mounted safeties, the Baby Eagle should probably be carried safety off. If you wish to carry the piece on safe, you must practice a great deal with a strong straight thumb action, whisking the finger across the safety on the draw.

The Baby Eagle is offered in .45 ACP. This produces a combination of a double-action first shot and a big bore in a relatively compact, comfortable pistol. The double-action press is smooth. Trigger reach and hand fit are excellent. The pistol is accurate, a common trait in CZ pistols. The trademark slide within the frame of the Baby Eagle produces a pistol with a lower bore axis and more straight-backwards recoil than the SIG, Smith and Wesson or Ruger double-action first shot pistols.

The Baby Eagle is also more controllable in rapid fire than any other double-action .45 I have fired. The low bore axis and steel frame design give the Baby Eagle every advantage. I have also used a full-size .40-caliber pistol extensively. This pistol is very pleasant to fire. The barrel of the Baby Eagle is unique in that it of a polygonal rifled type. This type of rifling is not friendly to lead bullets but produces a good pressure seal for velocity and is often very accurate. The polygonal barrel will produce twenty to thirty-five more feet per second in velocity than a conventionally rifled barrel of similar length and causes less bullet deformation in the barrel.

Despite its well shaped, comfortable grip, the Baby Eagle .45 carries a ten-round magazine in .45 caliber. Overall, I am impressed with the Baby Eagle. This pistol builds upon the CZ but has certain improvements that are worthwhile. The extended dust cover gives the pistol a Magnum-like appearance, and the quality of assembly and fit are outstanding. Overall, the Baby Eagle is my first choice in a double-action big bore handgun.

Armalite AR-24

The Armalite must be mentioned as a new version of the original CZ 75 9mm pistol, but with considerable improvements. The company did not wish to market an inexpensive version of the CZ 75 pistol but rather a premium pistol. They have succeeded and succeeded well. The AR-24 features a variation on the lockwork that allows the piece to be carried hammer down and safety on while maintaining the original cocked and locked carry option. The slide is slightly recontoured to resemble that of the SIG P 210 pistol, a classic design renowned for its accuracy.

The AR-24 is very well finished and more accurate than most CZ pistols. My personal Armalite 9mm is among a very few handguns I own equipped with adjustable sights. I have used the pistol as a workhorse in testing a wide variety of loads. I have been favorably impressed by every aspect of the AR-24. If you prefer the original CZ 75 pistol design, the AR-24 is probably the best choice available as far as fit, finish and value go. My example is an excellent handgun in every way. The AR-24 may well be the best 9mm available today. While the AR-24 is presently available only in 9mm, it is very pleasant to fire and even with the most powerful +P+ loads is a controllable handgun.

Heckler & Koch USP

I have enjoyed good results with the H&K Universal Service Pistol, or USP. The pistol has several design features that are 1911-like, including the grip frame angle and the ability to be carried cocked and locked. (There are also double-action only and decocker-only versions.) The H&K is accurate and reliable and offers good performance and handling.

I think that my first choice in combat handguns will remain the 1911, the High Power and the CZ 75 in that order. Nevertheless, the H&K USP is a pistol I could live with, and I am a demanding individual.

Armalite's AR-24 is among the top three best CZ-type pistols in the author's opinion. Fit, finish and accuracy are excellent.

The HK USP is an accurate handgun, reliable and well-made. The handling does not always inspire but some find the pistol suits their personal preference.

The recoil buffer design incorporated into the recoil spring system makes for a long-lived handgun, with lighter recoil than handguns of comparable weight. Female shooters have remarked the H&K USP is easier to rack, cock and manipulate than similar types, an important advantage. However, the H&K has not enjoyed the acceptance by shooters that the SIG and Glock have. Perhaps price is one consideration. Some shooters report that the safety of the H&K is prone to being activated while firing by certain hand sizes and grip styles. I have experienced this problem myself and it is a surprise to find that this problem passed testing and evaluation by H&K. Yet, with a minimum of acclimation, I find the safety issue is resolved. The USP Compact features slightly different geometry. I never have a problem with bumping the safety with this pistol. I think perhaps it is ex-1911 types who have the majority of problems with the USP. The double-action first shot version is a very versatile handgun. Not only is the piece a selective double-action allowing either hammer-down and ready or cocked and locked carry, it features a decocker, all in the same

mechanism. This outclasses the CZ for versatility. The DA first shot option is fine for holding felons at gunpoint or for short range use. The hammer may be cocked for a deliberate first shot.

I keep a USP on hand for training. My choice is the USP Compact in .45 caliber. The polygonal rifled barrel gives good accuracy and the piece is very accurate. I recently fired a 2.5 inch, five-shot 25-yard group with Black Hills 185-grain JHP ammunition. The polymer frame makes for a light handgun, especially for the caliber. The grip is a little square and less comfortable than the Glock's to many shooters. The heavy slide on top of a light frame seems to contribute to shooters firing low with the USP.

Heckler & Koch shooters are loyal but others tend to try the H&K and then gravitate to the Glock. For those who take the time to master the USP, it is a rewarding pistol with the advantage of a positive safety.

The Glock

The Glock was not the original polymer frame handgun but represents Gaston Glock's idea of

The long Glock 34 is probably the closest to 1911 handling as far as balance in a polymer pistol goes. Those who own the Model 34 swear by it.

handgun perfection. The pistol features a double-action only or safe-action trigger action. The actual action type is debatable; some regard the Glock as more of a single-action type. When the Glock's slide is racked, the striker is partially cocked or prepped. The trigger is prepped forward at the same time. To fire the handgun, the trigger is pressed against spring pressure and the striker is pressed fully to the rear and the piece fires. A true double-action-only that requires that the trigger both cock and fire the piece will have a heavier trigger press. The Glock trigger usually breaks at a relatively light five and one-half pounds. The Glock has proven reliable in my experience and demonstrated good hit probability in service. The standard frame Glock is offered in an effective caliber, the .40 Smith & Wesson, in a relatively compact pistol.

The original 9mm Glock is easy to use well. But the 10mm and .45 caliber versions are too large for most hands. This limits the use of the Glock combined with the big bore cartridge. The modern SF or short frame pistols reduce trigger reach by 3mm, often resulting in much better fit for certain hand sizes. My problem with the Glock is a light trigger action not combined with a manual safety. I am not blind to change, and I realize the Glock outclasses

some pistols in combat performance. But other polymer frame pistols including the Heckler & Koch USP, the Smith & Wesson Military & Police, and the Taurus 24/7 are available with a manual safety. Time will tell if they perform to Glock standards.

Range testing seems to show the Taurus 24/7 approaches the Glock in reliability and offers superior handling and features in most particulars. Those who use the Glock must practice, master the trigger action, and maintain rigid trigger discipline. The grip must be held firmly to avoid limp wrist malfunctions. The polymer frame gives a little in recoil and this may reduce felt recoil but by the same token the shooter must maintain a firm firing platform in order for the pistol to use its recoil energy to properly cycle. For those who practice and keep their head straight the Glock will produce good results.

Among the recent entries in the Glock stable are the various models in .45 Glock Auto Pistol (.45 GAP). This is a special short cartridge case variant of the .45 ACP. The purpose of the .45 GAP is to allow the chambering of a .45 caliber cartridge in a smaller pistol than the large frame Glocks. The Model 37 .45 GAP adopted by the New York State Police neatly solves the problem of hand fit with a .45 caliber Glock. It is unfortunate a young officer had to die after hitting two felons multiple times with the 9mm to instigate this change. The .45 GAP is not as powerful as the .45 ACP despite the hype and many writers' attempts to make the caliber seem attractive. It is a reasonable substitute for service just the same. Realistically the Glock will remain in service for many years but I think that there are better choices.

What is important is using the handgun properly. The author has fitted custom sights to this Glock and found it quite accurate at moderate range once the proper trigger press was learned.

SIG P Series

The SIG is a milestone handgun. It was introduced in the midst of a general rearming of European police. Tactical doctrine called for special teams to rely mainly upon the long gun. The pistol was the backup. The handgun needed to be as simple as possible with no manual safety.

The SIG features a long double-action trigger, which is considered a safety feature. The doctrine was something like this: the long press is safer when holding a suspect at bay, but after the first shot, you are in a gunfight and need the advantage of single-action fire. The SIG also features a positive firing pin block or drop safety and a well-placed decocker. It is often stated the SIG has no manual safety but safety features. This is true. The SIG also was designed to be accurate enough for hostage rescue shots at moderate range; the SIG is among the most accurate of service pistols. Finally, reliability had to be exceptional. The SIG P220 met all of these criteria. The original pistol was a single-column-magazine 9mm Luger pistol. SIG developed .38 Super and .45 ACP versions expressly for American sales. The P225 was a compact version of the P220 9mm. The P226 was the first high capacity pistol in 9mm, while the P228 is a compact P226. The P229 is chambered for the .357 SIG and .40 Smith & Wesson.

While other SIG pistols have a stamped slide, the P 229 features a machined steel slide. As a result, it is as heavy as the full-size SIG despite its compact dimensions. Many SIG fans feel that the P229 is the finest of the SIG pistols. I have a deep appreciation for the P220 but keep a P229 on hand also. I have served with an agency that authorized the SIG and nothing else and carried the P226 and the P220. I have my personal favorites among handguns, but I did not feel undergunned when carrying the P220 and .45 ACP Federal Hydra Shock hollowpoints. (The 9mm P226 9mm was loaded with the 124-grain Hydra Shock +P+.)

The SIG features a smooth double-action first shot and a well-shaped grip. The bore axis is fairly high, inviting muzzle flip, but the grip angle is such that the pistol kicks straight back into the hand. The P220 in .45 is a good service pistol and so is the P229 .40 caliber. This is a well designed double-action first shot pistol that solves many problems

The SIG series are among the most accurate of handguns out of the box. This pistol features the typical SIG double action, decocker, and good sights.

with issue handguns. It is simple to use. The pistol is proven reliable.

The Ohio State Patrol test program may be the single most exhaustive test of service handguns, ever. Some 228,000 rounds of ammunition were fired. When the smoke had cleared the SIG P226 in .40 Smith & Wesson was proven the single most reliable handgun tested. There were other criteria, including hand fit and combat accuracy in a variety of shooting drills. The SIG came in at the top of the heap. This particular pistol was a double-action-only variant, so that system is validated as to reliability in the SIG line.

The SIG is often the most accurate service handgun in any test. I have fired a 25-yard 1.5-inch group with five rounds of the Federal 124-grain +P+ Hydra Shock with my personal P226 and a 15/16-inch group with a P220 and the Black Hills 230-grain JHP. That is extraordinary handgun accuracy. To achieve SIG-like accuracy in a 1911, you have to go to the high end pistols such as the High Standard G Man, Springfield Operator or one of the Wilson Combat pistols. Few other pistols are comparable to the SIG in accuracy.

The SIG is a good double-action pistol and an excellent service pistol. There are other handguns I prefer for personal use but if I were equipping a major agency, many criteria make the SIG a good choice. When the brass choose a SIG pistol, you know they have not gone with the low bid. The SIG might not win a pistol match against a 1911 due to muzzle flip and its double-action trigger, but it is a reliable and accurate pistol that will serve well.

While the P220 .45 is my first choice for personal defense, I am able to fire the P229 a little better.

Beretta 92/96

The Beretta is my least favorite service pistol but I admit it has merit. The Beretta is usually well-made and -fitted and reasonably accurate. The pistol incorporates a manual safety but it's a slide-mounted safety lever that is difficult to manipulate quickly.

The Beretta 92 is basically a modified Walther P-38 with a high-capacity magazine. The external drawbar and open-top slide design as well as the oscillating wedge lockup originally used on the Mauser C96 are all Walther-like. But the original Walther P-38 featured a safety with enough length to manipulate quickly if need be. The Beretta's safety is smaller than the P-38's. The Model 92's long pull double-action trigger is difficult to use well. The Beretta exhibits less muzzle flip when compared to the SIG and other pistols, which is a plus. The slide lock and magazine release are easy enough to manipulate. The pistol is only a little more difficult to handle in .40 caliber than in 9mm, so the larger caliber should always be chosen for personal defense. The Beretta is usually reliable but in extensive tests such as the one conducted by the Ohio State Patrol and other agencies, the SIG usually proved out more reliable. In the US Army test program that chose our service handgun in 1981, the SIG P226 equaled the Beretta 92 in every regard but the Beretta was purchased on the low bid.

I think that little consideration had been given human engineering in that test program. Ergonomics are important and the size and bulk of the

This is a well-worn but reliable Beretta 92. Some practice must be given in actuating the slide-mounted safety.

Beretta is a drawback. The oscillating wings that provide lockup were once prone to eccentric wear. A design change helped produce a more reliable and long-lived pistol. When we come to the bottom line, the Beretta 92 is the archetypal over-large double-action 9mm that everyone loves or loves to hate. The pistol has served well enough in police circles.

We have to give the Beretta credit in that it seems to record the fewest accidental discharges of any type. Its positive firing pin block, double-action trigger and the safety and decocker, as well as a loaded chamber indicator, seem to promote safety. True safety lies between the shooter's ears but the Beretta's record speaks for itself. The Beretta requires the user to learn two trigger actions, double-action and single-action, and to learn the use of a safety/decocking lever that is awkward for most of us. In the end, the Beretta is a reliable pistol and accurate enough but suffers as a dated design.

Smith & Wesson Military & Police

This is a new pistol from Smith & Wesson that bears watching. First of all, the Military & Police name has a proud heritage, so Smith & Wesson had better have a winner on their hands or the designation is sunk. The Military & Police features a comfortable grip angle and a double-action-only trigger action. This is not my type of pistol, but if we must use a double-action-only polymer frame pistol the Smith & Wesson has promise.

The addition of a manual safety is a great advantage. An automatic pistol with no safety abrogates several important advantages of the type. I have fired the .40-caliber version extensively with good results. Do I prefer the M&P to the Glock? Slightly, but at this point the Glock is more proven. When you throw in the manual safety and the fact that the M&P in .45 is more comfortable than the Glock .45 to handle and use, there is really no contest. But I am concerned with the longevity of the type. I think we need we need to address the fact that this is a new design, not a warmed-over SIGMA. The SIGMA is among the most difficult handguns to use well I have encountered. I attempted to use the pistol but found it lacking. The SIGMA was a poor substitute for the Glock while the M&P seems to be a rule-beater and an improvement. Time will tell.

The Taurus 24/7 is a remarkable mix of efficiency and economy. It works well and has proven reliable in the examples the author has tested.

Taurus 24/7

My #1 choice among polymer-frame pistols, the Taurus 24/7, has been approved for private purchase and official use by a handful of domestic agencies just as Taurus is enjoying major orders from foreign police with their PT92 line. Taurus acceptance in the shooting world is growing. The 24/7 offers a smooth double-action-only trigger action and a manual safety. A manual safety! Why is that so hard to understand? If you do not wish to use the manual safety of the Taurus you can ignore it at your own risk or preference, but the safety of the Taurus is frame-mounted. It is not one of those slide-mounted safeties that works backwards and is difficult to manipulate. The safety falls under the thumb readily. The grip frame is very comfortable, not only in 9mm but in .40 and .45 caliber as well. The frame is comfortable enough and is covered in pebble grain rubber in order to enhance the grip. The Heinie sights are custom quality and a great addition to any handgun. The LS version (Long Slide) is a five-inch service pistol that has proven quite accurate and easy to control. This is a handgun I have tested in 9mm, .40 and .45 with good results.

I have been listening to input from the field and so far input is good. However, the 24/7 is still a relatively new design. I like that; the pistol is among a very few fresh designs to come along in the past few decades. But it is not as proven as the Glock. It is at least as proven as the Smith & Wesson Military & Police. I am waiting for the Taurus polymer frame pistol to be invited into a major police service pistol test and see how the pistol fares with different testers firing thousands of rounds of ammunition in a compressed time period. I am of the opinion the pistol will fare just fine and perhaps prove a rule-beater. Time will tell. As for range performance and my impression of the pistol, this is a good handgun.

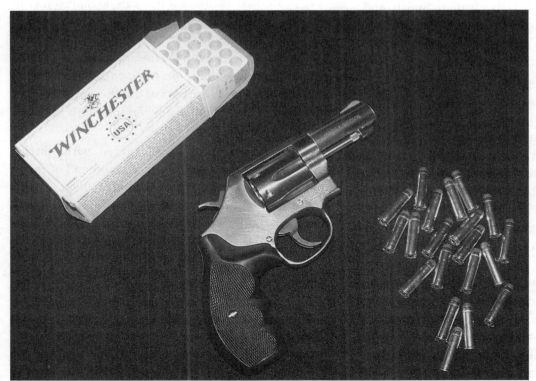

This is a plain vanilla Smith and Wesson M64 that will do the business in trained hands.

REVOLVERS AND OTHERS

The S&W Combat Magnum

There will always be those who believe the revolver is the superior personal defense handgun. In many circumstances, the revolver has advantages. In an intimate range battle, the revolver can be pressed against an opponent's body and fired repeatably, a situation in which an autoloader would jam. There are those who find the rolling action of a double-action revolver gives them excellent control. Since they do not know exactly when the trigger will break they neither clutch the trigger nor flinch in anticipating the shot.

Revolvers are often more accurate than the best semi-autos and definitely more accurate than the general run of autoloaders. A quality .357 Magnum revolver from Ruger or Smith & Wesson can group five shots into three inches at 50 yards. All are not that accurate, but the better pieces are more accurate than a human can hold. The revolver can be kept ready, loaded, for indefinite periods. There are no springs depressed when the revolver is at the ready; therefore the handgun is not unduly stressed. The revolver usually has good sights and reliability is simply not an issue.

The revolver that suits my needs best is the medium-frame (the so-called "K" frame) Smith and Wesson .357 Magnum known as the Combat Magnum. While no longer in production, many are available in the used market and a comparable model is available from Taurus as the Model 669.

The Combat Magnum revolver is well balanced. The sights are excellent high visibility types and when the Combat Magnum is equipped with an orange insert front sight, the hit probability is even higher. The action of this revolver is always smooth. With a bit of polishing by an expert gunsmith, it can be even smoother. The Combat Magnum can be fired with inexpensive .38 Special ammunition for practice but loaded with the powerful .357 Magnum cartridge for protection. Many have deemed the .357 Magnum the best manstopper we are ever likely to produce. I have seen the effect of the Magnum over my own gun sights, and it is immediate. The Magnum has plenty of power and enough velocity to ensure the jacketed hollowpoint bullet used in this cartridge works as designed.

The momentum of such a powerful cartridge can take its toll on the mechanism. A steady diet of .357 Magnums can loosen up the Combat Magnum over time. You have to keep your hand in with the full-power loads to stay in practice, but I recommend a ratio of ten .38 Specials for every Magnum fired if you want to make your Combat Magnum last as long as possible. My first choice for a defense cartridge in the .357 Magnum falls between two proven performers. The Winchester 110-grain JHP is easy to control and usually produces excellent effect on living targets. A reduced Magnum load, it still breaks 1,300 fps. This is a loading designed to afford good control while producing immediate effect on motivated attackers. Penetration would be on the light side for police service.

For more power and penetration, the Winchester 145-grain Silvertip is rated at about the same velocity, but with a better balance of expansion and penetration. The often-touted 125-grain JHP is no more effective than the Silvertip but produces incipient wear on the Combat Magnum. The problem of excess powder gas cutting and the damage possible when fired in light handguns makes me leery of the 125-grain Magnum. It isn't well known, but author and accomplished shooter Mike Cumpston pointed out a decade ago that with proper load practice, 140-grain .357 caliber bullets can be moved just as quickly as the 125-grain pills, with better accuracy, a more complete powder burn, and less chance of damaging the revolver. I sometimes carry the Combat Magnum by choice on my own time, especially when bad animals are part of the threat profile. The handgun is that good. My experience with the Magnum is excellent.

Some years ago, I was charged with putting down a large dog that had bitten the end of man's finger off. I found the big cur a half mile or so from the scene and fired a single shot at the running animal. The bullet struck this beast in the shoulder, and the effect was dramatic and immediate.

The Combat Magnum is a very versatile revolver, and offers a sub-load option. Those not fully confident with their ability to control the Magnum may load their revolver with +P .38s until they feel they have mastered the Magnum. I recently tested the Cor-Bon PowRBall round in .357 Magnum in not only the Combat Magnum but also a snubnosed

Taurus with excellent results. The recoil is less than that of heavy-bullet loads but the expansion is excellent. With sensible sub-loadings using well-designed bullets, the Combat Magnum and similar revolvers are good choices for personal defense.

Overall, I find the Combat Magnum an excellent all-around handgun. When carrying my example I certainly feel no ballistic inferiority complex nor do I feel disadvantaged in the least. But then I have used the Magnum for real. There are no shortcomings to the revolver, but the operator must be able to handle this one. There are alternatives to the Combat Magnum that make a reasonable substitution. The Ruger GP 100 is larger and heavier, making it slower into action, but it's a very strong revolver.

A four-inch-barreled heavy barrel revolver with fixed sights is a good choice for all-around defense use. Taurus makes several handguns that offer adjustable sights and a fixed sight service version as well.

Smith and Wesson M65

This is another revolver that is out of production but often found on the used-gun shelf. The Model 65 is a stainless steel, three-inch-barreled, round butt .357 Magnum revolver. This is a rugged, no-nonsense revolver with fixed sights. The blued version, the Model 13, was once standard issue of the FBI. The FBI liked the two-tier power system, issuing the .38 Special +P for general use and authorizing the .357 Magnum for special use. The Model 65 is brilliantly fast into action from my Blackhawk! holster and is a very well balanced revolver to boot. This is among the few revolvers I practice with often, and it's an important part of my home defense plan. All family members including visiting responsible adults are familiar with this revolver's action, making it an indispensable piece of equipment. I most often keep my personal Model 65 loaded with Glaser Safety Slugs.

The author puts great stake in his Smith and Wesson M21 .44 Special. For various duties this is a fine choice.

Smith and Wesson Model 21 .44 Special

Smith and Wesson recently reintroduced their big-bore fixed-sight revolvers in the Classic line. These revolvers are not true reproductions but improved models as they feature transfer bar ignition, the new action lock, a round butt in some versions, and excellent workmanship. These pencil-barrel revolvers are much lighter than a comparable .44 Magnum. The revolver's receiver tapers to a thin barrel with no underlug, and the revolver weighs only 37 ounces compared to well over 45 ounces for a .44 Magnum with its heavy barrel and fixed sights.

This is lighter than a 1911 and with proper care in holster selection; many users are able to conceal this handgun, at least with winter clothing.

The Model 21 is a very smooth revolver. Its light weight makes it surer into action than the large, heavy Magnum revolvers. The broad fixed sights will not be knocked out of whack and the revolver stays on target in the hands of someone who has mastered double-action fire. For those who do not trust the automatic or simply prefer the simplicity of the revolver, the Model 21 is a first-class revolver with much to recommend it.

The snubnosed .38 is a good choice for intimate range combat. At close range a contact shot will enhance the modest power of the .38 Special cartridge.

COMPACT PISTOLS AND REVOLVERS

The Two Light Revolvers

There are two leading revolvers for concealed carry use: the Smith & Wesson Model 60 family and the Taurus Model 85. The modern Model 85 often has better sights and a smoother action than its domestic competitor. The five-shot .38 Special caliber revolver has advantages of simplicity and ease of use. A short range weapon, the snubnosed revolver can be fired surprisingly well by those who understand the beast. This is the #1 backup revolver available. Snubnosed revolvers are light and handy and the advantages in intimate range encounters are obvious. There are examples in steel frame and aluminum frame and also Scandium versions. And there is a special breed with a longer cylinder and heavy barrel chambered for the .357 Magnum cartridge. I do not care for the .357 Magnum examples. They offer excess recoil and ear-splitting muzzle blast. Much of the power of the Magnum cartridge is lost in this combination. The slower burning powders used in the Magnum cartridge cannot fully develop their energy from a short-barreled handgun. Even worse are the ported barrel versions, which offer a further loss of velocity and greater blast.

The five-shot .38 is generically known as the J frame. While at their best with the square butt and steel frame, there are round butt aluminum frame versions available. A particular advantage of the snub .38 is that the weapon is among the best tools to consider for short range, intimate range combat. Often the fight for your life turns into a fight for the handgun. When you have your hand on the ample grip of a snubnosed revolver, you have excellent control. The gun-grabber has little to hang onto in a snubbie. I stress again that the revolver may be pressed against the opponent's body and fired repeatably.

There are many reasons for choosing a snubnosed .38. Simplicity and ease of operation are among them. While the .38 is demanding of a good hand for best performance, this is a genre we cannot do without in our battery. Take your time and choose the grip frame that fits your hand best. There are surprising differences in hand fit among snubnosed revolvers.

Taurus/Rossi .357 Revolver

This is a revolver that is reasonably compact but takes the sting out of the .357 in lighter revolvers. When I was a youth there were two basic types of snubnosed .38s. One was the Smith and Wesson J frame, a small-frame five-shooter, and the other was the Colt Detective Special, a small-frame six-shooter. The Smith and Wesson was a pocket revolver if left with the original grips intact and not fitted with over-large stocks. The Colt was really a belt gun although the Colt Agent, an aluminum framed Detective Special with an abbreviated grip frame, was a good try at a pocket revolver. The two competed for several generations but the Colt is no longer manufactured. It is uncertain whether Colt small frame revolvers will return. If you have a vintage Colt in good condition, you have an excellent all-around light revolver.

With its relatively complex lockwork, the Colt is a little more complicated to get right than the Smith and Wesson. When foreign companies copy an American snubnosed .38, it is almost always the J frame that is cloned. The two most successful producers of J frame clones have been Taurus and Rossi of Brazil, two companies that are now affiliated.

When Taurus acquired Rossi, there was an immediate upgrade in quality and some crossover in manufacture. Rossi followed the same path as Taurus had done; their first revolvers were clones of the Smith and Wesson line. Taurus was acknowledged to have the better product among these Brazilian makers. As time went by, both companies steadily increased the quality of the product and found that consumers were willing to pay for quality. I do not recommend 1980s or earlier production from either and use caution in choosing Rossi revolvers made before the Taurus/Rossi venture. The new breed is clearly marked Rossi/Taurus.

While both produce a J frame copy, Rossi produces a small revolver that combines the best features of both Colt and Smith & Wesson revolvers.

The Colt featured a six-shot cylinder but the revolver was on a frame smaller than the Smith & Wesson Model 10, S&W's legendary K frame six-shooter. The Colt is light but much easier to shoot well than the five-shot Smith & Wesson revolver. Rossi produced a six-shot revolver of similar dimensions to the Colt. The Rossi uses Smith & Wesson type lock work including the familiar S&W cylinder latch and cylinder rotation. I have used several of these revolvers and keep one as a general beater, for outdoors and personal defense use. This is a holster gun, not a pocket gun. My example features the elongated cylinder and heavy barrel that makes the piece suitable for use with the .357 Magnum cartridge.

I originally intended to fire this one with .38 Special ammunition and nothing else. However, I have found that the revolver is not unbearable to fire with Magnum ammunition. The large rubber composition grip makes for real comfort. The grip sets the hand off from the steel frame and allows a bit of a cushion. This is a good choice for backpackers and outdoorsmen who wish to deploy the most power for the ounce possible in case of animal attack. Many of the animal attacks that have been successfully stopped with pistol fire have ended up in a situation in which the handgun was pressed against the beast's neck or head and fired multiple times. I feel that a .357 Magnum revolver loaded with a good high-penetration load such as Federal's 180 grain Cast Core would be an excellent choice in this duty.

The Rossi revolver is a great shooter. The piece has every advantage discussed in favor of the snubnosed .38 but has greater heft, better balance, a smooth action and good sights. The revolver is pleasant enough to use, so informal practice is encouraged. After all, a revolver that bites our hand will be used less. This is an excellent compromise revolver, lighter than a Combat Magnum but larger than a snubnosed .38 and able to do the business in good hands.

Colt Detective Special

I do not like to mention handguns that are no longer in production. By doing so I may leave myself open to the gunwriter's pitfall:"I do not buy my guns; I have my guns." Just the same the Colt bears mention as the type is occasionally seen at gun shows and in well-stocked shops. Everything I said about the Rossi six shot revolver applies to the Colt Detective Special except for the Magnum chambering.

The Colt is a good shooter, smooth and accurate. However, be certain that the example you purchase is in good working order. After all, the type was in-

troduced in 1926. Not long ago I purchased a Colt that seemed smooth enough but in the end my daughter and I disassembled the piece and found eccentric wear throughout. I was able to peen some parts and replace springs and the Detective Special became a reference piece suitable for practice and little else. On the other hand a good Colt Agent, an aluminum frame revolver with an abbreviated grip frame, is often used by the author as a backup and occasionally as a primary piece.

The Colt revolvers were smoother than the Smith & Wesson on average but there is a price to pay. The Colt hand remains locked to the cylinder when the hammer drops and the revolver fires. The Smith and Wesson hand falls away before firing. The Colt's system is more accurate. The Smith and Wesson is less rigid. But the force of firing and recoil is transferred to the Colt trigger mechanism. Not a minor point: Colts went out of time more often than Smith and Wesson revolvers. The Rossi combines the size and weight of the Colt with the advantages of a Smith and Wesson mechanism. I would not wish to be without my Colt Agent but then there are better choices today.

Ruger SP101

This Ruger five-shot revolver was introduced in 1988 and has become a favorite of those who favor the rock-solid Ruger revolver line. The SP101 will never be accused of being a pocket revolver. This is a holster revolver to be carried on the belt. All of the advantages of the snubnosed .38 enumerated previously apply to the SP101. The SP101 has an advantage over any other light revolver in the handling of heavy loads for long periods. It is practically unknown for this revolver to go out of time or suffer damage from powerful .357 Magnum loads.

The SP101 is a fine choice for backup, for primary carry for those who prefer the revolver, or for protection against animals. This is a well-balanced revolver that offers good shooting characteristics. While many shooters carry the revolver with .38 Special +P ammunition, the .357 Magnum cartridge is not too bad to control in the SP101 largely due to superior grip technology. I normally recommend the Winchester 110-grain JHP, a mid-range .357, in compact .357 Magnum revolvers.

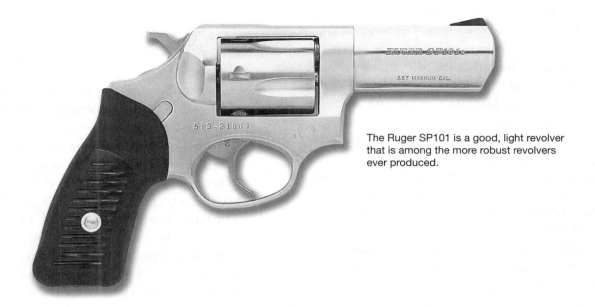

The Ruger SP101 is a good, light revolver that is among the more robust revolvers ever produced.

Some care is needed in purchasing a used SP101. The original was chambered for .38 Special only and that is fine if you prefer the .38. When the first few examples were offered in .357 Magnum the barrel was stamped "125-Grain Only." This simply meant the chamber was too short to accommodate the 140- to 158-grain loads. The 180-grain Federal Castcore I prefer for outdoors carry and defense against animals was out of the question. Later production features a longer cylinder that is suitable for all Magnum loads. The .38 is just a .38 and the 125-grain-only Magnums are not as versatile as later production. Overall the Ruger is a good revolver that is popular with hardened revolver men who fire lots of heavy loaded ammunition. It is a good choice for female shooters, especially as a house gun, as it is among the lightest-kicking and most trouble-free revolvers ever manufactured of its size and caliber.

Smith & Wesson Airlite Revolvers

I believe these revolutionary handguns deserve considerable ink. I am a professional who relies primarily on semi-automatic pistols for defense with a number of choice revolvers as backup. Smith and Wesson's modern revolvers have raised the bar considerably in handgun technology. Part of the reason for their being is to offer a powerful handgun for dealing with large animals. This is the reason some are chambered for the big bore Magnum cartridges. As such, the revolvers are not hunting handguns but revolvers designed for close range defense.

The Airlites sometimes feature fiber optic front sights for rapid sight acquisition. The lockwork is typical Smith and Wesson. The great difference is that the frames are of a mixture of aluminum and light alloys. The frame is scandium and the cylinder titanium. The J frame .38s weigh but 12 ounces and the .44 Magnum revolvers weigh about 28 ounces. As may be expected, recoil is greater than with similar revolvers of conventional steel frame construction. The revolvers are more expensive than other Smith and Wesson products primarily due to the exotic construction. Their intrinsic accuracy should be as good as any other Smith and Wesson revolver.

Practical accuracy depends upon the user's ability to withstand recoil. When firing the J frame .357 in rapid fire with standard lead bullets such as the Black Hills .38 Special 158-grain SWC at about 800 fps, recoil is heavy. I am used to the airweight Colt Agent, so I was prepared. With the Black Hills .38 Special 125-grain JHP defense load, recoil was more noticeable. I touched off a Black Hills 125-grain .357 Magnum and was ignorant enough to keep firing until I expended the cylinderful of ammunition. I suffered a blister on my thumb. This is a revolver that will be carried much and shot little but it needs to be fired in order for the shooter to acclimate to its action.

There is a competent, intelligent and loyal group of shooters who appreciate the big bore revolver. For these shooters, there is no better choice for personal defense than the Airlite .45 ACP. Smith & Wesson's 325PD is chambered for the powerful .45 ACP cartridge. You can load this brute with moon clips. Originally developed for use in the Smith & Wesson 1917 revolver, these moon clips fasten into the extractor groove of the automatic pistol cartridge and allow the use of a rimless cartridge in revolvers. This also creates a very rapid loading system. The cartridges are positively ejected with a single push of the ejector rod.

While recoil is there with this handgun, it is not in the category of a steel-framed .44 Magnum. Overall, this is the revolver in the Airlite line that makes the most sense. If you do not like moon clips, both Black Hills and Cor Bon now load the .45 Auto Rim. This is a rimmed version of the .45 ACP specifically for .45 ACP revolvers. The .45 Auto Rim case is stronger than that of the .45 ACP and advanced handloaders can really make the .45 AR talk.

The final Airlite worth considering as a defensive handgun is the 329PD, a .44 Magnum version. There are two sets of grips supplied, wood and rubber. Use the rubber grips. Trust me on that one. Loaded with the Cor-Bon personal defense loading in .44 Special, this is quite a revolver. Recoil isn't bad at all, about in lightweight .45 ACP territory. But if your mission profile calls for .44 Magnum ammunition, you are in for a wild ride. The 300-grain Black Hills JHP is a fine choice for personal defense against large animals. This load goes across the screens at nearly 1100 fps from the 329PD. I literally had to rub my wrists after three rounds. I did not fire single-action as I would jerk the shot, and only by attempting a smooth rolling double-action shot did I manage to get off a cylinderful. If you are on a fishing or hunting expedition to Alaska or other far north destination and wish to be prepared for a bear attack, this light weight .44 Magnum is a good choice. At bad breath range, you won't notice the recoil.

The Airlite Smith & Wesson handguns are wonderful examples of revolver technology. They are light, reliable, accurate and well made. They are also brutal kickers. Only those well indoctrinated into Magnum revolvers need apply.

Taurus Tracker

The Tracker is a new idiom on the shooting scene. The Tracker is advertised as a field gun. Examples are available in the gamut of handgun calibers beginning at .22 and ranging to .45 Colt. Depending upon the barrel length and caliber options they range from docile to brutes to fire.

The five-shot .41 Magnum offers unprecedented protection and hunting ability from a light package. My favorite, however, is the Tracker in .45 ACP. This is a five-shot revolver that is light enough, well balanced, and accurate. While five shots is cutting it close in a defensive encounter, the Tracker is lighter and neater to carry than a six-shot big frame revolver. It is fast into action and easy to control. The five shot moon clips supplied with the Tracker are superior to the speed loaders that must be used with conventional revolver cartridges. Overall, the Tracker is one of the outstanding outdoors and defensive revolvers of this century. The Tracker in many ways introduces a new baseline in revolvers. The construction, accuracy, and utility of these revolvers is challenging to competitors and welcome to shooters. Big frame six-shot revolvers are a stretch for the author. The smaller Tracker fits my hands well. I was disappointed that the .45 Tracker would not accept the .45 AR cartridge. The cylinder is headspaced for .45 ACP only. But that is OK; the revolver is a good, purpose-designed all-around shooter that delivers good performance.

Light Automatic Pistols

Most compact pistols of any power are cut-down service pistols. The Officer's Model Colt, as an example, is a cut and chopped Government Model pistol. True compacts with a shortened slide and butt include the SIG P229 and the Glock Model 23. Very often these handguns are among the best suited to personal defense. While lighter, shorter and more compact than the service pistol from which they sprang, they retain the advantages of reliability and good handling often associated with service-size handguns.

You can go too far when downsizing. The mini Glock pistols are interesting and fill a need, but the shortened butt and short sight radius make the pistols more difficult to handle than a Glock 23. They are a good choice for hideout but we should carry a true compact when possible. The compact version of the Baby Desert Eagle and the CZ 75B are excellent examples. But there are also purpose designed compacts with no service pistol as a parent. We will look at a number of these as they are credible defensive handguns.

Kahr

The Kahr pistol has many outstanding attributes. Among these are reliability and smoothness of operation. Even the feed ramp is especially designed with an offset in order to produce the most compact handgun possible. I have often remarked that the Kahr shows Europeans that Gun Valley can get it right. The Kahr is not a high-capacity pistol. The six-shot .40 caliber version is light and thin. This is an adequate cartridge reserve for what it is designed to do. The trigger action is smooth and can be used well once the shooter picks up the proper cadence of fire. The pistol is accurate enough to take advantage of its good sights to 25 yards or more.

I have been enthusiastic about this handgun from its introduction. The pistol has been authorized for off-duty use by the New York City Police Department, among others. I have not tested every model but I have seen quite a few in use. The reputation of the pistol is secure. The only problem worth mentioning is an occasional light primer strike that is detected in the break in period and easily fixed by the factory.

Kel Tec PF-9 9mm

The Kel Tec PF-9 is a fresh design with much merit. The parent is the P11, a compact double-column magazine 9mm. The P-11 has good sights and a smooth trigger action. But the PF-9 is the best purpose-designed hideout handgun in 9mm caliber yet produced. The pistol is light enough at 14.5 ounces to produce significant recoil with the 9mm Luger cartridge. The pistol is easier to shoot well than most airweight revolvers and impossibly flat with a slide just .880 inches wide. The grip features a special pattern that must have been influenced by Florida Alligators.

This is about the lightest 9mm pistol we are likely to see. I carry mine often either as a backup or when the southern heat limits outer garments. The pistol demands proper lubrication and much practice but in return gives an unprecedented level of

protection for the weight. I did experience difficulty in handling the piece during the first few range sessions. I caused several malfunctions by allowing my thumb to contact the slide in recoil. I took two hundred rounds of Winchester Personal Defense 115-grain JHP ammunition to the range, determined that the PF9 and I would work out our differences. There were no malfunctions and I learned how to do the business. I earned a blister or two on the firing hand and actually cramped my hand from the death grip I was forced to maintain. This is a reasonable sacrifice to master the PF-9. Keep these demands in mind when choosing an ultra-compact pistol.

Heckler & Koch P7

We have looked at quite a few practical and affordable handguns. Now we will look at a handgun that is quite a bit different. Once very expensive on the used market, the P7M8 retails for nearly $2000. But as of this writing hundreds of PSP or P7 pistols are available on the used market. These West German police trade ins are available for less than $1000. The Heckler & Koch P7 is a unique handgun with a manual of arms and operating procedure different from practically any other pistol. There are shadows of the P7 in Astra pistols and the Savage automatics, but the H&K P7 is a unique handgun.

The P7 is a result of the same German police trials that introduced the SIG P220. The P7 arrives at its simplicity of operation by using a cocking lever. There is no manual safety of any type. The pistol is inoperative until a cocking lever located at the front of the trigger guard is pressed. About 13 lbs. of pressure is needed to cock this lever but only a pound or so to keep the lever closed. If you are loading the pistol from slide lock, the squeeze cocker also drops the slide. The advantages of the squeeze cocker operation are many. If you drop the pistol, it is immediately made safe when the squeeze cocker is released. When the squeeze cocker is in operation the trigger press is a very light and crisp 3.5 lbs. This squeeze cocker met the safety and simplicity requirements of German police agencies. Also among the requirements of the pistol for the new German police forces was that it be accurate enough for hostage rescue at moderate range. The P7 clearly meets these requirements.

Another step taken to produce a slim and light pistol is most unusual. The P7 is a blowback pistol. Normally blowback pistols are suitable only for small caliber cartridges. But the P7 incorporates a gas piston into the design. While gas pistons normally operate a firearm's action by giving the action a kick, in this case the gas piston is actually used to retard the opening of the slide until pressure from firing abates. The system works and works brilliantly. The P7 has earned a reputation as one of the world's most reliable handguns. An advantage of the P7 is its low bore axis, a result of the innovative design.

Another advantage is the P7's 110-degree grip angle. I have run the P7 through any number of combat drills with excellent results. The P7 is friendly to either hand and completely reliable even when not cleaned or lubricated for long stretches.

The P7 has certain idiosyncrasies. The operation takes time to adapt to. The unique P7 probably is a better choice for the one-gun man than for anyone who chooses to own a brace of handguns. When firing the P7, the frame in front of the trigger guard heats up considerably. This is due to gas action and the location of the gas cylinder. Within a hundred rounds you will find the frame hot enough to produce a blister if you are not careful. This is another good recommendation for wearing gloves when training. Naturally we will not fire one hundred rounds in combat. All handguns heat up when firing, even my USFA single-action .45. But the HK heats up in a potentially uncomfortable manner quickly.

The P7 has proven reliable with every standard-pressure loading I have fed the pistol. Since it features a shorter than average 3.8-inch barrel, ammunition performance is critical. I have tested a number of loadings. I find the Speer Gold Dot 124 grain Short Barrel load a good choice. Speer has introduced several loads that are not +P rated but that use a bullet with a softer core for better expansion from short barrels. Another good choice is the Black Hills 115-grain EXP. The EXP is an extra power-rated load that is faster than most standard pressure loads but does not break into +P pressure. This load uses a well-designed 115-grain jacketed hollowpoint bullet. Since the P7 uses a polygonal rifled barrel, velocity is on a par with the average four-inch-barreled service handgun.

The P7 is a good handgun, an excellent example of the gunmaker's art. I find that those who adopt the P7 as a daily carry pistol are often very serious handgunners who feel that it gives them every advantage. The P7 is quite compact but offers performance comparable to any full-size pistol. The expensive P7 is a fine handgun well worth its price.

6 Combat Drills and the Combat Mindset

When working up this book I have attempted to produce more than a series of ramblings. I think that the best information I can provide is useless without a good attitude. This means a good attitude in instruction and also a force of will called the combat mindset.

An individual who has a bad attitude on the range may be a good person but he's a person not interested in what he is doing. He might practice drills that are not challenging. He might not strive to address problem areas. By the same token, some instruction is good and some bad and other instruction is mixed-up at best. In my home state an instructor managed to kill a student during a class when using a loaded handgun to illustrate a point. Incredible as it sounds, it happened. The title instructor does not automatically qualify one as a "good instructor." Some of the better instructors go by the book and understand doctrine very well. Doctrinal issues are solved by others and the application of doctrine is their main concern. The problem arises when you meet a bad guy who has not read the book!

Training gives the individual a foundation of skill that will apply to the decision-making process. You need to fully grasp every practical skill. Your survival in a critical incident will depend largely upon the

This is a picture of control. This young officer has touched off a cartridge. The case is smoking into space and the pistol is quickly back on target.

training you have received and how well you apply this training. The process of instruction is repetitive and must continue past initial training and qualification. Proficiency is gained by constant drills and occasional "Eureka!" moments. I occasionally find the same exhilaration among students. Devising a plan of instruction and a plan to carry you through an incident is imperative. If your plan includes rapid double taps on each adversary you had better be able to demonstrate seamless double taps on the range. Physical training is important. What foods you eat and don't eat and regular exercise affect your performance on the range. Don't skip workouts. The firearm should never be your only recourse. Open-hand techniques must be part of the plan.

Demanding physical training will answer this question: when push comes to shove how will you perform? How will you react? There is no looking back once you are dedicated to defend yourself. How much effort you have put into training and the drills you have put faith in as well as the decisions you have made will have considerable consequences if you are sitting in the mall when an eighteen-year-old Goth with a warped view of life opens fire. Being aware of your surroundings and possible threats is called situational awareness. You may have little warning of an attack. A shrug of the shoulder or a targeting glance may be the only sign of an attack coming. Nothing tells you, "You will be attacked on November 9, 2012." Recognition and reaction are what will save your life. You are at a disadvantage as the bad guy has chosen the field to fight. You must show no mercy as you meet aggression and adrenaline with a cold and somber response.

Many people are involved in high-risk behavior. Peace officers are one category. Those who frequent rough bars, drink, do drugs, frequent prostitutes or become involved in lover's triangles are also at risk. Criminals are at high risk. I have never met anyone in the former categories who woke up one morning and said, "I am going to die today." But many have. No amount of caution eliminates chance – but we may lessen our chances of being assaulted. I realize that some of you may not have been touched by violence. When death occurs unexpectedly to someone who lives on the rough side, well, it is not completely unexpected. Random acts and the death of persons living a sane and decent

life is difficult to explain to the family. Violence is a real part of life in America.

Among the latest reports I have on hand is the Uniform Crime Report by the FBI from 2006. It is interesting that violent assaults number in the millions, with over 1,400,000 reported that year. Another agency has documented 2.5 million assaults against women in a space of a few years. I have examined numerous crime scenes and know well those involved in violence and those whose lives were changed forever. Investigating crimes of violence taints your worldview.

A decent person cannot help but feel anger toward a perpetrator. Often the anger is non-directional, simply a fist shaken at the world, but other times we feel animosity toward the beasts who savage our young and elderly. Many of them are evil individuals who inflict injury rape and torture on others for the sheer pleasure of causing human suffering.

For some of us who deal with these criminals, it is only with considerable effort we do not take this anger home to our family in the form of depression or disgust at the world we see. The answer is simple: the world may be going to hell in a handbasket, but not the whole world, and we must not be part of that handbasket. In one way or the other if you do not deal with the criminal element, they will deal with you. The first step – and it is a big one for some people – is to accept reality. It can happen to you. The next step is to decide that you will fight back.

Situational awareness and a fighting mindset are important tools. An example of situational awareness is the observation of dress. A coat in sweltering heat means someone is hiding something. The object being hidden may be a weapon or perhaps the individual is shoplifting. When aware of the danger signs, you may be able to avoid violence.

It is best to avoid conflict. A fight may go 50/50 at best with either side having an equal chance at death. Within the week I have seen a pasty white ex-con, decorated with a dozen or more jailhouse tattoos, cursing his teenage son at the flea market. To call him down or attempt to educate him at this late date would have been futile. The son, alas, hasn't a chance in this world; Dad has made certain of that. In a confrontation I have much to lose; the ex-con, nothing. My family and I moved on.

Violence may be precipitated by a wrong word or gesture. You do not have to be a physiologist to understand evidence of drug use. If you have ever wondered why street people have such overinflated egos, this is a byproduct of cocaine use. Their highly developed egos are often a product of mind-altering drugs. As the drug addict comes down off of that high, agitation and paranoia overpower the individual. This is a deadly combination that manifests itself in violence every day in America.

I am spending more time on our adversary than you may have expected but you need to have a good grasp of the threat you face. The opponent will not be a piece of paper. He may be a 280-lb. ex-con who has spent the last five years working out and engaging in the most confrontational lifestyle you can imagine. Accoutrements are good, but awareness is vital. Your psychological evaluation of the threat is a significant component of your understanding of the

problem. The opponent is not a Joe or Jenny like you who is simply having a bad day. All criminals are sociopaths. Some are schizophrenic. Many are bipolar. Others socialize by combining drugs and alcohol. When I discuss these criminals, remember that I have dealt with hundreds and still do on practically a daily basis. Some are currently imprisoned and their present address is a result of my efforts. Some are paranoid schizophrenic with cocaine or meth dependency. Many would escape from their current homes at the first opportunity.

I am currently involved in a profession that demands that I size people up quickly. Their appearance is one indication as is their pupil dilation and even their smell. You might say their reputation precedes them. But some are more devious and do not wear their history on their sleeve. My suppositions are just that, but often a supposition will lead to a fact. Subtleties lead to facts. Visual imagery is important

This is an unrealistic scenario but the shooter is learning speed and accuracy under the press of time.

and feedback gives me information that allows me to avoid an altercation. Are we profiling? No, we are assessing risk by actuarial data. It is called going with what we know.

Cops make wrong decisions. I have heard wild speculation at crime scenes but in the end experienced cops "know the lick." They either develop good situational awareness or they pay with injury. When we look at the outstanding motivations people have for murder, remember, it may happen to you over an imagined slight or simply because you are different and do not fit in. Being a decent citizen in life and appearance may make you a target and object of hatred.

A sure clue to danger is inappropriate demeanor. Is the person of interest sweating profusely in a cool indoor situation? Do they have an uneasy calm in a volatile situation? I have often said a critical incident is much like a vehicle accident. It comes at you quickly. Sometimes the time dilation effect kicks in and time seems to pass in slow motion. You do not see it coming but the bad guys do. They have been known to point an individual out to their cohorts with the comment, "There's my next victim." How you are chosen varies. You may have fallen victim to happenstance, but then there are relationship issues that lead to unhappy circumstances and attacks.

Your demeanor is important. Arrogance is not a desirable trait. But a confident attitude with your head held up straight and a steady pace is likely to make a criminal choose another victim. Look around you and be aware of where you are and where you are going. Those who shuffle through life with their head down unsure of themselves are natural-born victims often chosen by our protein-fed ex-con criminal class.

It is a quantum leap from talking about homicide or reading about homicide to becoming involved in it. When a homicide occurs in your family or in your circle of friends, you realize how irrevocable this act is. I cannot recall the number of places in my home town where homicides have occurred. In many places they have become morbid mileposts, landmarks of murder. The neighborhood is traumatized and depressed as a result. On the other hand, places where citizens have successfully defended themselves remain successful and viable communities. Folks who defend their home continue to live in the neighborhood they have made safe. This is food for thought.

That is enough on the mindset. Let's look hard at vital skills.

The last criteria you should apply as a measure of combat ability is the ability to fire small groups at 25 yards. I appreciate an accurate handgun as much

This is a good target with the SW1911 and Winchester hardball. With attention to detail and the shooting basics, there is little excuse for a miss.

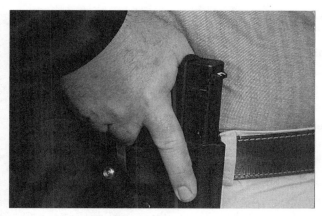

When drawing, it is important to sweep our covering garments back and also keep our fingers off the trigger as we draw.

as anyone, but a small five-shot group at 25 yards is not a requisite of a combat handgun. The pistol need only be accurate enough to consistently strike a man in the chest at 25 yards. Actual fights will be much closer. The time involved in getting a hit is what is important, and making the bullet fly to the correct place on the anatomy is another important skill. The most important advantage in shooting is familiarity with the handgun. You must be intimately familiar with the handgun's controls, grip, trigger press and sights. You must practice on a regular basis and attain sufficient skill to place all of the rounds into the X ring of a B27 silhouette at 10 yards. This is done offhand, with two hands, and taking plenty of time. Good shooting is not fighting. Next you are ready for combat drills. As always let safety be your guide. Keep the finger off the trigger until you fire.

On the range we will be relaxed, calm and fully anticipating firing. When attacked on the street, an attack will precipitate the draw. There will be no bell or whistle. Just the same, realistic drills may be used that offer a reasonable approximation of the stress of combat. We can outpace the ability of the handgun or the shooter by rendering a contested drill so difficult only the most masterful handgunner will be able to achieve the goals. "What if five terrorists attack McDonalds" is an interesting scenario for an IDPA match but not realistic. Drills should be played out at realistic ranges, with the gear we carry on the street. If the pistol is primarily for home defense, then it should be at ready in the condition of readiness the handgun is normally kept in. If the pistol is kept chamber empty in the home, then range drills should begin chamber empty.

Over time the dense forest of interlocking branches of experience and judgment will give you both internal and external confidence. Those who see this confidence will not wish to test you. An encyclopedia could be written on successful tactics. I am attempting to condense forty years knowledge into a single book of less than five hundred pages. What I would like to do is convince the reader to think a few seconds ahead and perhaps realize that his pet tactics are not the ones that will save his life. We must crawl before we can walk and that means taking our time. Speed comes only with smoothness. You can go too fast and your movements become jerky and choppy.

First, the essential elements of marksmanship must be mastered. These are traditional and things become traditional because they work. Here are the elements that must be understood and applied. I risk repeating myself but these precepts are very important. Previously I mentioned grip and hand fit mainly as an aid in choosing a handgun. Let's take a hard look at these needed skills and how to direct their use to save your life.

The proper grip is very important in handling a .45-caliber handgun such as the Kimber Operator .45.

GRIP

The grip must be firm and consistent. A good firm handshake is often described as the proper handgun grip. A gauge of the proper grip is to grasp the handgun with all of your strength until your hands shake and then back off. That is your combat grip. The hand should meet the back strap properly in order to allow the trigger finger to reach the trigger and the pad of the finger should lie on the trigger face. A number of handguns are too large for some hands and nothing can be done except to change handguns.

The proper grip is essential to handgun accuracy. The competitor's grip is a two-hand grip that relaxes the firing hand more and often results in excellent accuracy. Sixty per cent of grip pressure is applied with the weak hand. This is an excellent all-around grip style.

STANCE

The firing stance is often described as a relaxed martial arts horse stance. The feet are about a yard apart with the firing side foot behind the other. We lean forward into the handgun slightly. We always use two hands except at very close range. The isosceles is simply the arms thrust forward to hold the handgun directly in front of our eyes.

The Weaver stance seems to have fallen into disfavor. I adopted the Weaver as a youth and this stance has served me well. The body is bladed to the target and the weak hand side elbow is slightly bent. The firing hand is extended and the weak hand pulls the handgun back to lock into isometric pressure that results in excellent shooting. The isosceles is faster to learn but with practice the Weaver is a very stable platform.

Our family member is practicing with the Taurus .44. This left-handed shooter can make the most of any available cover.

SIGHT PICTURE

This is the sight profile seen as we address our target. The sights should be clear with the front post in sharp focus as we allow our focus on the target to blur. Even if you do not perfectly align the sights, the front sight will carry the day. The six o'clock hold is holding the front post slightly under the aiming point, with the target partitioned as if it were the face of a clock. Some handguns are sighted for the six o'clock hold others work with the dead-on hold. Some handguns fire a little low or a little high in relation to the sights and we must practice with the handgun we carry. But the sight picture is always important.

SIGHT ALIGNMENT

Sight alignment is the proper relation of the front and rear sight. The front post must be centered in the rear notch. There must be an equal amount of light on each side of the front sight. Sight alignment is much less difficult with a good set of sights such as the Novak Lo Mount.

TRIGGER PRESS

Of all the skills necessary to becoming a proficient pistol shot, trigger press is the single most difficult to learn correctly. The trigger must be pressed cleanly and evenly as straight to the rear as possible. Consistently pressing the trigger is an art. You may have perfect sight alignment and jerk the trigger and miss by a mile! Learn to control the trigger by regular dry-fire practice. Do not jerk the trigger. If you are having problems with the trigger press, go to a remedial drill and use a good .22 until you are up to par.

I think that the single greatest fault among shooters who think they have mastered the trigger press is to push the handgun just before they fire. They do this in order to combat recoil and this push – not quite a flinch – is detrimental to accuracy.

FOLLOW-THROUGH

The handgun recoils while the bullet is still in the barrel. As the barrel recoils upward, the bullet is directed upward as well. Sights compensate for this to an extent but if you do not grip the handgun tightly as the piece fires, the shot will be off. Avoid the tendency to lessen your grip pressure after you release the trigger. Keep the pistol gripped tightly in order to not only keep the bullet flying straight to the target and also to prepare for the next shot. Control is critical. Follow-through is a keystone of handgun control and handgun accuracy. Follow-through is simply maintaining the grip.

ACCURATE SHOOTING

If you go to the range often or attend police qualifications, you will realize that most handgunners are not very good shots. I think that writers and trainers are responsible for not pushing shooters more in the accuracy department. Most handgunners are primarily interested in personal defense. They feel that the ability to strike a silhouette target at three to ten yards is adequate.

This type of complacency is a terrible waste of potential. You will feel much better about yourself if you excel with a handgun. You will be better prepared for a defensive encounter but just as importantly more able to appreciate the shooting sports as an enthusiast and perhaps a competitor. You will need a quality handgun. While price is not the only factor in choosing a handgun, remember: quality remains after the price is forgotten.

A service-grade handgun often sports adequate sights. You do not need target sights on a defensive pistol but you need good sights. Good sights and smooth trigger compression are a great aid. There are many variations on sights but Novak's Gunshop remains the company that produces the sights by which are others are measured. One of my Springfield pistols is fitted with a special wide rear notch and a gold bead front. Another Novak sight features a red fiber-optic front insert. This combination helps with aging eyes. A tight sight picture is counterproductive to true precision shooting. You need enough light to allow your eyes to center the front sight in the rear groove. Various combinations including three dot sights exist. The dots are a marginal aid to marksmanship and may be a hindrance in precision shooting, depending on the light conditions. The standard square post front and wide notch rear is often the best choice in combat shooting. The "2 2 2" sight picture exists when the rear notch and front post are of equal proportion. I prefer the "2 1 2" profile in which the front post is more narrow than the rear notch.

Two of my favorite handguns are fitted with Wilson Combat night sights. These sights are available on high end Wilson Combat handguns but are available for retrofit to the 1911 and the Glock. They give a good sight picture favored by seasoned shooters. Not long ago I decided to fit my much-used .38 Super with Wilson Combat sights. The difference was literally night and day. The pistol once was usable in good light now it is effective with no light. For best performance, a pistol has to have good sights. An example of poor all-around sights are found on the Glock pistol. These blocky sights have a sight picture too tight for anything but coarse shooting at close range. If you own a Glock, the Wilson Combat sight, much superior to the original Glock's, should be installed. A person who knows the way around the Glock may find that the Glock can become a 50-yard rather than a 25-yard pistol with the proper sights and proper trigger compression.

An important warning is that some stainless steel handguns have sights too bright for use in bright sunlight. Nickel-plated handguns are also a problem. Conversely, bright blue handguns also have a problem when the front sight is well worn and sunlight glints in reflection. These handguns often fire off a bit even at moderate range due to the glint, usually moving the proper point of impact in the opposite direction of the glare. In other words, glare off the left shoulder will move the point of impact to the right.

AVOID AREA AIMING!

One of the more counterproductive aiming problems is area aiming. I don't think anyone would aim at a whole deer when hunting. Rather we aim at the smallest part that will do the most damage. Similarly, aiming at the silhouette rather than the X ring produces poor results. Even with a matte silhouette with no clearly defined X ring you will aim for the center. In training, always aim for a relatively small area such as the heart lung area. The aiming point should be perhaps half the width of your front post. By aiming for a vital area and aiming for a small portion of the target, you will learn marksmanship faster.

By concentrating on the trigger and sights, your ability to engage small targets is greatly improved. The repeatability of your marksmanship will be established. Always keep this in mind, no matter how fast you are attempting to fire or how large or small the target. Aim for that minute area of the target that will show the most effect.

VARIETY

Always firing at the same type of target at the same range produces a dull and unskilled shooter. Fire at different types of targets at known and unknown distances. Firing from a solid benchrest is a good means of mastering trigger compression and sighting the piece in but has little to do with combat. Try the Uncle Mike's Dartboard Target for recreation and the realistic Law Enforcement Incorporated tactical design targets for practice. A bad habit is to consistently practice a certain drill because we are good at it. It is satisfying to grab the brass ring with consistency but you become a one- trick pony. If you are pleased with mediocre performance then you will remain a mediocre shooter.

For many years I was kept busy handloading just to keep up with my practice schedule. It was not unusual to fire five hundred rounds of .45 automatic in a week. I thought this was the fast train to Georgia. I learned rapid manipulation and gained real speed. This skill served me well in a half-dozen incidents. But I have come to realize it is not about making brass. It is a good rule to pretend that you have only one cartridge and that the shot you are firing is the only one that counts. When using the eight-shot .45, this is a useful totem to worship. I admit that I occasionally carry the 10mm or .38 Super and find the availability of an instant second shot appealing. When carrying the Browning High Power, I have a useful reserve of ammunition. But often as not I practice the one-shot, one-hit doctrine. That is the only doctrine that is really acceptable. A string of fire is not a string of shots fired as quickly as possible. It is a cadence of carefully aimed shots. Each shot in the string must be an aimed shot.

HANDGUN DRILLS

The following drills will build skill if properly practiced. Keep track of your results in a notebook in order to record your progress.

A simple but important drill is to draw from your chosen concealment holster and fire a single shot at seven yards. You must hit the X ring and you must do so in 1.5 seconds or less. Another drill is to draw and fire five rounds at the same distance. All should be in the X ring. Time is not as important when first beginning. Another useful drill is a double tap at seven yards in 1.8 seconds and a double tap at ten yards in

2.2 seconds. A single hit at seven yards in one second is a good standard that takes years to achieve. The author has achieved a consistent .92/second time to draw, fire and hit after many years of practice. These increments of .1 second or so are hard-won. Do not be discouraged. You can go too fast.

SMOOTHNESS

Smoothness is a product of much practice and the elimination of wasted motion. The first drills we should practice begin with the pistol in hand, held in front of our body. Drawing the pistol should be practiced only with an unloaded weapon until we are completely comfortable with using a "hot" pistol in self defense routines. Repetition is the mother of all smoothness and confidence and speed will build with good practice skills.

Beginning Drills

When we begin practice, our goal is to fear no man. That doesn't mean we will be arrogant but rather confident in our ability. That means diligent practice. The handgun will be held in front of the body. We will be squared to the target. The target, a man sized silhouette, will be placed at the seven yard line. This is not a completely realistic engagement, but by the same token we don't throw a young driver into freeway traffic, do we? We begin with standard loads that offer the lightest recoil in our handgun. This would be .38 Special 148-grain wadcutters in the .357 Magnum revolver, 230-grain generic ball in the .45 and 115-grain ball in the 9mm.

Be sure to save your brass. You will be firing hundreds of rounds of ammunition in practice. Winchester White Box or USA brand as it is known is a good practice ammunition source. Once you have accumulated at least five hundred brass cases you may choose to ship these cases to Black Hills ammunition (among others) for a terrific savings on remanufactured ammunition.

The First Shot

With the handgun at ready, we will raise the pistol to our eyes and fire a single carefully sighted shot. The bullet should land in the X ring. If not, remedial instruction is needed. Practice until those bullets eat the X ring out. One second is plenty for each shot. Five seconds, five shots. This is plain shooting, sure, not the type to win a contest, but it will save your bacon. Practice until bringing the handgun from ready, disengaging the safety, and pressing the trigger as the sight picture is held steady are second nature. With time, you may increase your speed. You are looking for smoothness. Addressing a stationary target that is squared to the shooter will build confidence in the handgun as well as muscle memory. The skills you learn at close range will transfer to advanced tactics at a later date.

Next, you will wish to move the target to ten yards. At the ten yard line, more accuracy is demanded of the shooter. The X ring now seems smaller. Our goal remains the same. Each and every shot must strike the X ring. There is no excuse for a missed shot, for with the proper attention to detail each shot will strike the point of aim. At ten yards, again work your way up the ladder in speed while maintaining accuracy. A good rule is that if the bullets are in a tight cluster, say, three inches or so, you are shooting too slowly. If the group is widely spread at eight inches or more you are shooting too fast for your ability. You will be able to gauge your results by this criteria. It is not a bad idea to save your targets, or at least the target centers. The targets will improve with time and you may discard earlier efforts as progress is noted.

The Double Tap

We are now ready to move to advanced tactics. The first tactic that I feel a shooter should use is the double tap. The double tap is best used at conversational range and may double the effect of a cartridge. The double tap is simply firing two rounds into the target as quickly as possible. Handguns are none too powerful and a second round, accurately delivered, is good insurance. Compared to a .223 rifle or the 12 gauge shotgun, the "weak" .38 and "strong" .45 handgun cartridges are more alike than they differ. Double tap when possible! The types of double taps and the differences in application should be understood. Never attempt to fire too quickly; we can all squeeze off shots faster than we can get hits. But with time and practice the double tap will be a formidable component of your defensive armory. Any target worth a shot is worth two!

The Double Tap is for all ranges past intimate range (three yards or more). The double tap is executed by firing in the normal matter at a target and then

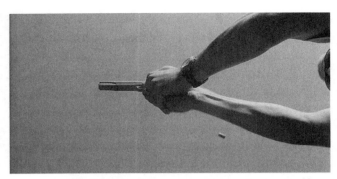
This shooter is practicing double taps with the 1911 .45. Note the case in the air and the pistol back on target.

bringing the sights back into focus as quickly as possible and firing again with a coarse sight picture.

The two shots may not impact in the same location but both will impact the threat. The front sight is most important in this drill.

The Hammer

The hammer is reserved for point-blank range. The pistol is thrust at the opponent at intimate range and fired twice as quickly as possible. I am aware of a case in which a defender fired in this manner and struck the adversary once in the thigh and once in the neck! Better control is needed but it worked for him. With the hammer, if an opponent is practically on top of you, two cartridges fired quickly will greatly increase your chances of registering an effective hit. The hammer is for ranges in which the shooters are practically nose to nose.

The Controlled Pair

The controlled pair requires more accuracy than the hammer or the double tap. The controlled pair means we will fire the first round with as much precision as possible, then bring the sights back into as sharp an alignment as with the first shot and fire again. There is an important distinction. A hammer hastily executed at three yards will miss. A double tap at ten yards could miss. A controlled pair is two controlled shots, suitable for any distance. Mastering the firing of two rounds as quickly as possible goes a long way in achieving proficiency with a handgun. If you do not bring the front sight completely back into alignment during recoil you will fire high every time. This is something that must be understood to be defeated.

Next, we will practice solving a problem from different angles. In all probability the threat will not be squared to you when the action begins. You may have turned your body away, always a good tactic. Moving the body to cant the shooting side away from the threat may introduce a level of surprise to the draw. Again, you are practicing with the handgun held in front of the body, not drawing from a holster at this point. You will walk along the range at three to seven yards and bring the pistol up to ready and fire quickly at the target. This is more advanced than firing from a position squared to the target and builds confidence in answering a threat originating from all angles of the compass.

THE DRAW

After we have built some confidence in handling the pistol safely, we will advance to working from the holster. This is a big step, so be certain you are completely ready. A great deal of dry-fire practice drawing an unloaded pistol should precede this decision.

You must feel completely comfortable in handling the pistol and safely drawing the handgun quickly from the holster. Speed is unimportant at this point and smooth motion is the ideal. There are a number of holsters designed specifically for this use. Called "range holsters," these vary from the simple belt slide to the retention screw rig from Nevada Gunleather. The Rogers style holster offered by this company is one of my favorites.

Range scabbards have little purpose beyond carrying the handgun on the range. They have a deeper offset from the body than service or concealment holsters and theoretically are safer to use. I am not willing to admit safety is anywhere other than between the ears, but these holsters do offer a simpler draw than concealed carry holsters. Beginning with a range holster is the recommended course. You can practice with a concealed carry holster with a triple-checked unloaded firearm until the concealed carry draw – a much more complex issue – is mastered. The range holster allows a beginner to practice with less frustration.

Remember, I am not creating a Wild Bill Hickock with this instruction but an interested individual who can save his or her life. Simple drills perfectly executed over a period of time will pay bid dividends in proficiency. The addition of the draw to the previous drills is a big step, one that must be approached with caution. With proper attention to the rules of

The concealed carry draw is demanding. We must be careful not to entangle the shirttail, gun and holster.

safety, the course is a safe one. There is an element of danger in range work but with proper precautions, all will be well.

An area of instruction that is often overlooked is the proper clothing. On the range when you begin practice you wish to deploy with attire that will not interfere with the draw. A shirt that rides out of your trousers or blousey shirtsleeves may be an impediment. Such attire deters your advancement in both a physical and a mental manner. You will advance to a concealed carry draw at a later date and deal with drawing from beneath covering garments. But when beginning to practice the draw, the less of a challenge to economy of motion, the better.

The Combat Draw

The draw is as simple or complicated as you make it. Simple is best. We begin to practice the draw standing perfectly erect and our hand in front of our chest. The elbow of our firing hand shoots to the rear. The hand scoops the pistol out of the holster quickly with a firm grip and continues forward to meet the support hand in front of our belt buckle. The support hand and firing hand lock on the handgun and the handgun is pressed forward. The handgun continues on to the firing position. The draw sets not only the hand grip but also sight acquisition.

The draw is very important to combat marksmanship. There are ruinous steps to be avoided. This includes going to the handgun, stopping, and then beginning the draw. A scooping motion works. The fingers come up under the handle and scoop the handgun from the holster. A variation on the draw is the one-hand draw and fire, eliminating the step of meeting the weak side hand. This is acceptable at very close range. The concealed carry draw is more difficult. I have executed a high speed draw from concealed carry under stress and fired an accurate and necessary shot. It is a difficult chore at best. If you have not practiced hard and often, this type of draw and shoot is impossible.

Specialized Draws

There are variations on the basic draw. As an example, when you are carrying the holster in an inside-the-waistband holster under a sports shirt or T-shirt, the gun hand goes to the handgun as the support hand sweeps the clothing up, allowing better access. In some cases the firing hand will go under the shirt and draw the handgun. When drawing from under a jacket from a strong side holster, the firing hand is bladed and slips under the jacket. The firing hand protects the handgun from snagging on outer garments.

The author demonstrates the crossdraw.

the crossdraw is handier for the adversary than the shooter, and there is some truth in this. But many gun grabs are rearward-originating as well. Some martial artists rely on the crossdraw and feel they are better able to defend the holstered handgun by using their strong side arm for blows and protecting the handgun with the weak side arm. There is some controversy involved, but the person who carries a crossdraw holster often is a very experienced individual who knows what he needs and realizes the shortcomings and the advantages of the type.

There is one disadvantage of the crossdraw that is difficult to address. When we draw from a strong-side holster, we draw into the adversary. In other words we draw against the length of his body. If we fire too soon we may strike a knee or if we fire late we may strike the head. When drawing crossdraw, we draw across the width of the body and a jerked shot has much greater chance of an outright miss. Add to this the slowness of crossdraw and there is a problem. But on the other hand you may not be able to draw from strong side at all when seated.

There are two crossdraw techniques, one the far superior but each is situational. The standard and seated crossdraw involves reaching across the body to the handgun. Remember you cannot simply place a strong side holster on the weak side and effect a crossdraw. The crossdraw holster must be properly designed with the correct tilt for a good sharp draw. Ted Blocker's classic crossdraw designs and the Haugen Handgun Leather Wedge each offer first class crossdraw designs. When the strong hand reaches to the handgun, the weak side arm moves out of the way. The pistol is drawn and then pivoted into a correct firing alignment and the weak side hand meets the strong side in front of the belt.

An alternative is much faster and sharper but requires tactical awareness to execute. The former draw is often practiced against stationary targets that we are squared to. If we are aware of a threat coming, a superior option is to blade ourselves to the threat. We simply reach down to the holstered pistol and present it straight up into the waiting hand of the weak side arm. The pivoting in front of the body is eliminated and weakhand travel shortened. For those who prefer the crossdraw, this is a first-class, sharp draw that meets many needs.

The shoulder holster draw is fairly simple but much of how well you succeed on the shoulder holster draw depends on the proper holster. In the shoulder holster draw the hand shoots across the chest and the support arm is directed straight up as much as possible and out of the way of the gun hand. Then, when the pistol is on the way toward the targe,t the support hand will meet the gun hand.

The crossdraw has been criticized and the shoulder holster draw can be criticized on the same counts. However, in some situations the crossdraw is an outstanding option. The crossdraw holster allows the wearer to be instantly ready for action when seated. Those who are seated behind a desk or in a vehicle for long periods of time are well served by a crossdraw holster. There is an argument that

If we draw from a position bladed to the threat and bring the handgun into the support hand quickly, speed and accuracy are much better.

When drawing from a conventional crossdraw position, the pistol sweeps across the target and a miss is more likely. Practice diligently if you adopt crossdraw carry.

If you adopt pocket carry, be certain to draw with a bladed hand. If you make a fist in the pocket, the draw will be difficult.

A final note: carefully consider your needs when addressing the crossdraw. We will address holster types at a later point but I wish everyone to understand the proper draw for each type.

POCKET CARRY

Pocket carry is very popular. I prefer belt carry, especially the inside-the-waistband, for concealed carry but so many armed citizens use pocket carry I would be remiss not to include this draw. The pocket carry draw is simple. Blade your hand into the pocket and carefully bring the pistol out with only finger pressure. Do not make a fist in the pocket. If you do you will not be able to draw the handgun. Blade the fingers in and take the proper grip as soon as the pistol's handle clears the pocket. Practice both the proper and the wrong way a few times and you will easily see my point. Blade the hand into the pocket and bring the pistol's handle out with only open finger pressure. Take the grip as soon as your hand clears the pocket.

I have used this draw extensively with Mika's Pocket Holster and it works well. If you must angle the holster against the pocket in some way to clear the handgun, be certain you do so in every practice draw.

ANKLE CARRY

I prefer ankle carry as a backup type of carry and do not recommend this concealment mode as a primary carry. There are surprising advantages of ankle carry, especially for the seated person. Ankle carry is a poor choice for most females. Women's fashion and body type usually do not work well with ankle carry. The proper ankle carry draw is to quickly go down on one knee, the strongside knee. The ankle holster is normally worn on the weak side with the handgun on the inside of the leg. Once we are kneeling the weak hand pulls up the trouser leg and the firing hand quickly runs under the trouser leg and draws the pistol. The weak hand engages the handgun with the strong hand and if necessary the shooter stands up. As may be expected this is not a draw that may be executed quickly.

An alternative if you have a wall, fence or vehicle available is to lean against the structure as you raise the ankle to the gun hand and draw the pistol. Alternatively the draw is very fast from a seated position. You may set calmly with your legs crossed when seated and have your hand on the pistol. As many seasoned cops know, when seated in a patrol vehicle the ankle draw is more accessible than the strong side holster. If you are knocked down you can bring your weak side to the firing hand and draw the pistol.

In closing I wish to stress that ankle carry is seldom the best choice for primary carry but is a number one choice for carry of the backup pistol. If you are going to use an ankle holster use a good one. I am currently using the DeSantis Apache with good results.

APPENDIX CARRY

Appendix carry is controversial but presently is enjoying a certain vogue. I have experimented with appendix carry and find that it works well with a compact handgun and properly designed holster. A tall individual may have more success with larger types of handguns. For a snubnosed .38 or Glock 19, appendix draw works well. The handgun is carried near the front of the trousers between the right pocket and belt buckle with the butt facing the pocket. To draw, simply raise the shirt with the weak side hand and draw the handgun. It is important you understand the need to offset the handle from the body and draw the handgun away from the body. During this time the muzzle is aimed at irreplaceable parts of the body, but then I do not wish a perforation anywhere on my person. The appendix carry seems to incorporate the best aspects of strong side and crossdraw carry and is a viable carry position and draw for certain body types.

DIFFERENT DRILLS

When experienced shooters discuss the draw they often neglect to observe that the draw is a lead-in to the proper grip and sight picture. Draw, grip, sight picture, trigger press, and you get a hit. Do not flinch from that conclusion! The handgun is drawn and the sights are moved into the focal plane and your shot is taken if needed.

I cannot remember where I first saw the draw diagrammed but there are well defined components of the draw that must be understood. This is a version reflecting the components of a one and one half second draw.

In quarter seconds these are the components of a draw:

.25 Reaction. The draw is instigated by an attack.

.25 The hand moves to the weapon.

.25 The grip is taken.

.25 The actual draw.

.25 The hands and the handgun are locked.

.25 The sights are aligned and the weapon fired.

Do not become married to the concept of firing every time you draw. Practice the draw without a shot and the draw with a shot so that the shot becomes a conscious decision.

With the basics and the draw in your arsenal of tactics you may move to the practice of more advanced tactics, always with a focus on the fundamentals. As we advance to firing at stationary targets from different angles we will build familiarity with the weapon. Absolute familiarity is the goal. The ability to quickly deploy the weapon and make a center hit is what counts. With constant practice and attention to the fundamentals, you will find that the work you have put into building competency is more important than the particular choice of weapon. Be familiar with the trigger action sights and controls of the chosen pistol.

There are other issues related to close quarters battle that we will address later. General tactics and marksmanship are addressed in this chapter. After a time, you will be surprised with the good results you achieve on the range. You will reach a plateau that will require considerable practice to rise above. Do not become overconfident at this point. We can all achieve better results and we all must practice to retain our skills.

When addressing the silhouette realize that this paper form is designed to mimic a man about 5' 10" and 190 lbs. It is fine for most practice. Reduced silhouette targets are good for reduced ranges especially in indoor ranges and may aid in building skill. You are always aiming for a specific point, not the whole area. No matter how close or how large the target place the bullet where it will do the most good. Area aiming will produce hits somewhere on the target but not necessarily in a part of the body that will produce good effect. A peripheral hit not only is seldom effective, it may supercharge the assailant with anger! Certain addictive drugs are based on painkillers and many criminals have a full medicine cabinet.

As we advance in practice, it is a good idea to partially obscure the target. Several target systems are available that will block part of the target, some even offer paper approximations of brick walls as an aid in simulating cover. The Duelatron targets offer changeable modules that are excellent for training. As an example, a man-sized target is presented realistically as a man wearing a suit and a pistol in his hand. By placing an overlay on the target, the gun becomes a harmless radio. This makes for excellent training in decision building. Shoot and no shoot drills are important. We must not be a robot and fire every time we draw.

There is every chance a felon will seek cover but remain a threat. You may be faced with only a small part of the adversary exposed. An elbow or an ankle may be your target. If this is the shot you have take it. It will be painful if not final and may end the fight. I have been struck in the lower leg by a 9mm bullet and while this was a light wound it was painful and my muscles immediately locked up in that limb. The core fully penetrated my leg and the bullet jacket simply lay in a trough in the wound. (It was a ricochet.) Suffice it to say, it got my attention.

Practice firing at small targets at moderate range, from seven to ten yards, advancing to fifteen yards in gradual increments as skill allows. I consider the ability to strike a knee, foot or elbow size target at fifteen yards an important skill. The gun and the hand may be stretched around cover firing at you, and this too presents a considerable difficulty in marksmanship. Most defense situations do not present a severe marksmanship problem. The difficulty is deploying the weapon quickly and producing a hit under stress.

Other situations while more rare demand much more from the shooter. Moving targets can be quite a problem if we consider motor-propelled targets at thirty miles per hour or more. But for most situations, the math is simpler. A person who is a threat will probably be stabilized and firing at you, but if he is on the move between cover, you should have skills on hand to enable you to connect. Consider the facts: this threat is unlikely to be moving at more than five miles per hour. At ten yards, a person moving at this speed can move four inches from the time you press the trigger and send a 800 fps bullet toward him. Most handgun bullets are faster than 800 fps, and the felon may not be moving straight across the line of sight; he may be running toward you or away from you while firing. The problem is usually not difficult. A person traveling at three miles per hour and facing a 1,300 fps bullet is even less of a problem. The solution is simple. Place the front sight on the forward leading edge of the target in the direction of his motion and squeeze the trigger. Do not stop leading when you break the shot. Follow the target with the front sight and even after you press the trigger continue leading. To lead, then jerk the shot and stop the pistol's motion is to ensure a miss.

Does it work? I have rolled dozens of old tires down a hill in practice to perfect this art and it works like nobody's business. I have also fired this drill on advanced moving targets at the range. But be prepared for an instant second shot. We don't spray and pray; we aim each bullet – but sometimes the ability to instantly recover and fire again is a lifesaver.

FAILURE TO STOP DRILLS

On many occasions the threat doesn't go down with the first or second shot. There are many theories on this problem. Small caliber failure is the most common reason for failures to stop. The only

constant we can be certain of is that failures occur. Failures to stop occur less with big bore cartridges and Magnums but they have been documented with practically every pistol caliber and even shoulder fired weapons such as the 12 gauge shotgun and .30-06 rifle.

There are two basic remedies to stop a threat that won't go down. First, we must realize that we may have missed! The first shots may not have hit the target or struck anything important. The first shot is the most important. There is considerable evidence that once the nervous system has endured an initial shock subsequent shots are even less effective. When this happens our only chance is for a nervous system hit. This means the spine or the brain. The head shot is sometimes criticized as very difficult but I am not certain that is true. If the adversary is firing at you chances are his head is stabilized as he looks over the gun sight. The head is no more difficult a target than the heart. But you must have sufficient time in to feel confident with this type of shot. The following failure to stop drills will address the problem, and you may develop your own drills as benefits your situation. Consider your likely scenario and your own level of expertise. But I believe that the drills I have set forth in these pages are a good starting place.

Once we have fired two rounds (a double tap) into the torso with no effect, we might reasonably expect that two or four more would serve no better. If the opponent is armored this is especially true. The point of focus is changed to the head and a cranial shot taken. The proper point of aim is the bridge of the nose. Higher or lower shots may not be effective. I am aware of a failure of a 110-grain .38 Special bullet to penetrate a skull in such a situation, but the shot did knock the threat senseless for a few minutes. The bullet fully expanded on the skull. In another case a .45 caliber 230-grain hardball bullet struck the skull at a curving angle and actually traveled under the skin exiting near the rear of the skull. Numerous examples exist of lower jaw hits without appreciable immediate effect. The head shot is a last-ditch effort that must be delivered to the right spot.

A second choice, especially for those less sure of their marksmanship, is the pelvic shot. There are heavy bones in the pelvic area that once broken will not support the body. There is some evidence that a pelvic shot is the most painful of body wounds. If the first shots to the chest do not take effect, the point of aim is redirected and two rounds fired into the pelvic area. This is also taught in a slightly different style by some as the "chicken beak shot" with an upside down triangle shot the ideal placement. Two to the belt line and one to the center groin.

When wearing body armor there are areas of the body that must be free of restriction and chafing. These exposed areas are the only target areas that will prove profitable when confronting an armored felon. Body armor is occasionally encountered among the criminal class. Some may have obtained conventional body armor and others may have home made surprisingly effective armor.

The drills explained and illustrated are fairly simple but practice is demanded in this implementation. At this point perhaps you should set this work aside and come back to it after a few days of range work. With sufficient range time invested you will appreciate the worthiness of the drills we have outlined. This is not a book to be finished in one setting. Take your time and absorb the basics. Do your range work and discuss the results.

ADVANCED DRILLS

We all have a weakness that we tend to ignore. For example, weak-hand firing is a challenge for the author. I suffered an on-duty injury that was difficult to recover from and to add insult to injury as a young man I had broken this arm and required two surgeries to repair the limb. As a result, weak-hand shooting is not my best point. But there are so many well-designed modern pistols that are fully ambidextrous I decided to go on a crash program and get up to snuff with the weak hand. I felt that weak-hand shooting would be an important addition to the book. This was the sweat and blood of the volume. I often carry my Browning High Power Practical Model in a Watch Six holster from Milt Sparks. The High Power is just a bit flatter than a 1911, allowing me to carry it without resorting to a handgun with less inherent accuracy when I need something thinner than the 1911. I wear the pistol strong-side but I can easily reach and draw the pistol with my weak-side hand. After a few weeks practice and plenty of ammunition I was surprisingly adept with the weak hand.

Just as the repentant have favorite sins they are loathe to lay aside, many of us lack certain skills and we are loathe to practice these to achieve proficiency. A fellow who excels at deliberate fire might ace qualifications with consistency and find the hostage rescue drill is not a challenge. A young lady of unusual dexterity might draw quickly and engage multiple targets with double taps in the blink of an eye. Both are very good at what they excel at, but are they good all-around shooters? We all like to prove ourselves capable on the range. But we also must practice those skills that challenge us in every way. Personally that means weak-hand fire. A quick canvas of my shooting friends and students shows that most of us who practice on our own time on our own dime do so to the exclusion of the weak hand. Some qualifications require a certain amount of weak-hand fire and this measure of qualification often plays hell with a perfect score.

All humans are naturally dominant with one hand or the other. (And one eye or the other as well.) Most shooters are right-handed. Left-handed shooters number about one in five. The natural incidence of left-handed individuals may be much higher but cultural mores and parental pressure often result in naturally left-handed people being trained as right-handed shooters. I write with the left hand and play baseball with the left hand but I use my right hand with handguns. Left-handed shooters are often far more capable with the weak hand than right-handed shooters. The reason is simple: this is a right-handed world. Vehicle stick shifts and public facilities cater to the right-handed person.

Left-handed shooters often progress quickly in weak-hand drills because they have been challenged by this right-handed world. I could cite numerous incidents in which the dominant hand has been injured or otherwise occupied, resulting in the need for weak-hand fire. I am aware of two incidents in which the combatants were shot in the gun hand in the first few seconds of battle. One was a shooting in Florida in which a female deputy was wounded in her gun hand but switched her Glock .45 to the weak hand and finished the business.

The affects of aging and injury also may indicate a need to learn to fire well with both hands. When considering weak-hand use I am primarily concerned with tactical on-the-spot transition. The injury I mentioned left my non-dominant side weaker than usual, resulting in a long climb to normal life and proficiency with the handgun. The normal ratio of strength in the strong side versus the weak side arm is about seventy-five percent of the strength in the weak side as is found in the strong-side hand and arm. At one point after my injury my ratio was about forty percent. Even today my ratio of strength in the weak side is lower than normal. As a result, non-dominant-hand fire has been challenging. I find it interesting I have not found recoil objectionable during this work and I have come to understand that pain is different from weakness. When practicing weak-hand fire, remember that tactical problems are train wrecks coming at you without warning. One advantage in being able to use either hand well is that you will be able to fire from cover with more versatility. There are times when you will need to use the non-dominant hand as when a right-handed shooter may need to fire around a left-hand corner. A left-hand corner presents different problems. We are not talking about producing small groups on paper targets with weak-hand fire but controlling the weapon and making hits at combat distance.

There are many reasons for learning to use the non-dominant hand. You may be driving or even aiding a wounded comrade and need to draw and fire with the weak hand. Quite a few agencies and shooting schools demand at least some indoctrination in weak-hand fire although one seasoned trainer tells me there is not enough time to cover the basic skills, much less a difficult skill such as using the weak hand well!

You cannot expect proficiency to come quickly. First, realize that the odds of becoming an equally good shot with either hand are slim. Those who lift weights and do pushups on a daily basis will have a great advantage. They exhibit far less bias between limbs. The best advice I can give in learning the weak hand is to forget all you have learned and begin anew. Practice the firing grip with the weak hand as if you had never held a handgun. Don't be frustrated; you are no longer an expert but you are a novice once again when learning non-dominant hand drills.

A warning: when using a light trigger action that is perfectly controllable with the strong-side hand, you will find that you might double inadvertently when firing with the weak hand. Firing the second shot when you do not mean to fire a double tap can be dangerous. Be careful!

SPEED LOADING

Quickly replenishing the handgun is a learned skill that is easily accomplished on the range. We load between each drill and if we fire often we become familiar with reloading quickly. But speed loading may also be practiced in the home.

Whether or not it is worthwhile for anyone not heavily involved in competition to learn to reload the handgun in less than two seconds can be answered only by that individual. I have debriefed numerous gunfight survivors including military men who have used the pistol. Two to three rounds is the rule. If you do not get your man with the first few rounds or get to cover, your battle is probably over. But this statistic reminds one of the person who drowned in a creek of an average three-foot depth: statistics are not very comforting to those in such a position. There have been occasions when a rapid reload was needed.

With the practically universal issuing of the semi-automatic pistol in police circles, there are more shots being fired per incident, but I am not certain the problems faced are significantly different. The criminal class definitely fires more ammunition and misses at ridiculously close range. We need to be able to quickly replenish the handgun if need be. I have often stressed that an advantage of the semi-automatic handgun is not necessarily that the automatic holds more rounds but that it is easier to keep in action. There is nothing wrong with carrying a revolver. But those who carry a revolver should carry at least one gunload as a spare. If I were carrying a revolver in personal defense, as a park ranger, or in armed security, I would carry two speed loaders. You are not serious if you do not carry speed loaders. Belt loops don't cut it!

Speed loaders are mechanical devices that hold a cylinderful of ammunition. You load the speed loader, twist a knob to lock the ammunition in place, and store it in an appropriate holder. Leather, Kydex and fabric speed loader carriers are available. The softer the better for concealed carry. These speed loaders should be carried on the same side as the revolver.

Let's go over a speed load for the revolver. I can almost guarantee you have been doing it wrong.

First, the revolver is fired empty. The thumb goes to the cylinder release and the weak hand moves into place to grasp the revolver. As the revolver is trans-

When making a rapid reload, we first angle the magazine into the magazine well and then. . .

. . .press the magazine home.

ferred to the non-dominant hand, four fingers from the weak hand go into the frame window where the cylinder was and the thumb moves on the outside of the frame to the open crane and presses the ejector rod. The revolver muzzle must be pointed upwards into the air at this time in order to ensure the spent cases are thrown clear.

Make certain all cartridges clear the revolver. Snubnosed revolvers with short ejector rods sometimes do not completely eject the case. The revolver may be wriggled to convince these cartridge cases to disembark. The strong side hand now goes to the speed loader pouch. Here is where most of us mess up! During this operation the muzzle of the revolver must be pointed straight down. Do not grasp the speed loader by the loading knob but run your fingers down to just over the speed loader body and partially onto the cartridges. This makes for much better control. Seat the bullets as far as possible into the cylinder and twist the speed loader retention knob. The cartridges fall into the cylinder. Drop the speed loader and snap the cylinder shut as the revolver is grasped in the firing hand. You're good to go!

SEMI-AUTOMATIC PISTOL SPEED LOAD

In a properly functioning semi-automatic pistol the slide will lock to the rear on the last round, indicating the pistol is empty. As the shooting thumb presses the magazine release and drops the spent magazine, the support hand leaves the pistol and moves to the magazine carrier. (Heel-clip magazine release pistols such as the Heckler & Koch P7 and Walther P-38 demand a different technique. The weak hand first pulls the magazine out of the handgun as the heel-based catch is operated.) The carrier is properly worn on the non-dominant side with the bullets in the magazine pointed forward. For concealed carry most of us carry a single magazine behind the hip.

If you use a double magazine carrier, the second magazine must be pointed to the rear or the magazine stop, the protruding sheet metal piece on the bottom of the magazine, will conflict with the other magazine. The support hand grasps the magazine with the trigger finger of the support hand leading down the side of the magazine. The hand moves to the handgun and the magazine is angled into the

magazine well against the flat of the magazine housing and moved briskly upward led by the finger of the support hand. The magazine doesn't have to be slapped into place. I cant the magazine into the magazine well at an angle and then press it firmly to lock. The slide lock may be released, or as I prefer, the rear of the slide pulled to the rear and released. The grasping and releasing of the slide are far less demanding of fine motor movement when you are under great stress. You are ready to fire.

The tactical reload is a different type technique stressed in competition. Many trainers feel that it is vital never to run dry during combat. In the tactical reload you have fired the handgun but not fired it to slide lock. You may not be certain how many rounds you have left in the handgun and you wish to replenish your ammunition supply. The magazine that is in the pistol is released and captured by the support hand and the support hand moves to store this magazine while drawing a fully loaded magazine and inserting it into the magazine well. I am not certain I have much truck with this type of load. I think most of us will shoot the handgun empty during a fight. I am not certain we will be able to count our rounds during a fight either.

I do, however, like the idea of instilling magazine discipline into a student. The tactical load is important enough to a number of trainers that I respect their opinion. The loading sequence should be practiced at every range session – what better opportunity? While a second gunload may not be needed very often, if you do need to reload you need to reload quickly.

VERBAL WARNINGS

At this point we will leave the mechanical behind and consider practical and mental aspects of personal defense. As a peace officer I often used verbal judo. I worked with good trainers who taught me how to communicate with street people and felons as well as ordinary citizens in trouble. As a twenty-one-year-old cop I had confidence but by the time I was twenty-three I sometimes thought I had walked into shoes two sizes too large.

One thing you must never allow the adversary to do is confuse your demeanor with determination. If he does not see determination in your eyes he will make a move. I also would like to warn those who feel they are formidable individuals, the 6'2" strapping types. As a peace officer I learned that those who challenge formidable opponents are usually armed. Most street toughs pick easier victims and only those who are armed pick on those who could fight back.

Some of us are more socially adept than others. When dealing with those who threaten us with violence, few of us know how to respond. Often an apology works, giving the individual nothing to continue complaining about. There are situations in which words can help or hurt.

Let's look at the serious business of de-escalating violence. Sometimes "drop the gun" or "get out of my house" works. Verbal commands are an important part of your personal defense strategy. Sometimes there is neither time nor need for words. If you are being shot at or the adversary is assaulting you, the time for words has passed. But there are times when you may have a favorable defensive position, such as behind cover. You may be able to avoid taking action.

During my time in uniform I used verbal commands practically every day. I have seen officers struggle and grapple with offenders because the offender seemed not to know what the officer wanted him to do. I have seen officers attempting to take down subjects work at cross purposes, with one pulling the man one way and the other officer another.

This experience reminds me of a bad joke:

Cop: Freeze! Drop the gun!

Felon: Do you want me to freeze or drop the gun?

Be careful of your words. Witnesses can go from hot to cold at the drop of a hat. As a rule juries are fair and intelligent but lean toward the underdog. No one likes a bully. Be clear and firm in your instructions. At home have an open 911 line as soon as possible if you have an intruder; this is a good recording device.

Be careful of the connotation of your words. "Don't make me shoot," sounds weak, as if you are not prepared. Far better is the statement, "Leave now or I will shoot!" There is no confusion in this statement. You are prepared. The subject must know you are competent and willing to stop him. Tell him clearly what you wish him to do. If we are attacked, we must stop the threat.

If the adversary is warned, he will usually leave. If you are not a law officer, do not pursue him. When verbal commands are followed by an incentive to behave, they work best. Incorporate these commands into your training sessions as your skill progresses. For many years the National Rifle Association has collected studies of self-defense incidents involving firearms. The NRA states that the vast majority of confrontations with burglars and robbers are decided in the favor of the armed citizen without a shot being fired. That is a good goal to reach for.

7 Malfunction Clearance Drills

Modern handguns are very reliable but there are variables in their operation. Let's face it: there is nothing perfect on earth. There are many reasons for a handgun malfunction and some of them are beyond the control of the shooter.

Environmental and ammunition problems can stop your handgun from functioning. Improper maintenance is the usual culprit but a poor grip, limp wristing and substandard ammunition can produce a malfunction, too. Fortunately, semi-auto malfunctions are simple to clear. True jams that cannot be easily cleared are rare. As for the revolver, the problems that will take a revolver out of action are more time-consuming to clear. We will discuss these. You could easily be shot while clearing a malfunction, so practice these drills and commit each to muscle memory. If possible, dart to cover when you experience a malfunction. Always carry a spare gun load of ammunition. If the threat level is low, many shooters who should know better carry only the load in the gun. While a high-capacity 9mm or a nine-shot .45 can be comforting, if you do not have a spare magazine you may not be able to get the pistol back in action if a jam is experienced. A second gun as a backup is never a bad idea.

SEMI-AUTO MALFUNCTIONS

The most common malfunction is a failure in the feed cycle. The pistol may short-cycle, with the round partly in the chamber but not quite seated. Another common malfunction is a spent case caught in the ejection port and the port closed on this case, creating a stoppage. (This is the so-called "stovepipe" jam.) Weak or improperly-sized ammunition is one explanation for this problem but just as often the shooter has failed to properly grip the firearm and provide a firm platform for it to recoil against. I have observed spent cartridges bouncing off the barricade and jumping back into the slide window, causing a failure to feed and trapping the cartridge in the slide.

This young woman is keeping her Kel-Tec turned to one side at close range in order to avoid a spent case bouncing back into the ejection port and to avoid contacting her body with the slide.

I am not certain what the odds are of such an occurrence but I have seen a dozen or so over the years.

Another problem is simply a dud round: the hammer has dropped and the primer has been struck but the cartridge has failed to fire. While most common with handloads, I have seen fresh, high-quality factory ammunition fail to fire on occasion. This malfunction must be cleared immediately. Occasionally you may find that the magazine is not properly seated and not feeding correctly. Poor holster designs allow the holster to contact the magazine release button, allowing a magazine to partially drop. Poor gunhandling also produces this problem.

The standard drill to address the common short cycle stovepipe and dud problems is the tap-rack-bang. This drill is as simple as it sounds. Tap the bottom of the magazine to ensure the magazine is properly seated, rack the slide with the pistol canted to one side in order allow the dud round or spent case to clear, and then bang as the trigger is pulled. Tap-rack-bang! A variation taught by Larry J. Nichols was shared with us in print in the journal *Voice of*

American Law Enforcement and deserves attention. The drill begins with ripping the magazine out of the pistol and inserting a new magazine during the "tap" component of the tap-rack-bang drill. This will cure any magazine related problems – but you had better have a spare magazine on your belt for this drill.

Let's go over the tap-rack-bang:

1) TAP the base of the magazine. Be certain the magazine is seated properly.
2) RACK the slide to clear the chamber. Be certain the chamber is cleared and a fresh round inserted.
3) BANG! That's obvious; press the trigger.

Some malfunctions are more complex. The extractor may fail to snap over a cartridge's rim so that it will not be pulled from the chamber, or a slide override may have tied a round up in the feedway. These are more difficult to address. A long thin Kubotan or dejammer type tool is useful for ramming down the barrel and clearing a bullet lodged partway therein. A dud round that leaves a bullet in the barrel is rare with modern quality ammunition, but it happens on the range with regularity, most often with contaminated ammunition. Such problems with handloads are far more common.

The tap-rack-bang drill covers most of what are known as Type 1 malfunctions. Type 2 malfunctions, the stovepipes, are more complex. I see stovepipe ejections pretty often. Quality ammunition of sufficient power to actuate the pistol and a good firm grip will prevent most stovepipe jams.

The first indication of the Type 2 is a dead trigger. A cartridge case will be caught in the ejection port. The best means of addressing a Type 2 is to tap the magazine, rack the slide and flip the pistol to one side to clear the malfunction. The rack and flip are done simultaneously.

Type 3 malfunctions, failure to eject, are much more involved. I have seen good shots with mediocre gunhandling skills stopped cold on the range with this one. Even those who have practiced the Type 3 malfunction clearance drill may be caught short when it actually occurs. The spent case is still in the chamber and a new round is attempting to feed from the magazine. This is a difficult jam that seldom occurs, but when it does you have more of a true jam than a mere malfunction.

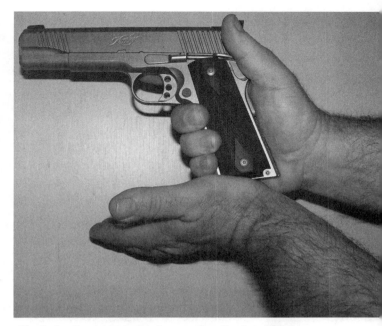

The first action taken in clearing a malfunction is to TAP the magazine.

Tap, Rack, BANG!

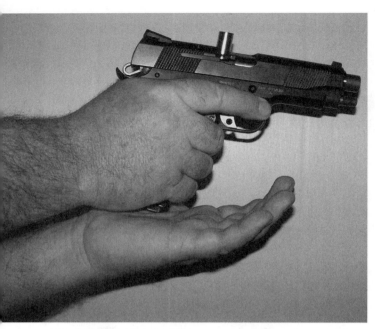

With the case in the ejection port, you may have to turn the handgun on its side to clear the case.

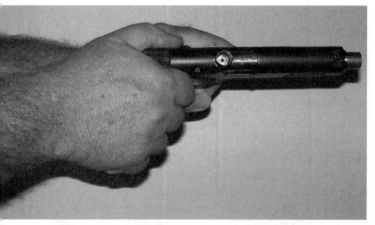

Here, the SW1911 is turned on its side to clear a spent case.

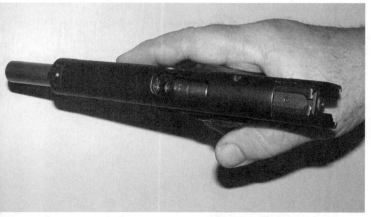

To clear a Type 3 malfunction, you first ascertain that a case had not ejected and you have a double feed. The magazine is removed first.

To clear a Type 3 malfunction, follow these steps. First, drop the magazine into the weak hand. Either secure the magazine in a carrier or pocket or place the magazine between the fingers of the firing hand. Determine which you are comfortable with and practice the same drill time and time again. After removing the magazine, rack the slide very quickly and strongly three times. Naturally if you see the case ejected once is enough but in practice I rack three times. This should clear the spent case. I recently tested a factory new pistol that refused to extract at least one round from each magazine. In every case a single rack cleared the problem. I was able to tune the extractor and cure the problem at a later date- but instant action drills saved my range time. If the case rim is torn off or the case will not eject, well, the long Kubotan or a very strong steel pen is a life saver. Or a backup handgun. Type 3s are rare in that I seldom see them but they are especially rare with high quality ammunition and handguns. Type 3s have been observed in practically every handgun type.

A malfunction that occurs fairly often in breaking in new handguns is a failure to go into battery – that is, failure for the slide to return to its fully-forward position. This can occur when using weakly loaded ammunition or when the shooter does not grasp the handgun tightly enough. An automatic pistol needs a solid platform to recoil against. When the slide does not go into battery, simply press it forward with the weak-hand thumb against the slide so as not to disturb your firing grip. If this malfunction occurs after the first one hundred rounds of ammunition in a well lubricated pistol using quality ammunition, something is wrong.

Never neglect to properly lubricate the handgun. Some miss an important point concerning lubrication. The handgun need only be lightly lubricated for carry. But for range work in which you may fire a hundred rounds or more, heavier lubrication or even grease is needed. A tip: if the handgun functions properly during the first few magazines then begins to short cycle, the pistol needs lubrication. If it malfunctions during the first few magazines and then smoothes out, it needed a break-in.

When you look at the problem of clearing malfunctions, consider what may happen and do not be caught flat-footed. You need to set up malfunctions

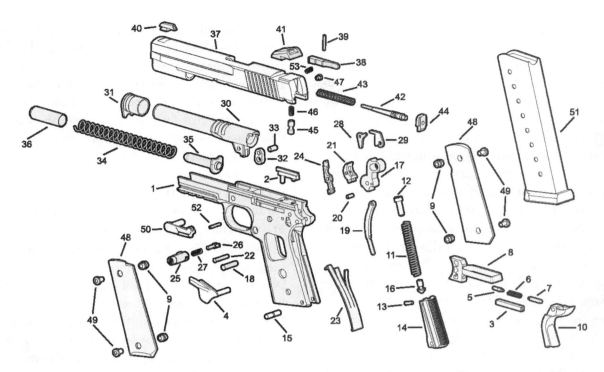

You really must be completely familiar with the handgun and how it works in order to avoid malfunctions and fix what comes up. An exploded drawing for each handgun (such as this 1911) is recommended.

with STI PRO dummy cartridges or a homemade dud round to learn to address these situations. (STI PRO rounds have an orange nose and shiny case and look like toy bullets although they are quite robust and last many chamberings.) Have a friend load one of these safety cartridges in your practice magazines at random. You will fire a few rounds and then have an unexpected malfunction. Learning to clear these duds is important. You say your handgun has never malfunctioned? Great! That is all the more reason to practice malfunction drills because you do not know how because you have never had to do it. When some thug who is one digit shy of a full zip code charges you and you draw and fire once and the pistol jams because you have limp wristed or tangled your Glock in your clothing, you need to be able to clear the piece.

REVOLVER MALFUNCTIONS

Revolver malfunctions seldom occur during firing but exhibit problems during reloading more often. The ejector rod should be checked periodically for loosening. This occurs most often under the battering of Magnum ammunition. As the ejector rod unscrews it extends to a longer length and will tie the handgun up if you are using the type of revolver that features an ejector rod that locks into a lug under the barrel. If the revolver will not open due to the ejector rod unscrewing, the only recourse is to carefully bring the hammer back just a little to release the cylinder and rotate the cylinder in the opposite direction of normal rotation until the ejector rod is tightened. This is time-consuming, and such a break in firing could be fatal if you're facing an armed opponent.

I have also seen a cylinder refuse to open when the cylinder release is actuated. This was independent of the ejector rod but occurred due to a hammer shifting on a worn hammer pin. I have seen this happen on the range and often the problem is cured immediately with a hard slap of the palm against the cylinder in the direction of opening as the release is held back. Not an ideal situation, and it may break small parts but it's worth a do-or-die effort on the street.

It goes without saying never to slam the ejector rod on a table or brick wall to eject cases or you will bend the rod. But I have seen shooters do just this when hot hand loads or occasionally factory loads will not eject properly. High pressure literally makes these cases adhere to the cylinder wall. I have seen a brand new, off-brand .357 Magnum revolver that was fired with 110-grain Magnums, not a heavy load by any means, that refused to eject the spent cases. I have seen an Astra forcing cone crack with domestic standard pressure .357 Magnum loads.

A malfunction that can be avoided but which we see often in training is the ejector star over a fired case. When we eject spent cases from a revolver, we should point the revolver muzzle upwards so that the cases slide from the chambers easily. If we are too fast and attempt to eject the cases while the revolver is held barrel down or at a neutral angle, the ejector rod may reach the end of its travel and allow a spent case to remain in the cylinder. The ejector star will then snap over the case. To clear this type of tie-up, the revolver must be pointed upwards, the ejector rod actuated and the revolver shaken so that the case can slide out of the cylinder. Manipulation by a finger or an edged tool may be needed. The cartridge must be angled out of the cylinder and past the ejector star. If you have more than one cylinder with a stuck case in this condition you are in trouble! The case rim under the ejector star is a result of fumbling and can be avoided with proper gun handling.

The best means we have to avoid malfunctions is to use quality arms and ammunition and to properly maintain and lubricate these tools. But even the best handguns and ammunition are subject to problems. For example, inadvertently pressing the magazine latch while the pistol is holstered can produce a malfunction when the pistol is fired. Take care of your gear and it will not fail you. But be prepared. The next few paragraphs will go a long way toward preparing you for conflict if the information is adhered to.

MALFUNCTION DRILLS

I have often stated that basic gunhandling skills are the most common shortcoming of new students. Even some whom we might call good shots are not the best at manipulation under stress.

It is obvious that a firearm must be properly maintained to function. But it also must be properly loaded. If the handgun fails during a critical incident, the implications are lethal. I prefer not to be found prematurely among the dead. When training, the goal is for consistency. We must take personal defense seriously whether or not we are engaged in a high-risk occupation. I have seen ham-handed, lazy and downright sloppy gunhandling by those who should know better. I have seen the pistol held in an improper manner and magazines shoved awkwardly into the pistol. I have seen pistols jammed under the arm or the belt on the range while the trainee awkwardly searched for a magazine on his belt. After I describe the techniques that have proven out for me, you may find something that works better. But let safety and efficiency be your guide. Be completely serious in considering what drills you will use in the future. Use the same drill consistently and with every firearm.

When loading the automatic pistol with a magazine, many shooters attempt to place the magazine into the magazine tunnel and slap it straight up. There is always a visual component to this; even the best shooters who claim they are not looking at the pistol sneak a glance. A superior drill is to angle the magazine into the magazine well. The magazine is canted to meet the back of the magazine well and then it is pressed into the magazine well until the magazine catch locks and the magazine locks in place. A slap is not necessary.

Practice the same way you will deploy the handgun. As an example, when loading a fully-loaded eight-round 1911 magazine into the 1911, if the slide is locked back the force needed is much less than to load against a pistol with a slide that is at rest. With the slide at rest and the magazine fully loaded, a slap may be necessary. So, always lock the slide to the rear before loading a magazine. Be certain you are aware of differences in the handguns you use. As an example, some do not like the looks of the CZ 75B's magazine stop and remove this thin plate from the magazine. This is a mistake as the magazine stop serves a legitimate purpose.

Loading

Rack the slide to the rear and lock it in place. Insert the loaded magazine and release the slide. The handgun is now loaded. I often simply grasp the rear of the slide to and let it fly forward and do not use the slide lock. If you use a variety of handguns with different slide lock designs, this is an especially valid technique. Make the piece ready by either lowering the hammer or actuating the decocker or applying a safety depending on the type of handgun. At this point you may choose to drop the magazine and top off a round to bring the pistol to full capacity. Personally I deploy eight rounds in my 1911s and thirteen in my High Powers.

Let's discuss different loading scenarios. At some point we will unload the pistol and set the magazine aside. We then take the round that was in the chamber and place it at the top of the magazine. When we reload, we will rechamber that round a second time. There is an alternative; reloading the magazine as it is withdrawn from the pistol, chambering a round, then topping the magazine off with the previously chambered round. In either case either the top round or the top two rounds are chambered repeatedly over a period of time. None of us leaves the pistol loaded indefinitely; we go to the range and practice with range loads and keep the pistol loaded with premium ammunition (at least I do). So the piece will be loaded and unloaded numerous times during its service.

Be certain to keep track of the ammunition used in the pistol. Be careful that the top rounds do not suffer a bullet setback in the case from repeated chambering. Pressures are driven up from a deep seated bullet, the case mouth seal is broken and water and solvent may invade the case. The best types of ammunition are very durable but some brands I would not trust for more than a single chambering and never carry them for personal defense.

Revolver Loading

You would think a revolver is simpler to load and it is but just the same use care in loading. Be certain each cartridge case fits snugly in the chamber or you may experience a failure to rotate during a critical incident. There may be a high primer or a dirty or scarred chamber. Likewise be certain the ammunition used in your revolver is high quality with a good bullet crimp.

When the Charter Arms Bulldog was introduced during the 1970s I found that most of the factory ammunition available was designed for light-kicking revolvers. The bullet was prone to jump the crimp and tie up the revolver. Practically all that was available at the time was the roundnose lead 246-grain bullet. This load plowed along at a leisurely 750 fps. Once I fired enough factory ammunition to obtain a supply of .44 Special brass, my handloads gave no problems, as I applied a good crimp with RCBS loading dies.

Such a jam would have been deadly in a gunfight. It was very difficult to drive the bullet back into the case to untie the revolver. I had to crimp the factory ammunition with my RCBS crimping die in order to finish out the factory loads!

Ammunition quality has come a long way but there are still loads not suitable for hard-kicking revolvers. Never use lead bullet loads in the Ultra Lite revolvers, for example. At least, do not use factory loads as the bullets are softer than the hard-cast bullets often used in hand loads. I have never experienced a problem when loading hard-cast bullets in heavy .38 Special and .44 Special loads in light revolvers – but then I am a careful handloader.

A RECAP OF IMPORTANT POINTS

- To load a magazine, angle it into the magazine well and move it in quickly to snap into the magazine catch.
- Carefully be certain all revolver cartridges are properly seated.
- In order to limit the number of feed malfunctions, the cartridges in a high-capacity pistol magazine should be properly loaded.

A word of warning: in agencies using both calibers, I have found 9mm ammunition in .40 caliber magazines and .40s in 9mm magazines. Each was a disaster waiting to happen. I have also seen 9mm cartridges fired in .40 caliber chambers. Most often, all that occurred was a burst case and a squib load. But worse scenarios exist.

LOADING MAGAZINES

Begin with the cartridge in the non-dominant hand. Hold the magazine in the strong side hand. Press the cartridge under the feed lips and to the rear of the magazine. Once you have loaded three rounds, tap the magazine gently on a wooden countertop or boot heel in order to insure that each cartridge is fully seated to the rear of the magazine. Continue until the magazine is loaded. When the last round is loaded, tap the base of the magazine to be certain that the rounds are seated properly.

Often we wish to check to be certain the piece is loaded before we go where angels fear to tread. Checking a revolver may be done visually: if there are cases in the cylinder it is loaded. To be certain they are live rounds we may point the muzzle toward the floor and open the cylinder. A rule you must adhere to is to always point the muzzle of the revolver down when loading or checking the cylinder.

The semi-automatic pistol press check involves moving the slide to a certain extent to view or feel the cartridge in the chamber. There are both tactile and visual means of checking the chamber. These checks simply do not work with all types of semi-automatics and must be tailored to the individual pistol. For example, my CZ 75B with the slide guarded by a long dust cover demands that the slide be pressed to the rear using the cocking serrations. The High Power and 1911 work well with slide pressure on the forward portion of the slide. The trick is to keep your hands completely away from the trigger and muzzle during the press check.

Remember, there are three rules in handling handguns:

- The handgun is always loaded.
- Do not allow the muzzle to cover anything you do not wish destroyed.
- Keep your finger off the trigger until you fire.

A press check on a pistol with a mounted light is difficult, but not impossible. You can reach over the slide and press the slide to the rear from the top. The Press Check once taught by Colonel Jeff Cooper and others for use on the 1911 has been criticized as unsafe. I can see the point; perhaps there are other drills that work well but with practice the original Press Check offers economy of motion and it works. It is also very 1911- and High Power- specific. With this technique you hook your thumb into the trigger guard and use the forefinger to press the front of the slide to the rear, exposing the round in the chamber or lack thereof. The grip is relaxed and the grip safety activated but the slide lock safety is off. An alternative is to use the weak hand to move the slide back in a slingshot method.

How important is second strike capability?

I have read any number of discussions concerning second strike capability. Here are two scenarios:

The first scenario: A cop presses his trigger and the piece fails to fire and is killed because of it. His handgun – be it a Glock, a 1911, or a similar type – did not have a second strike capability because the slide resets the trigger action after the cartridge fires.

The second scenario: A cop fires a DAO semi-auto with second-strike capability-practically unknown a few years ago. His first try produces a click, a misfire. His second press on the trigger fires the round and saves his life.

Is second strike capability a life saver? Not always.

If you carry a revolver you do not have second strike capability. You have the only advantage worth having, an advantage far superior to second strike. If the first round does not go off, you simply press the trigger again and a fresh new round is introduced to the hammer.

In my experience, if a round does not go off with the first blow of a properly functioning hammer, it will not fire the second time. There are exceptions but the proper course is the tap-rack-bang. Second strike is okay as far as it goes and the Taurus 24/7 is a laudable design. But I prefer to rely on what I know. In time you will almost certainly encounter a dud round unless you fire premium defense cartridges exclusively.

But the only thing that a second strike will cure is a light firing pin strike. Ammunition failures are not likely to be cured by a second strike.

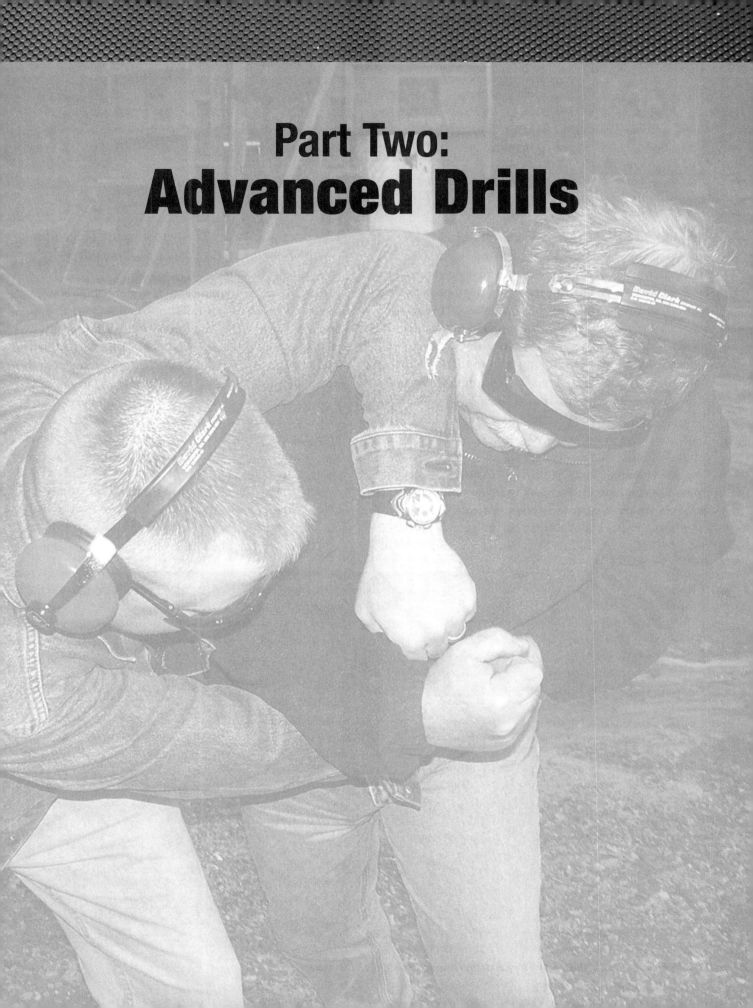

Part Two:
Advanced Drills

HIGH-SPEED, LOW-DRAG DRILLS

With one son and the military and the other son's wife currently serving in Iraq, I have been exposed to the military way. Overall the drills have been profitable. The Army Way must be understood. If the Army wishes for its young officers to learn something, it will send them to a school where they practice language or computer skills day in and day out for as much as a year. My son has seen training from both the enlisted and commissioned side and understands the dedication needed from both groups.

I have been exposed to trainers who feel that high-visibility sights on a handgun are a detriment to malfunction clearance drills. Their drills go far past the common tap-rack-bang. These men feel that a high visibility sight with its smooth profile prevents the snagging of a sight on the belt or bootheel and racking the slide sharply to clear a malfunction.

This is a radical piece of advice known as high-speed low-drag gun handling. I am going to explore the issue in this chapter.

Let me assure you if you are in the sandbox in a battle and your pistol fails to function, you will appreciate these drills. You must also realize that there is no good reason to execute these drills with a pistol loaded with live ammunition. Using dummy rounds works just fine for practice and removes the danger. Sure, there is an element of danger in every type of live-fire handgun drill but when we are able to eliminate danger we should. When conducting high-speed, low-drag drills, as I call them, you will occasionally cover your body with the muzzle of the pistol. This is sometimes a mistake but at other times unavoidable. Properly executed, you will not cover the body but then we are not perfect as we begin practice.

There are certain handguns that simply cannot

This is a good example of a desperate maneuver that just may work with sufficient practice.

be used with the high-speed, low-drag drill. Some feature snag-free sights that will not hook on the belt. Then, there is the problem of a very stiff recoil spring. High-speed, low-drag drills work best with full-length service pistols and military uniforms. But they should be included in your tactical repertoire.

Beginning Drill

The basic high-speed, low-drag malfunction drill focuses around the problem of clearing a malfunction with only the firing hand. We may be firing from cover or we may be wounded or our weak hand may be holding a prisoner or a communication device. The ability to quickly clear a malfunction with one hand makes sense.

The Type 1 and Type 2 malfunctions are readily addressed but the Type 3 is another matter, although it too may be successfully addressed. These drills are sometimes called wounded-officer drills. Make no mistake, if you are involved in a fist fight you might be struck with a fist. If you are involved in a knife fight you might be cut and if you are involved in a gun fight you might be shot. It is necessary to perform numerous one-hand drills in order to maintain all-around proficiency. However, one-hand shooting is more difficult and the shooter should always be aware of the need to grasp the pistol properly in one-hand fire. We must know our limitations. It is more difficult to maintain a proper firing attitude with one hand. If the handgun is a little too large for your hand, it shows up more in one-hand fire, especially if you must resort to weak-hand fire. This is definitely an advanced student problem as those with little experience have no business attempting to execute these drills. Rather, these drills should be addressed once gun handling skills are well established.

If you wish to embarrass your friends you might ask them how many of them practice malfunction drills and how many practice these drills with one hand, on their back, or behind cover. If you are shot and you involuntarily fire while the hand is not properly grasping the handgun, it will probably malfunction. In a truly desperate situation I would hate to have to clear a Type 3 malfunction. The first thought that would come to my mind is "Feet don't fail me now."

Let's look at the high-speed, low-drag drills. I am also going to expound on training, especially mirror image training.

The basis for cooperation is wired into the human hard drive. When working toward a common goal, humans often excel. A good trainer looks past his paycheck and a good student looks past his certifi-

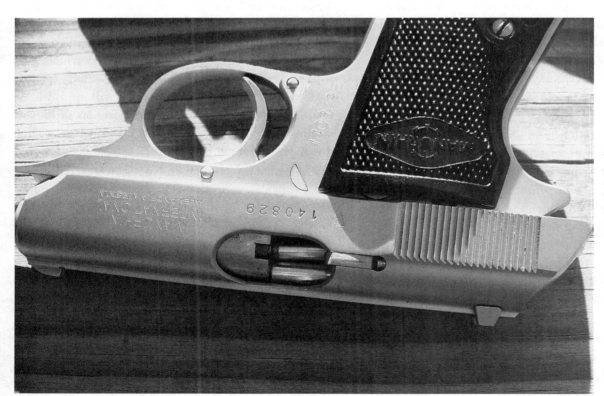

Type 3 malfunctions are especially difficult to clear in small handguns without much slide leverage.

According to some, a GI 1911 is the most reliable of all handguns and the easiest to clear when it hiccups.

cate. A student must have a good attitude and ask questions. Speech is the favored human communication but not always the appropriate model in handgun training. Skills that require coordination and manipulation are best taught by demonstration. Words may be too clumsy. Non-verbal communication is especially appropriate when the skills being taught require unconscious repetition.

A good illustration is to observe that pointing is much quicker than expecting the student to look at something by staring or jutting your chin. Humans quickly pick up a focal point but the extended finger is a great compass. We need to recognize the others intent and copy their movement. Knowledge of how to properly perform a drill comes from practice and seeing the drill properly executed. By performing mirror image with the instructor we are beginning to understand drills and tactics.

One person's body movement often mimics another's on a subconscious level. It is termed involuntary impersonation. This is the basis by which children learn language and is the basis for adults to learn

complex skills. The desire to copy is so great we sometimes pick up counterproductive movements from others. An example is what psychiatrists term the "first truth." This is a term usually applied to erroneous perceptions of preschoolers but which also applies to beginning shooters. Point shooting, unsighted fire, the myth that the .45 will spin a man around with a shot to the arm, relying on skills you cannot demonstrate – these are all first truths that the instructor must deal with.

Several of my students have encountered dubious tactics such as operating the decocker, safety or slide lock with the weak hand while the pistol is held with both hands. When one of my students asked this instructor what to do if the weak hand was disabled he was met with a blank stare. The one-hand gun should be manipulated with one hand with the support hand there just for that – support in firing and to aid in reloading.

When working in the mirror image, be certain your partner is up to speed. You will pick up bad habits otherwise. A task approached by two individuals

Jacking the slide against the body or heel should clear the jammed cartridge or cartridge case, but plenty of practice is needed.

is more quickly accomplished. An hour of dual training with feedback from each shooter will prove more beneficial than several hours of solo practice. A cooperative relationship in training is vital. The rule in mirror image training is perception, action and understanding of the drill. The unconscious cognitive processes supply the rest.

Recently I was asked my opinion of a course that favored rapid unaimed fire. Now, to fire from chest level quickly at a target a few feet in front of the shooter is one thing. But from seven feet or so on the sights must be used. This is the flash sight picture we learn in rapid fire drills. I will stand with Colonel Cooper on this one. Use your sights! And mirror your instructor. Mirror image training is often essential. In the aforementioned course the instructor attempted to convince the shooters to use unaimed fire past five yards. They shot with the sights first and all did well. But when they adopted the instructors point firing program hits and speed suffered. He told them they would groove in with practice. Sounds to me like a monkey trying to write Shakespeare. Highspeed, low-drag is high level training performed with

one hand for the most part – and use your sights when you are up and running.

ONE-HAND MALFUNCTION DRILLS

The one-hand malfunction drill will begin with a triple-checked, unloaded handgun that has been properly staged with a dummy cartridge. The handgun is held in the firing hand at the side. When the handgun is brought to eye level, the student immediately notices the weapon is in a disabled condition. The pistol is moved rapidly to any part of the covering garments that offer sufficient leverage to rack the slide and clear the malfunction. The rear sight is caught on a heavy belt, for example, and the sight stabilized. The pistol is forcibly racked open. The dud round clears and the next round up properly loads. (Be certain to load a second STI PRO dummy round in the magazine or the slide will simply lock open.) If you are kneeling or behind cover the handgun may be quickly transferred to the boot heel and the same malfunction drill executed off the heel of the boot.

Variations exist. While originally envisioned as a one-hand drill, there are high-speed drills that

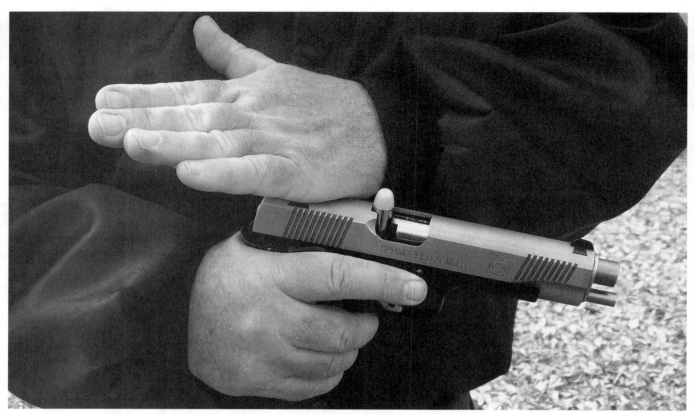

When using the sights as a fulcrum point, be certain to stop and get your grip on the sights.

Aggressively rack the slide to continue clearing the pistol.

require the use of the weak hand. One of these involves the weak hand ripping a stovepipe jam out of the slide. The weak hand rushes across the slide and comes to rest on the jammed case. The stovepipe round is used for leverage and the slide quickly jacked to the rear and a fresh round loaded. This drill can be executed by a Marine I know well in the blink of an eye.

Another malfunction drill involves ripping the hand across the sights to clear a malfunction. At least it appears this way. What is done is this: the hand rushes to the handgun and flies across the slide but stops at the rear sight, acquires leverage, and continues. The malfunction is cleared. This is a quick and solid drill for those who are able to master it. The problem is this drill can be hard on the hand if not done correctly. If you really ripped the hand across the sights the palm would be injured and the slide would not budge. The proper drill is move, stop, and rack. While these drills work just fine with GI .45s and stock High Powers, they will not work at all with the majority of commercial high end pistols that are fitted with Novak, Wilson Combat, or Hienie sights. These sights offer an excellent sight picture and give the shooter much greater accuracy, not only in terms of slow fire accuracy but also in terms of speed through rapid acquisition of the sights. It is up to the shooter to decide which is most important.

One hand reloads are simple and straightforward. They require some thought. The handgun is run dry and the slide is locked back as I practice these drills. When the pistol goes to slide lock on an empty magazine, the magazine is ejected and the pistol is jammed into the waistband pocket or holster depending up the garb and how the shooter's gear is configured at the moment. The firing hand reaches for a magazine and slaps the magazine into the pistol. Next, the pistol is drawn from the waistband or pocket and the slide lock actuated to load the pistol. Be certain to practice actuating the slide lock. If you use the weak hand to release the slide by pulling on the cocking serrations and releasing – as I

often do – working the slide lock with the firing hand may prove difficult. Ripping the sights on the belt to release the slide is another option.

REVOLVERS

One-hand loading of the revolver is a neat trick. Since the spare gun load for the revolver is normally carried on the gun side this is not as difficult as with the automatic. The revolver is fired dry and then the muzzle is pointed upwards. The thumb actuates the cylinder release and the trigger finger presses the cylinder out of the frame as the other fingers firmly grasp the pistol through the frame. The thumb hits the ejector rod and the spent cases fall free. The revolver cylinder is left open and the butt is jammed into the waistband or pocket. A snubnose is handle-heavy and secure positioning must be practiced. Sometimes the handle should be jutted into the waistband. A long-barreled revolver may be jammed in barrel-first quite securely. Be certain to determine which is the best for your revolver. The speed loader is then drawn from the pouch and inserted into the cylinder. The speed loader is then firmly held and twisted as the gun load is inserted. The speed loader is dropped and the cylinder shut by pressing against the body. The revolver is then grasped in a firing grip and is ready for action. There is some potential for a fumble and this drill should be practiced often.

CONCLUSIONS

In my youth there were any number of true story magazines available for hairy-chested men and the rest of us. A recurring theme was that somehow a soldier was trapped in rubble, wounded, or otherwise incapacitated and had only one hand available. In that hand was most often a Colt 1911 Government Model .45 carried chamber empty. The story revolved around the protagonist somehow managing to rack the slide with one hand. I recall a special military holster with a block in the body for racking the muzzle of a .45 against the holster. I think we are better off to properly carry an automatic handgun chamber-loaded, but just the same the various one-hand drills are worth practicing.

Close Range Battle

All handgun work is close-range, but in this chapter we are truly up close and personal. We need to determine at what range rapid action and even unaimed fire trumps the two-hands-on-the-handgun aimed fire we often stress. Do we need to learn to use the handgun without sights? Will we behave instinctively at close range? The bottom line is that unaimed fire is acceptable only at four to five feet.

The speed rock is one of the few examples of unaimed fire I actively teach. The obvious use of the .38 caliber belly gun is another example. The revolver is jammed into the opponent's body and fired. Even at very close range all other scenarios call for some type of body aiming. I have dealt with point shooters on the range and in training. Many of these people miss a silhouette at ridiculously close range. Walk-ing bullet holes into the paper or onto the X ring is not acceptable or possible in real life. Moreover, such practice sessions are not applicable to reality. I have little patience for those who advocate ill-conceived concepts that may results in the death of good guys and girls.

There are tiers of training that must be understood. At the bottom level are basic skills. These are shooting or marksmanship skills. Quite a few shooters who have these skills believe they are well prepared for combat. They simply know how to shoot. The second tier of knowledge involves advanced skills. This is what we will cover in the next few lines, the thinking person's climb up the ladder from mere competence. There are even higher planes of learning that demand interactive training. It is always one step at a time.

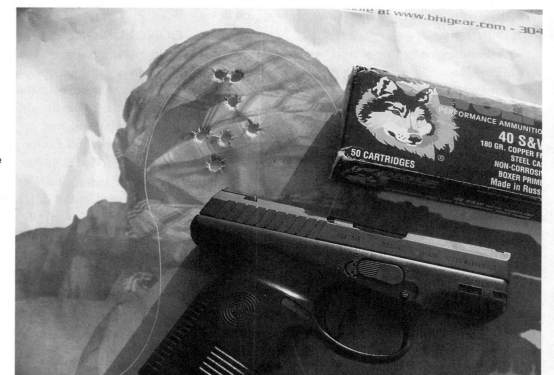

Marksmanship problems are not severe at close range. The problem is moving quickly and keeping your nerve. This group was fired with the Steyr at a relatively long ten yards.

THE SHOOTING STANCE IS DICTATED BY RANGE

My first ideas on the variations in shooting stances at different ranges spring from Bill Jordan's seminal work *No Second Place Winner*. The hardware featured in Mr. Jordan's books is dated by a half-century but the common-sense advice and practice regimens are not. I alloy this work with the recommendations of Colonel Rex Applegate. Colonel Applegate developed the Applegate drills for use at very short range. For what it is worth, the Colonel's drill incorporates the use of sights, if only the front sight. In the day when the Applegate drill was developed, most pistol sights were poor for accurate shooting. The Colt Single Action Army had only a trough in the top strap and a round front sight that defied a shooter to find the top. Double-action revolvers were little better. Military handguns featured small sights that were difficult to acquire quickly, although some were precise if properly lined up. I believe the major reason so many point shooting styles were developed in those days was a lack of good sights on the handgun. You simply had to go with what you knew. If the pistol's sights severely limited marksmanship, then some type of unaimed fire or fire concentrating on only the front sight was needed. As custom handgun sights were developed and the factories took notice, the situation improved dramatically. But old habits die hard.

The modern technique as taught by Colonel Jeff Cooper demands good sights. By the time Cooper was gaining prominence for his work in promoting serious combat style pistol competition, we had the Combat Masterpiece .38, the K-38 and the Colt Python but still no factory semi-automatics with good sights (excluding the Gold Cup, a target pistol). The revolvers had first-class sights and when this technology was applied to the automatic, we had something. My recommendation to get both hands on the pistol and use your sights is borne out in pistol competition. Take your time – in a hurry. Get on the target get a sight picture and execute a good trigger press as quickly as possible.

Competitions really changed the shooting world. Let's look at the practical lessons.

When you have a large target, you may take a coarse sight picture and still hit a vital area. If only the head or feet are exposed then you have a great-er demand for accuracy. I recommend practicing to keep all shots on a target about 8.5 x 11 inches out to twenty-five yards and practicing on smaller targets the size or a head or heart at closer range.

At very close range you can draw and fire using a technique known by several names including "meat and paper," "steel and paper" and "combat silhouette." At this range you draw the handgun and cover the silhouette. The outline of the handgun is against the paper and all you see is paper on all sides of the handgun. You are using the handgun for a visual reference. This is an intimate-range tactic that can work wonders. The handgun must be completely square against the target. The front sight should protrude on the top but little and you should not see the flats of the slide or the long flutes of the revolver cylinder.

At intimate range, with an attacker practically on top of you, the Speed Rock is the ultimate development of the belly gun tactic. In this drill you draw quickly from the holster and fire as soon as the handgun clears the holster. The shot is angled

This young shooter has learned the Applegate point and understands its practical application.

The author finds the speed rock an excellent technique for survival in intimate range fights.

directly into the opponent's body. You are basically shoving the handgun into his belly. A revolver may be fired repeatably into the opponent's body, but you need to practice keeping the automatic far enough away from the target that paper and other debris from the target are not blown back into the slide, jamming the gun.

Let's look at the Applegate Drill, as this is still a viable drill that gives a new shooter a real advantage as they learn gunhandling skills. In the Applegate Drill, the shooter begins with the handgun at his or her side. (The draw comes as we add experience.) When the handgun is out of the holster and by the side, take a step forward with the gun side leg and bring the handgun on target. The eyes have drilled the target and when the front sight breaks the plane between the eyes and the target, the handgun is fired. At moderate range, ten to fifteen feet, this technique is very fast and works well with a minimum of practice. The execution of the Applegate Drill is similar to a martial arts strike.

Bill Jordan's work stressed the difference in firing stances at different ranges. Jordan had the problems worked out to a science through long, hard practice,

and he made valid points. His recommendations are worth our consideration. At very close range the handgun is extended from the body with the arm braced against the ribs in a position similar to many in the martial arts. Beyond arm's reach, the hand is extended and the handgun fired when the front sight is on the target. At longer ranges Jordan recommended two-hand fire, concentrating on the front sight at relatively close ranges of five to seven yards and then going to the sights and more deliberate fire at seven yards and back.

After a bit of time on the range, you will realize that we have time to assume the two-hand hold at practically all ranges. If you are close enough to the target that the muzzle blast rips the target, that is another matter. At this range even a wounded felon might attempt to grab your weapon and weapons retention becomes important. This brings to attention a need to create distance when drawing, which we will discuss in detail later. At present we have to understand that we will not hit past intimate range if we do not use the sights.

A final word on point shooting: I would not wish to be the trainer called to testify in court that I taught a shooter not to use his sights. In the case of a missed shot hitting an innocent bystander, this would be a difficult pill for a jury to swallow. And perhaps an expensive one for all concerned.

WEAPON RETENTION AND OTHER CONSIDERATIONS

If an armed individual comes to understand close range combat, he needs to understand weapons retention. Everything we discuss concerning proper weapons use means nothing if the attacker gains control of our weapon. Little if any weapons retention is discussed in most concealed carry handgun classes. Peace officers receive some training depending on the agency and its dedication to personnel.

The problem of an assailant gaining control of your weapon is real. About one in five peace officers killed each year is murdered with his own weapon. No other skill addressed in this book is worthwhile if you cannot maintain control of the handgun. One of the simplest rules of handgun retention is to keep the handgun away from the adversary's line of attack. Let's look at some of the most important considerations in handgun retention.

Belts and Holsters

A properly designed holster and a good belt should always be chosen. A holster with good retention attached to a rigid holster belt goes a long way. As an example, the Blackhawk! Serpa CQB line provides excellent retention with a degree of speed. Extra practice is required but we must look at our own needs. If I were working as a school recourse officer, a mall security officer, or as a bouncer in a crowded bar I would definitely combine common sense with a good retention holster.

Most of us choose an open top or thumb break for concealed carry. This is fine as far as it goes, but be certain the holster passes a minimum shakedown. Jump up and down with the handgun holstered and triple-checked unloaded. Be certain you do not dislodge the handgun with this minimal effort. Some years ago I was wearing a quality inside-the-waistband holster when I was literally bowled over on my back during a fight as I tripped over furniture. I brought my legs up over my head and did a back flip to get back on my feet. My handgun did not budge. The handgun and holster should lock together with security.

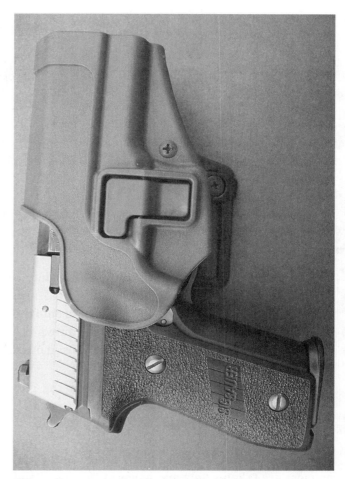

If the author were involved in a day to day occupation that involved working in crowds while visibly armed, this Blackhawk! holster would be the ticket for security.

Be Alert!

Do not be caught by surprise. Some of us go though life asleep, and this can precipitate a tragedy in personal defense. Complacency and a lack of situational awareness are not acceptable but we are not all at Condition Red 24/7. If you are in an environment with the possibility of a high threat level you need to maintain a higher level of alertness. The ability to think one second ahead is priceless.

Fending Off a Gun Grabber

The single most important tool in preventing a successful gun grab is to maintain distance. Gun grabs are a hands-on tactic. Maintain at least arm's length with a threat and those you encounter in public as much as possible. Remain perpendicular to the threat if you are able. Move quickly from the line of attack. When you move out of the line of attack you force the adversary

In this illustration the author is simulating a gun grab attempt. He has drawn his backup from the weak-side pocket.

into an elliptical pattern. This will force him into a position advantageous to your defense. The weak arm comes up in defense and the strong side locks onto the holstered handgun. The handgun must be drawn upwards in most cases and blocking the upward motion protects the handgun from a gun grabber.

When faced with a situation in which the gun grabber has managed to get his hands on your holstered weapon, you need to have tactics in place to combat this threat. When practicing such drills, there is potential for injury so take steps to ensure the maneuvers are taken safely and never at full speed and full power with an untrained individual. Never use a real firearm. The red composite ASP training gun or the aluminum cast Odin Press fake handguns are ideal. If nothing else, go to a flea market and purchase an eight dollar plastic Glock or 1911.

I like to do a set-up and allow the training partner to get a hand on the holstered pistol and come in at that moment. Obviously if he has progressed this far in the disarming attempt, something has gone wrong. The attacker has made his way through our outer defenses. As he clamps onto the pistol, slap your own hand down hard on top of his. If the pistol has an exposed hammer you may be able to grind his palm into the hammer. At the same time execute a full-power strike into his face with the open palm of the other hand. Immediately change direction after this strike and move the weak hand to the opponent's wrist and apply a wrenching effect. Put your hips into the twist and wrench the hand down and away. It is possible at this time to trap the opponent's hand and wrist and execute a takedown that will put the adversary on the ground.

Peace officers are at a disadvantage in a gun grab situation because they carry their pistol openly. It is more likely that civilians will be forced into a fight for the pistol after they have drawn the handgun. If the opponent has managed to get both hands on the pistol, you probably should pull the trigger. The pistol may jam and the shot may not disable the adversary but the handgun will not be used against you if he cannot clear the jam. The attacker has provoked a deadly force encounter by attempting to forcibly take your handgun. He is not going to take it and admire the finish!

If the pistol is being forced either up or down, press the trigger. The attacker may be powder burned or startled but in any case if he has hold of the slide the pistol will malfunction. One of the great techniques is to quickly press in the opponent's direction to take him off guard and then quickly extend your weak side arm as high as possible and bring it smashing onto the opponent's wrist. Two rules apply: retain the weapon and damage the adversary.

The specter of a thug gaining control of your handgun is yet another reason not to draw the handgun until you are certain you are going to fire. I am aware of a New York City detective who was engaged in a struggle for his handgun. His finger was in the trigger guard and the skin of the first joint was peeled away to the bone as a thug attempted to wrest his Colt Detective Special .38 from him. But our man retained his weapon. On March 11, 2005, a man on trial in Atlanta for rape escaped, obtained a weapon, and killed four people. I am not certain retention skill or a security holster would have helped. But the fact is when the adversary gains control of your weapon, there is hell to pay.

There have been times when officers have advised me that a sharp front sight is a wonder against soft palms in a gun grab. The old Smith & Wesson undercut target sight commonly found on the K38 was a good example. I don't know about that, but I do know that if the handgun is too large for your hands it will be much easier to grasp the pistol out of your hands. By contrast, a handgun with a well-shaped handle that fits your hand is another matter.

This is particularly true if the handgun has a relatively short barrel. With an ample grip to hold onto to and little for the adversary to grasp, short-barreled handguns are often ideal for personal defense.

A motivated individual can gain control of a handgun quickly.

Remember, a good joint block should be part of your defensive skills.

This is a desperate maneuver – but if you are going to be shot anyway it's worth a try!

As a final exercise I will describe a tactic that is often taught to disarm an armed individual at intimate range. Always use a fake pistol when practicing this drill. This technique works well in the dojo and should be part of your tactical repertoire. When the adversary is close enough at almost point-blank range, use an uppercut-like motion to slam the handgun up and away and the muzzle away from your body. Even if the assailant presses the trigger, the shot should go into the air. Be certain you are prepared for the shot. The handgun is forced up and the pistol forcefully rotated violently in the opposite direction of the grip. If the attacker is right-handed, rotate right in the opposite direction of body center. If the trigger finger is on the trigger it will probably be broken by this violent action. Continue to rip the handgun from the adversary's hand and continue the movement to the gun-hand side and run past him and behind him. You now have control of the weapon. This tactic may be turned against you if you allow the adversary to close distance, so it cuts both ways.

10 Creating Distance

There are considerable problems involved in parrying with an enemy at intimate range. The closer the range, the less advantage a skilled marksman has. Mere chance may decide the encounter. The person who is able to get his weapon into action first has the advantage. At grappling distance, an adversary can interfere with the draw and prevent us from bringing our handgun to bear. They may even gain control of the handgun. A marksman has the greater advantage as distance increases. Few felons have sufficient skill to produce center hits at extended handgun range but they really do not need this skill when robbing good folks at a few feet distance.

There are tactics that may be executed profitably at intimate range. I have used these tactics in incidents that did not turn into gunfights. The step back and the slap are two I have found work well. The slap cannot be overrated. To bring your open hand across an adversary's face with a full power blow can be disorienting and cause him to lose his balance. Not a casual fake slap across fatty cheeks but a full power slap to the side of the head or lower jaw can be very effective. The hand is open and the palm cupped for greater effect. In addition to the open palm area giving a hearty blow, the larger area also gives us a much greater chance of contact.

When faced with an attack at close range you cannot always draw your handgun. A quick strike to the adversary is a way to escape, at least briefly.

The open hand is superior to the closed fist in almost every situation. I have rarely engaged in fisticuffs but when I have, afterwards I've found my hands swollen and red. Friends have broken bones in their hands in such actions. The open hand can be directed in a short sharp blow to the jaw. If the front of the jaw is contacted the jawbone may set a vibration in place that may result in unconsciousness. A sharp blow to the nose may produce tears and can be quite painful. The point of the jaw seems to be the preferred point of impact for a palm strike, however.

To gain distance, we have to get away from the attacker. Strikes at intimate range may do that. Footwork is also important. As we strike the opponent we execute what is known as the step back. I have seen this tactic demonstrated many times and suspect it dates to Trojan times. It is effective and worth study. To execute the step back, you can plant a punch or slap to the opponent and then rapidly step back by placing one foot to the rear and rapidly moving the other. Even if you do not land a blow, the step back will allow you to move out of the opponent's reach

and into a safer area. If the opponent is close enough to interfere with your draw and you are justified in drawing a weapon, the step back is a good tactic. You should step back with the gun side foot. The preferred method is a long slide that avoids tripping. This tactic places the gun side hand farther from the attacker. I also practice tilting the body away from the attacker so that the gun is away from his immediate grasp. I continue to extend the weak side arm outwards so as to fend off any interference with the draw. You should develop an arsenal of open hand tactics as well as tactics with firearms. The tactics I describe are related to getting the handgun into action and protecting the handgun from a gun grabber.

Another technique for gaining distance is a simple one. If the opponent is running toward your position or aiming at you, simply step out of the line of attack. (Or line of fire.) If you are stepping to cover, that's even better. Remember, a right-handed shooter may swing to his left and your right much easier than he may sweep the muzzle to the right. Demonstrate this for yourself with a triple-checked unloaded handgun

Striking and backing while drawing is a good tactic that should be practiced.

Simply moving out of the way of an attack is a good tactic.

The author has moved out of the way of an attack in this illustration.

or even a pointed finger. Stepping out of the line of attack and tilting the body to one side as you draw may be a lifesaver. A blow received from the side to the ribs or upper arm or shoulder will be far less conclusive than a wound to the front of the body, with the vital organs just under the surface.

A concrete wall is equivalent to three hundred yards of distance as far as safety goes. I have studied after-action reports from the FBI, NYPD and the LAPD. For fifty years, reports have been constant. Critical incidents occur at an average well inside twenty-one feet. The marksmanship challenge is not severe. Presentation from the holster and gun-handling problems are the real challenge. Often no cover is available, so tactical movement is vital. The distances involved may range from three to twenty-one feet. This is bad breath or conversational range. The essential element involved in these encounters is movement.

Movement out of the line of fire is important but I have seen tactics recommended that are as difficult to learn as a rumba or tango for the average shooter. If your legs are made of rubber, fine, but otherwise you will have to learn to move both naturally and quickly. You must achieve automatic motion in your movement without conscious thought. You simply cannot learn as you go along during a gunfight. I have a number of friends who did just that, learned as they went along, and most were injured along the way. Practice and sweat are easier than knots on your head.

Stance and movement are important. A natural stance should make it easy to maintain good balance. Something on the order of the boxer's stance or the martial arts horse stance is ideal. It is not difficult to maintain a relaxed stance with the feet about shoulder-width apart. You should be able to quickly change direction or side step from this stance. When

This young lady is too close to a threat. She should be a room's length away, even if the burglar has surrendered.

confronted by an attack, the fight or flight response is strong. It is difficult to impossible to restrain – and that is a good thing. Fight or flight is the only choice. To freeze in place is to invite a closed-casket funeral. When an attacker is moving in to assault your person, stepping out of the line of attack and redirecting it is vital. If the assailant is armed with a knife or impact weapon you may not have time to draw if he has closed the distance. You should step in to one side and sweep your arms across his to redirect the force of the attack. Step to one side and then smash or sweep your arms against his to keep him moving in the opposite direction.

Stepping from the path of an attack to draw your own weapon must be practiced. Keep in mind the draw conflicts with movement and movement conflicts with the draw. If you draw on the move, neither movement nor the draw will be optimal. Just the same this is often the preferred tactic. Practice diligently and adhere to tactical movement.

If trouble can be seen coming, you have every advantage. One tactic is to make a hasty exit from the attack zone. When forced to stand your ground but able to engage in verbal judo, the interview position, a staple of police officers, is ideal. In this stance you are ready for trouble but still in the final stages of verbal argument. In the interview position the knees are slightly bent and the arms held loosely in front of the stomach. The body is bladed at a forty-five degree angle to the threat. If the attack comes we will attempt to redirect the force. If we cannot redirect, we may need to use the weak arm to deflect the blow as we draw our weapon. I am aware of a case in which an officer used his weak arm to blunt blows from a baseball bat. His arm was severely injured but not crippled from repeated blows. The assailant took three .45 caliber hollowpoints before succumbing.

In case of attack by an edged weapon or in some animal attack scenarios, the weak arm is sacrificed for want of a better shield. The weak arm becomes the only cover we have. Standard military doctrine supports this tactic. I am not happy to feed my non-dominant arm to an animal or accept a knife but this is preferable to lethal injury. A pit bull may sink his fangs into my arm with less permanent effect than if he were to rip into my throat. When you understand the necessity of movement and maneuver in critical defense, you are more prepared to blunt an attack.

The main fault in some stances is that stability is not maintained during movement. That is why some karate moves that require sweeping movements are not credible for personal defense. The danger of slipping on wet pavement or uneven surface is real. The simplest means of creating distance remains stepping out of line with a strong, simple movement. Remember, the lower half of your body takes care of itself. The difficulty is found in maintaining a stable firing platform with the upper body. The trick is not to fire when either foot is off of the ground. Fire only when both feet are the ground. With practice this is something that most of us catch onto quickly.

THE SPEED ROCK

Two methods of creating distance are essential to learn. Both have an element of danger and should be practiced extensively with a triple-checked unloaded handgun or better still the dummy handgun. The speed rock and the step back are similar but just the same very different. The speed rock has more of a sense of urgency about it and was an important part of police training in the 1980s and 1990s. It remains so in many agencies. It is an answer to violent short range attack. Several variations exist but speed and decisiveness are important components.

The speed rock is often practiced as an answer to gunfire from inside a vehicle, such as when a peace officer experiences a bad traffic stop. In some drills the officer quickly backs away and throws the ticket book at a suspect as he draws and fires from hip level. In other drills the officer quickly slaps the target as hard as possible with an open hand or undercut from the weak side hand. The essential component is to immediately draw back the weak hand before firing. As the initiative to draw is taken, the body is bent at the waist to the rear and the gun hand draws and fires immediately from the hip level. The handgun is aimed simply by thrusting forward. This is a two- or three-feet range technique.

The speed rock is an all-or-nothing drill not designed to bring the gun out to hold the assailant at bay, but to quickly save your life. There is a theoretical advantage that has been discussed concerning angling the muzzle upwards to strike vital organs. As delivered, the speed rock will result in a gut shot. Some claim that an abdominal shot is not as effective a target as the heart and lung area. Others feel that the abdomen shot produces more pain than any other shot and often results in immediate incapacitation. If you are worried about wound ballistics tilt the muzzle slightly upwards as you fire and the bullet will take a longer path, damaging more tissue. The speed rock is not perfect but this tactic should be studied and practiced. This drill is simple, it's effective and it may be a lifesaver.

THE STEP BACK

The step back is similar in that the weak hand delivers a smart blow to the opponent's jaw or face. The main difference is that the strong side leg is thrust backwards and the individual executing the drill steps back. Next the weak side sidesteps and you have created considerable distance. This is an excellent drill to address the problem of an assailant who has closed the distance and does not give you room for movement. If the legs are slid rather than taking a step, you reduce the likelihood of objects tripping you as you execute the step back. Obstructions and drop offs may be a real danger, but the student should be aware of his or her surroundings. The step back creates distance quickly and if the adversary is sufficiently disoriented by the slap and move, the step back restores your initiative.

Finally, when considering the best means of creating distance, never underestimate a good sprint. Discretion is the better part of valor. If you are able to run and guard your six o'clock while doing so, so much the better. Distance is your ally.

When backing and drawing, issue a verbal warning and be prepared for further action.

Firing in Urban Scenarios

Fighting is fighting, but many different environments exist in which we may be called on to fight. Any battle may have severe consequences. Firing in a crowded environment is difficult and should be avoided. Take-over robberies, school shootings, mall gunfights and even shootings on buses erupt on a regular basis. Not long ago in my hometown, a group engaged in an argument in a local mall and took the fight outside. Dozens of shots were fired but no one was hit! The potential for injury of an innocent person was great, perhaps greater than the potential for injury of the person being fired at.

Nearly fifty years ago I witnessed a common-sense tactic used to take out a dangerous individual and at the same time protect bystanders. A large, disorderly drunk knocked a guard down at a public event. The guard was stunned and the drunk reached for and drew the guard's revolver. An older man in overalls drew his pocket pistol and squatted near the larger man. He fired five shots rapidly into the offender's torso. The man fell to the ground. I am not certain but I believe the revolver used was a break-top Smith & Wesson, caliber .38 Smith & Wesson. Current loads produce perhaps 650 fps. It worked. As a pre-schooler. I was highly impressed.

When handgun action occurs, the barrel of the handgun is usually tilted downward to a certain degree. Seldom is the bore perpendicular to the ground. The bullet may miss or pass through the target but usually finds the earth within a hundred yards or less. Test this theory by firing at a target set up at the range. I have fired in the normal stance and position and found that due to the geometry of the handgun's relation to the eyes and the manner in which the handgun must be held to be used efficiently, most bullets that pass through the target meet the earth within twenty-five yards.

Just the same, it is a significant worry that a pistol bullet may travel far beyond the specific area of the problem. By adopting the crouching position, you maximize safety and limit the penetration of the bullet. Crouching to fire and firing upwards into the heavy bone structure will work well in close quarters battle. If the bullet does exit it will probably find its way into a roof, not into bystanders.

The overpenetration problem is considered by most trainers, but it is seldom a problem in actual encounters. There are cases of overpenetration by bullets injuring innocent individuals, and some date to the days of the old west. When the FBI shot John Dillinger in 1934, several women were wounded by

No one has more experience with urban shooting than LAPD SWAT. They practice moving carefully, firing accurately and moving with the finger off the trigger.

Never forget to use cover. This shooter is using his own vehicle as cover, making good use of his Kimber PDP.

ricocheting bullets and sued the FBI. Al Capone paid numerous hospital bills in Chicago when bystanders were wounded during an attempt on his life. But by and large the problem is not as severe as some would think. Modern expanding bullets either stay in the body or exit with little velocity left.

When the time comes to fire at close range in an emergency, the crouching position can be a lifesaver. By crouching, I mean a deep crouch that literally has the shooter firing upward to shoot an adversary. Crouching is not only a strong position but also offers a smaller target. The long bones of the arm and leg are placed in front of the soft vitals if the stance is executed properly. Be certain to aim slightly lower than is the norm in order to direct the bullets to the opponent's vital organs. The shot is angling upwards and by aiming for a lower spot on the body, the bullets will be properly directed. Naturally we are talking about firing at practically point blank range. If you fire for the heart the bullet may miss and run a path above it. By firing slightly lower than the heart, the bullet will find its way to the vital organs. Nothing else will equal an immediate shutdown.

When shots break out in a crowd, you are under no legal duty to attempt to stop the shooter if you are not a peace officer. But none of us would like to stand still when we could prevent a massacre. Remember, the parties involved may be engaging in mutual combat and you could be running into a battle between drug dealers. But random shootings, mall shooting and workplace shootings seem a common danger. Being aware of your surroundings means much, but the shooter may be difficult to identify. Have you ever looked for your family in a crowd, such as at the circus, and picked them out? This is a skill that you would do well to develop in picking out shooters from the crowd. To take out a dangerous active shooter, I would first take cover. Then I would take careful aim to prevent adding to the danger with my own misplaced bullets. This is a true saving shot. Pray for the best, train for the worst.

An overlooked firing position that lends great stability and minimizes the body profile is the prone position. The prone is not used as often on the range as others because it is uncomfortable and dirty. If you are afraid to get dirty, shame on you! To assume

With a bit of thought and foresight, it isn't difficult to set up a course of fire similar to an urban situation. Corners and street scenes will be skeletons of their true self but appropriate for practice.

A street scene from the French Quarter in New Orleans. Be on the lookout for both danger and cover.

Kneeling fire makes for a smaller profile and increases accuracy. This is a good urban option.

When it is all boiled down to the final ingredient, marksmanship is what counts. The author counts a high capacity 9mm with +P+ loads as a good urban defense piece.

the prone position, move quickly with the handgun in the strong hand and allow your weak-side hand and elbow to support the body as you scoot your legs out flat behind the body. Move smoothly, not heavily. The head is rested on the firing side bicep and the hands support the handgun. Do not attempt to raise the head; vision is blurred by blood flow constriction in this uncomfortable attitude. You may even become lightheaded if you raise your head. Rest the head on your firing side arm. Very good shooting may be done from prone and if you are prone behind cover you are in the catbird's seat in a combat situation.

Another shooting position that is useful is the kneeling position. Kneeling fire may be very accurate, especially if braced against a vehicle or a light post. When kneeling, the weak-side knee is up and you rest the elbow on the weak-side leg. The bones of the weak-side arm are lined up with the bones of the leg and the strong side controls the pistol. Accurate fire may be used from kneeling but doing so restricts your movement. An advantage of kneeling fire is that you can break out of kneeling quickly.

All of the above stances maximize accuracy, which is the whole concept in urban shooting.

BOUNCING OR RICOCHET

When you are firing in urban situations, bouncing or ricochet should be understood. We cover ricochet more thoroughly in the chapter on cover. Keep in mind that peace officers are often disciplined by the administration if they fire at anything but a visible target. Firing into a dwelling or through a door with no clear field of vision is not allowable. But there have been cases in which a bounced shot is a lifesaver.

If the opponent is firing at you or a loved one, you need to understand ricochet. We deploy modern expanding bullets that have limited ricochet factor but almost all except the Glaser and Extreme Shock will bounce at a sufficient angle. Since vehicles play such a big part in urban battle, we need to address the problem of an adversary behind one. We should practice quickly moving under a vehicle and firing at the area just even with the opposite side door. The bullet will then strike and sail away just above the ground. If the felon is on the other side of the vehicle firing at you, he will be struck. Be certain of your backdrop and use this tactic only in extreme cases. But it can be done.

Firing under a vehicle is an option we should all be familiar with. This is a simulated urban street scene.

FIRING IN CROWDS ON THE MOVE

It is likely that you will face multiple assailants on some occasions. Firing at one or two or more threats who are in a crowd of innocents firing at you requires the utmost skill. Remember, the threat will not be stationary as they are at the range. There will be linear stringing of the targets and innocent persons involved. In this type of action you must very quickly achieve a good sight picture and perfect rapid trigger compression. Certain drills and IDPA competition stress this type of skill. You must concentrate on the target, get a good sight picture, and compress the trigger very quickly but also smoothly. Then move to the next threat immediately. You really need to find cover but if the only cover is the body of innocent bystanders, then you are in a bad situation. You must stand on your feet and deliver. Even a thin metal seat or a curb on the sidewalk might constitute cover. Among the only justifications for firing in such an environment is if the adversaries are massacring the people around you. If you are thrown into such a situation you must call up every skill you have and fire perfectly.

When you are in this situation you will never leave behind your training in trigger press, sight picture and sight alignment. But what you will do is exercise your skill in a tightly compressed time frame. You will get on target, execute a perfect trigger press, and then move smoothly to the next target. If you have not practiced heavily with realistic scenarios, the situation will be hopeless. Consider the pitfalls and advantages of firing in urban situations. Take a look around you as you travel your route to work and to entertainment. An advantage of urban areas is that there is often much opportunity to find cover. The disadvantage is that the scenarios will often be crowded. It is a problem worth your deepest thoughts. As you enter an urban environment, think ahead a second or two. Is there cover nearby? What does the street ahead look like? If you are in the habit of walking down dimly-lighted streets in strange cities there is little I can do to change your attitude. Think ahead and do not go through life asleep.

Squatting and firing upward into a threat's body can minimize the danger to innocent civilians.

12 | The Knife vs. the Gun

If you train only for gunfights, your training is limited and lacking in important points. A large number of defensive actions do not involve felons armed with firearms. A number of attacks in my experience involve blunt trauma and edged weapons. Meeting an unexpected attack is what training is all about. Meeting the unavoidable problem head-on and prevailing is the mark of a skilled combatant.

Anyone interested in personal defense must have a good understanding of edged weapons. Edged weapons and impact weapons are an important aspect of personal defense. We must understand how to defend ourselves against these weapons and also how to use these weapons if need be. Be certain to consistently and correctly train for close-quarters ac-

tion with edged weapons. Often a hand-to-hand fight erupts and you are unable to access your sidearm or a firearm may be an inappropriate answer for the attack. Those of us who are familiar with edged weapons are aware of their potential. Knives never jam or run out of ammunition. In intimate range combat, edged weapons have advantages.

Let's look at the situation logically. If you draw on a person who is attacking with only his hands, you are in a debatable position. You are not justified in firing and the attacker may even make a play for your drawn weapon if you present it too soon. A wrestling match for the handgun will ensue, and the assault may result in a negligent discharge. If the attacker is armed with a knife, that's a different mat-

At this range the woman with the .44 Special will be in a world of hurt if she has not delivered one or two good hits.

ter and you may rightly fire – but what if you press the muzzle of your automatic against his body and the disconnect prevents the piece from firing? The pistol will not fire or it may fire once and jam. You need to prepare for such a situation.

I am aware of a nurse who found herself in a very bad spot. An assailant intent on rape kidnapped her as she walked in the hospital parking lot and forced the woman into a vehicle. She was armed, but was brutally beaten and assaulted after her .380 automatic jammed on the first shot. Despite a contact wound, the offender continued the assault.

Hand-to-hand combat calls for strength training and a good knowledge of open-hand technique. The greatest predictor of such a test is prior training. An advantage that becomes obvious of the knife over the gun in such training is that it is much more difficult to grasp a knife and whisk it away than a firearm. Carrying a defensive knife makes sense for a gun carrier. If the attacker does grasp a knife, he won't hold it long. A knife wound often produces a physiological shock and retreat. The felon may cut his losses and leave if he receives a knife wound. Gunshots are unpredictable but much deadlier than a knife wound. A knife usually produces a degree of deterrent. I have been stabbed more than once and while I was not seriously wounded it is not something I wish to repeat.

Most defensive knives are relatively short. Even the tactical folder lacks sufficient blade length to be immediately effective. But then again, who would want a one-inch-deep trough across his chest or abdomen? Few of us will carry a KA-BAR or Ek Commando knife concealed. I have been asked why bayonets were once so long and fierce-looking. Reach is one answer and another is that until about 1930 bayonets had to be long enough to reach the vitals of both men and horses, as horses were an important part of the military equation. Pistols had to be able to drop a horse with a single shot, hence the .45 Colt and .45 ACP cartridges. Perhaps warfare has suffered since. In any case, while the shorter pocketknife or folder may be effective if sufficient force and repeated cuts are caused, the fact is the common concealed-carry defensive knife is capable in some ways but seldom immediately deadly.

Any number of peace officers have played down the effectiveness of the blade compared to the stick

and gun. I am not one of them. The edged weapon can seriously injure and inflict a lethal wound and also leave hideous scars. My own scars add character to my appearance (according to one editor) but I could have done without them just as well.

The accompanying table was developed for use by British Commandos and shows just how long you are likely to survive a knife strike with a serious blade to a vital area. The penetration of the knife is calculated from various angles. As you can see, there are differences in potential and severity just as important as the differences between point of aim and penetration when it comes to handgun bullet effectiveness. The knife may be deadly and brutal but not always instantly effective. If you are stabbed you will be able to fight back and save your life unless a Commando knife has penetrated your heart. Most wounds received in a knife fight are relatively light, but the following table is a sobering thought.

Time from Stabbing to Death

Carotid artery	1.2 seconds
Heart	3.0 seconds
Subclavian artery	3.5 seconds
Brachial artery	1.5 minutes
Radial artery	1.5 minutes

We should also be aware that edged weapons might be a terrific asset in weapons retention. There is some controversy on defensive knife types. There are perfectly suitable folders but when you are able to deploy a fixed-blade knife, you should. In some jurisdictions even a concealed carry permit holder is not allowed to carry a "dirk" and some fixed blade knifes may be described as a dirk. Double-edged daggers are also prohibited and several southern states prohibit hawkbill knives for carry. For the most part a quality folding knife such as the Spyderco Military is ideal. Some prefer a smooth-edged weapon while others prefer serrations. I have to admit that serrations are less likely to skid off garments such as slick rain suits and windbreakers, and a slash from a serrated edge may produce a complex wound that is difficult to repair. But a sharp blade produces a deeper wound. A ragged wound may heal more cleanly than a wide slash that separates the bone and flesh.

Let's look at knife defense tactics that work in the real world.

Beware of legislation labeling a fixed blade knife a "dirk" in some jurisdictions. Just the same, the Columbia River Knife and Took First Strike is a first-class defensive knife with much to offer. The fixed blade is superior to the folder in most respects.

We need to understand the deadly aspects of knife defense and also the use a good defensive knife may be put to. First, lets look at the Tueller Drill. This drill is named for Dennis Tueller, a respected trainer. Tueller is a great mind in police training who pioneered training and understanding of the reactionary gap. At the time Tueller was perfecting his thinking in this regard, police training was a great wasteland with few exceptions. Tueller recognized the problem. Officers were being cut, stabbed and even killed because the blade was not taken seriously by trainers. An officer who shot a felon armed with an edged weapon, especially if the range were more than a few feet, might be in serious trouble. Tueller's experiments changed our perceptions.

The Tueller drill is an eye-opener that clearly illustrates that the handgun does not always beat the knife at close range. The drill is built upon an earlier exercise. At the time, officers were trained to draw, fire and get a center hit on a man sized target at twenty one feet in 1.5 seconds or less. Many officers have considerable difficulty in meeting this standard, while those who practice constantly with good gear may reach the one second mark. A consid-erable amount of effort is demanded to reach the one second standard.

Sergeant Tueller tested his own theories of edged weapon danger by placing volunteers at each end of a 21' distance, one with a knife and the other with a holstered sidearm. (Fake handguns and knives should be used in performing this drill.) While some shooters are faster than others and some attackers are quicker, an average attacker could close the distance before an officer could draw and fire his weapon. It has been demonstrated that even overweight and out of shape individuals can move pretty quickly.

The Tueller Drill gives us a documented danger zone. I have worked through difficulties with the drill and find it challenging to any shooter. The added stress of having the threat bear down on you impedes the draw. You must practice redirection of force and other life saving techniques. Twenty-one feet isn't a danger zone and twenty-two feet is out of danger. Twenty-one feet is in the zone and depending upon the assailant and your personal speed, longer distances may be well within the zone. I am aware of a case in which the court ruled a shooting justifiable at thirty feet, but each incident is unique.

At this point the knife wielding adversary should be addressed by handgun fire – but is she up to the marksmanship demands?

If he makes it this close, it's all over.

The bottom line is this: if you shoot a threat who is armed with an edged weapon, particularly if he is not in motion, at a distance greater than twenty-one feet, you may end up in jail yourself or have a hard time justifying the action. There is much to be said for drawing and keeping him covered as you back up. If he follows you and keeps up the attack you go with what you know. A tactical withdrawal looks good to trainers and jury alike. When practicing executions of the Tueller drill it is obvious that even if you fire and strike and kill the assailant, his forward motion can carry him into your body and drive the knife into you. You need to fire and sidestep.

If your tactical awareness is working properly and you are able to draw and cover the threat, your Peacemaker may make the peace without sounding loud and clear. If the fights stops at the sight of that long tunnel in the end of the .45, all is to the good. Some scoff at the thought of bringing a knife to a gunfight but the edged weapon is nothing to make light of. Few shooters will consider taking cover a viable option against an edged weapon. They are wrong. If you have cover, the edged weapon wielder is helpless and he might be persuaded to put the edged weapon down and give up. If not, well, with cover between you and the attacker he hasn't a chance if you have a drawn pistol and are able to shoot straight.

MORE KNIFE FIGHTING: THE REVERSE GRIP

There is a technique often taught in the schools and one that looks very cool in knife advertisements: the knife is held in the hand with the edge forward and jutting from the bottom of the hand. A powerful uppercut blow should be devastating. But is it all it is cracked up to be? My son is a military intelligence officer. His training indicates the reverse grip may be effective but he has also seen the reverse grip turned upon the practitioner by experienced trainers. A skilled operator can step into the assault and gain control of the attacker's wrist and push the arm carrying the reverse grip back onto the attacker's body. The defender presses down and the point of the blade held in the reverse grip ends up in the victim's thigh. Not a very good ending for someone adopting a popular grip style. Use caution with the reverse grip.

On the other side of the coin, remember that the person advancing on you with the reverse grip may be a very skilled martial artist. Or a neophyte who has seen too much television.

This young lady can run and she can swing a machete. A machete is a common weapon these days – and a very effective edged weapon. At this range we need to quickly fire and fire accurately.

THE KNIFE AS A RETENTION AID

I have often stated that anyone who carries a handgun should carry a knife. The knife is a great aid in handgun retention and as a backup for the handgun. There are few situations that would call for a knife and not a gun but one such situation concerns weapons retention. When a gun grabber attempts to gain control of your firearm, there are several tactics he uses. One is the rearward-originating attack. While the knife may be used defensively in many ways, the blade is a great tool in retaining the primary weapon during this type of action. An attack from the rear may be accomplished by a confederate of the felon you are facing or an assailant who is striving to gain control of your weapon. The rearward-originating attack is often practiced in prison as surveillance photographs prove. The attack will wrap the left arm around the throat of the victim and lean to the rear to bring the victim's feet off solid contact with the ground while the right hand goes to his holstered sidearm. This tactic is primarily intended to gain control of the holstered sidearm of a peace officer but could be used against an armed civilian just as easily.

The first impulse in such an attack is to grapple with the arm that is around the neck, but seldom will we have sufficient strength to dislodge a solid lock around the throat. Very quickly our brain is deprived of oxygen and our vision blurs. Soon after, we will receive a bullet in the back or brain. If the gun is drawn, we might aim behind our body and shoot the attacker but if the handgun is holstered and we are being lifted off of the ground, we might be able to quickly draw a defensive folding knife and rip the blade across the arm that is across our neck. I cannot imagine anyone not moving the arm at this moment. You can then pivot and strike again if necessary. While some disciplines might stress defending the weapon with the strong-side hand, there is a need to very quickly address the problem of losing consciousness and we will indeed lose consciousness if the arm remains around our neck.

DEFENSIVE BLADES

There are good choices in defensive blades. The humble Spyderco Native is an affordable knife with good features. The Spyderco Military features a rug-

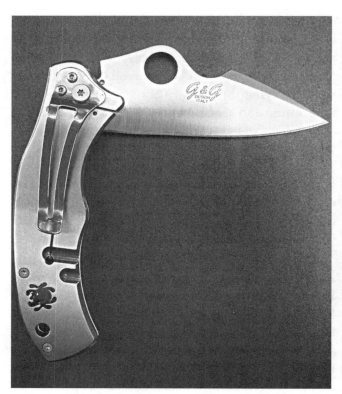

The Spyderco Volpe is just one of Spyderco's folders and an excellent folder with more than a little flash – and a razor sharp blade. Highly recommended for personal defense.

ged nonslip G10 handle and a sharp blade. The patented Spyderco opening mechanism is among the better choices in rapid deployment. The thumb simply finds the thumbhole and snaps the knife open, aided by a flick of the wrist.

Kershaw offers a true rugged hard-use knife in the form of the Zero Tolerance line. I am very impressed with these knives. At present my son favors the Kershaw Stephen Segal knife. While there is some flash involved, the Stephen Segal knife features a well-designed blade, fast opening, and a ray skin underlay that gives excellent support. This is a first-class folder.

It behooves us all to practice drawing the defensive blade. I carry my folders point up. I quickly grasp the handle and draw the knife, running my thumb to the opening device as I draw the knife. The thumb opens the blade as the wrist gives a snapping movement that aids in opening the blade. Some practice is needed to achieve a degree of confidence and speed, but once learned, a minimum of practice keeps you "sharp."

In this illustration the adversary has his arm around the author's neck and the author will lose consciousness if he does not react. A quick slash (applied in this case with a Spyderco SALT training knife) will do the business and enforce compliance – the arm will move.

Night Combat

When we consider standard tactical doctrines and balance them against some of what is taught, we may have conflict. As an example, tactical illumination is not something that I strictly adhere to in every situation. Nor have I been overly enthusiastic about turning my handgun into a beacon. Just the same we do not wish to be blind in a fight in the night.

I remember reading an account of a shootout in a dark warehouse in one of the great northern cities. I was a child in elementary school and while I cannot recall the author's name, the tense account of shots fired and the feeling of a muzzle flash in the dark sending a bullet your way was palpable. The account made quite an impression on me. This was not a gun story but a human story. The tension and terror of

nocturnal combat with no clear target available was well stated. The cop faced three burglars. He related the pop of a small caliber pistols and his own attempts at return fire that eventually wounded one of the burglars. The officer fired in their general direction until he had only a single round left and had wounded one of the felons. The others surrendered. The writer related that he dared not turn his flashlight on for fear of the adversary's bullets homing in on him. Perhaps this fear was well-founded and clinging to the dark side of a structure may make good tactical sense. Perhaps we must realize that darkness can be our ally if properly understood.

Don't get me wrong. Illumination has its place. The #1 advantage of illumination is target identification. During the War Between the States a Con-

The author demonstrates marrying the handgun and the light with a Taurus .44 Magnum and the Inova light. This is the Harries technique (discussed above).

federate general remarked after a night action, "We have killed one another in great number." He was referring to friendly fire and mistakes made by his own men during the night action. General Stonewall Jackson died from wounds received in a mistaken-identity shooting. The same type of tragedy has dogged combatants from Trojan times to Afghanistan. Some of the most capable commandos have fumbled their weapons in the darkness and others have made terrible mistakes.

A good light is a great tool for illuminating a threat in the home. We must be certain we are not dealing with a family member or the drunk down the street. I despise drunks but last I heard it was not a capital offense to become inebriated.

Do we wish to mount a light on the gun and always point where the light goes? Some feel that the gun light is an evolutionary step in handgun effectiveness. Does the light blind an opponent temporarily? If the scene is sufficiently dark, yes it does. Night blindness will occur quickly. But the shooter may be handicapped as well. I was once involved in an incident during which I dropped my flashlight in a field. My eyes were adjusted to the light and when

I dropped the light I was helpless for the few seconds it took for my eyes to adjust. I had not yet drawn my pistol so I would not have been able to use a weapon-mounted light had they been available at the time. As it turned out, the situation was resolved with a single round and the aid of night sights. It was a lesson but not as costly as it might have been.

During my time in uniform I used lights but at any time it was feasible I relied upon what I considered highly developed night vision. I often turned the lights off on the dash of the cruiser and sometimes stood outside it when running radar or staking out trouble spots on lonely stretches of highway. I felt that my night vision was good. I remembered reading about Marines assigned to night duty who sometimes moved about in the day with a bandage across their eyes to develop night vision. Since they were facing individuals who had grown up without electricity, they needed every advantage in night vision possible.

Lets look at some of the things I have learned that may be applicable to your personal situation. Lesson one: darkness is your friend, not your enemy. Criminals seldom carry a flashlight. A burglar

This young lady is the wife of a JAG officer. She is practicing in dim light and can take care of the situation if need be.

needs to stay hidden and not alert neighbors or the police to his unauthorized presence. Most are seldom without a cigarette lighter and this is what they use to look through drawers and closets. The light is ambivalent, natural, and less likely to cause suspicion than a flashlight. A penlight or flashlight is another matter. Only the most sophisticated burglar will carry a flashlight. Often the light is carefully shielded.

A few words on burglars, since they are the likely adversary in a night battle. Often they are someone familiar with the home. Many burglars are acquaintances of drug and alcohol-addicted family members. These rogue family members think much more of their pill popping and drinking friends than they do your life or that of your children.

When you are in the home and under cover of darkness, you can easily see into a lighted room while those in the light cannot see easily into darkness. I would not be shy about illumination if the identity of the threat is in question. For this reason I keep a pair of SureFire lights near the bedside. If the threat turns out to be a spouse or roommate, you will be glad for the illumination. The utmost discipline is required not to tangle your fingers and press the trigger when holding both the gun and the light. A handgun light switch and handgun trigger may be confused if you have a weapon mounted light. Remember, the first few minutes you are awake after rising from a deep sleep are not your prime thinking moments. The illuminated person may be a threat but he may not have offered an attack at this point. If he is warned and refuses to leave your residence or advances on your position, you have little choice but to defend yourself.

A different proposition is presented if you have children or elderly dependents in the home. In this case you have to have some idea of how to clear the area. (We must assume that you think enough of your children not to simply run into the yard and cry for help. I am aware of a number of cases in which parents have escaped the home and left children to fend with burglars.) When moving in a search you wish to keep as low a profile as possible. Keep one shoulder against the wall or nearly so.

Practice is required to avoid producing a scraping sound as you move in this manner, but you wish to remain close to the wall. If you are close to the wall you are not likely to be bowled over if the burglar

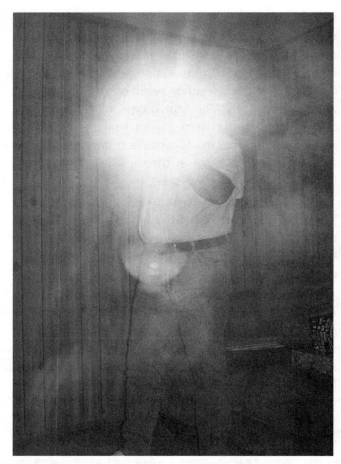

These are formidable tools: the Taurus 24/7 in .45 ACP and the SureFire combat light. This is a blinding light that works quite well.

takes a run at you and you are less likely to trip and fall. Always be alert to scraping noises and remember the adversary will be in the dark as well but you are familiar with the layout of the home.

When moving and illuminating in the home, the first rule is to avoid being outlined or illuminated yourself. Be aware of the danger of being backlit by house lights. Move into a room by sliding in one side of the doorway, not walking in through the center. A doorway is a sure target indicator. A punk in the other room with a .32 cannot miss a 200-lb. man coming through a doorway if he's backlit by the dining room chandelier. Do not become an outlined target!

You should have a good flashlight and illuminate as needed. Your toddler may have made his first escape from the crib. Or you may be facing a serial killer. You must have considered the situation and have tactics available to handle the scenario. If you are reading this book you are interested. Learn the necessary skills and you will be confident and calm. The alternative is to be helpless.

HANDGUN AND LIGHT COMBINATIONS

Few battles occur in inky blackness. The arena may be a living room, the alley behind your shop, or a bank parking lot as you make a night deposit. The theater of battle may be dimly lit but jet-black darkness exists in few places, including the wild. While some of us avail ourselves of the latest light rail and weapons light technology, others will marry the flashlight to the handgun with a special stance. Others will fight without illumination. In many situations at close range you can see the opponent in dim light and the conventional stance and grip you have mastered on the range will carry the day.

While the sights may be blurred, simple body positioning will work for you. Drawing and going to the proper stance and addressing the target quickly are vital to survival. But there are other considerations and among these is the eye and light combination. Marrying the light to the handgun with a stance is a fairly simple operation but must be practiced until muscle memory exists to support the tactics. I prac-tice flashlight tactics often and they are second nature to me after many years of practice. The main goal is to marry the light to the handgun in a manner in which accurate fire may be directed.

When the light and the pistol are paired correctly, both are addressed to the same point: the vital zone of the threat. We often use the light independently but when the time comes to fire, the handgun and the light should be on the same aiming point. A tip when searching: if the flashlight is aimed directly at an object there is a certain amount of glare. In practice I aim the flashlight at a doorway or a doorknob. If the light is directly on the doorknob you will not be able to discern details as well as if the light is aimed to one side or the other. Practice the proper target illumination.

As for the proper light, a plastic-body combat light for personal carry or a three-cell police model for the home is ideal. I often carry one of the Sure-Fire lights on my person. I have used SureFire prod-ucts for many years with satisfaction. These lights

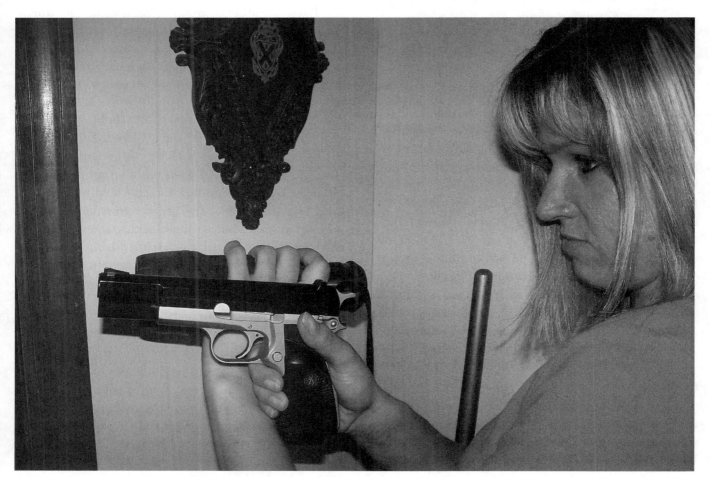

This young woman is using an inexpensive Dorsey light that works for her.

You really need to use a carrier for the combat light. This is a Gould and Goodrich belt carrier, a first class piece of kit.

are designed by leaders in the tactical field and get the job done. They are well suited to the problem of compact carry and illumination. The main criteria in choosing a light is that it works and that it fits your hands well, with a switch that is easily manipulated. Practice in activating the switch is mandatory. To marry the handgun and the light is to use the handgun and light in such a manner that they are aimed in the same direction and do not conflict. Practice is demanded so as not to compromise the handgun's action with the support hand. If you are willing to obtain and use a handgun with a rail, the Surefire X300 is the current top of the line, well suited for critical use. The X300 is more powerful than previous lights but also lighter. It's all we can ask for in a combat light.

Let's look at some of the tactics for use in marrying a hand-held light to the handgun. At the same time we must realize that the SIG GSR and X300 light will eliminate the need for some of these tactics.

THE HARRIES GRIP

Developed by respected trainer Michael Harries, the Harries grip is arguably the most successful hand and light combination ever developed. To execute the Harries grip, lock the backs of the hands together with the bulb side of the flashlight protruding from the bottom of the support hand. The thumb of the support hand is used to press the momentary switch of purpose-designed combat lights, or it can slide to the switch of conventional small flashlights. In either case the proper technique is to fully extend the firing hand and then slide the support hand under it and bring it up into contact with the firing hand. The backs of the hands touch, but when the technique is properly executed the back of the support hand is hard against the wrist of the firing hand. This practically secures a solid firing position – not quite as solid as the standard two-hand grip but sufficient for the work to be done at close range. The stance may be adopted very quickly with a minimum of motion.

There are other techniques but they are not worth the effort as they do not work as well as the Harries. There is no need to muddy the waters. At one time a technique generally taught at the police academy included holding the light far out at arm's length and the handgun in the other hand, with the operative premise being that the opponent would aim for the light rather than the officer involved. This is a difficult technique to use with any degree of accuracy. Such a hyperextended position is unnatural. Other stances I have examined include holding the gun and light in front of the shooter in a more or less aligned position but without locking the wrists. The Harries is the best and works well during movement in restricted quarters. The others are clumsy.

BODY POSITIONING

When we talk about body positioning while shooting in dim light, we are dangerously close to advocating point shooting. Always use your sights! But if your sights are only dimly visible, you have a serious problem. By the same token, all shooters cannot afford a SIG with night sights and the newest Sure-Fire. If there is not enough light to see the sights clearly, then try to find at least the outline of the slide or the top of the front sight. If you cannot aim, you probably should not fire at all.

When using the light and the gun, you might not always wish to point both the light and the gun at the perceived threat – it may be a family member. Practice the Harries Grip shown.

The author demonstrates the Harries in this view, with the arms high for better illustration.

Some advocate the finger point. The best point-shooting techniques (I do not consider these techniques unaimed techniques as we are using the body or slide to aim) use the same stance in night shooting as in firing in good light: we plant the feet and look toward the target. The handgun is held in the normal firing position and we aim for the target. If you have practiced and are a capable shot, you just may be able to place good hits at seven yards or so with this type of shooting. If you have not practiced, hits past fifteen feet are pure luck. In a true dim light situation, the slide (or cylinder) of the handgun can be used as a substitute for a sight.

NIGHT SIGHTS

Self-luminous iron sights are commonly known as night sights. Night sights are simply iron sights with a vial of radioactive tritium mounted into the sights. The glow ranges from a dull green to orange or yellow color, depending upon the type of precious stone used to focus the radioactive glow. The three-dot system is now universal. At one time there was some concern of misalignment with the fear that the front dot might be misaligned with the rear, in other words the sight picture might be completely wrong. In practice this is unlikely and, if necessary, the shooter may order his night sights in contrast. A competing system with much merit is the Heinie Eight Ball. The front dot is larger than the rear of two dots and when aiming the large front dot is superimposed over the rear dot. This is a good alternative that many shooters swear by.

Still another system that has enjoyed some popularity is the XS Sights Express Sight. This is a single large tritium ball on the front sight. I have used this sight extensively and returned to the three dot for all-around use. This is because my handguns are all-around handguns, used for competition and hunting as well as personal defense. As a pure personal defense system for use at moderate range the XS system has much to recommend. Night sights are an option I would not wish to be without, and it would behoove all of us to make certain our personal defense handgun is fitted with night sights.

LOW FLASH AMMUNITION

Practically all American-produced ammunition is treated with a flash suppressant or is loaded to produce a full powder burn. A full powder burn virtually eliminates offensive powder flash. For example, 230-grain .45 ACP hardball usually produces a few sparks and little muzzle flash. A 185-grain JHP in the same caliber uses more powder and often produces a warm orange glow. A full-power .357 Magnum load often produces a brilliant orange fireball that may produce night blindness with a single shot.

While there are other criteria in choosing a personal defense load, a minimum of muzzle signature is desirable. Winchester's SXT loadings are of high quality and often demonstrate a full powder burn in all calibers. This is a guidepost for choosing a loading. Most generic ammunition is intended to be used for practice and may produce more muzzle flash than service ammunition. That is just fine, as it meets the need for low-cost, reliable ammunition. A few shots fired in gathering dusk at the range can give you more insight into muzzle flash.

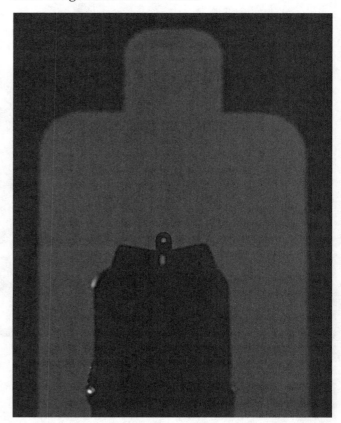

This is the XS Big Dot night sight. This sight is a good choice for nocturnal combat.

14 | Home Defense

All handgun work is close-range work. In a home the longest shot would be across your longest room or hallway. The marksmanship problem is not severe, but the tactics are worth consideration. Let's look at a number of incidents in which homeowners made decisions based on their own knowledge or tactics, good or bad.

In one case a homeowner heard a noise outside his home and went to investigate. This foray was not wise. Our hero was silhouetted by police flashlights and ordered to drop his firearm and assume the prone position. He was lucky that a calm and experienced officer was on the scene rather than the all-too-common hyper type. A neighbor had seen the real prowler and called the police. The homeowner was fine but spent a little time face-down on his lawn before he was positively identified.

In other cases homeowners returned home to find side doors open. One rushed through the mental process immediately. "Are the children home?" he asked. What could have happened? As it turned out the children had left the door open. We are human and leave the water running and doors unlocked from time to time, but just the same an open door may have serious consequences.

In yet another case a mother was suspicious of an open door and entered the dwelling after retrieving a pistol from her vehicle. She found her daughter

This young military intelligence officer is practicing firing in a simulation of a dwelling. It works well in acclimating the shooter to firing in tight quarters.

being assaulted and shot and killed one thug while wounding another. This incident had a satisfying ending but the mental and physical health of the good girls involved was put at risk. Take-over robberies and home invasions are increasingly more common. Nearly everyone taken hostage or held prisoner during such an event is killed or raped if not released within the first few minutes of such a crime. In July of 2007 I was particularly distressed by the brutal assault and rape of a mother and her two young daughters. Rescue must be immediate.

Awareness and alertness go a long way but the old .38 under the pillow looks good at close range. How exactly are we to proceed? We have to plan for the worst. We have to live scenarios in our mind's eye and practice tactical movement on the range and

This young woman is investigating a noise in the home. It might be a child moving around or her Boston Terrier. Note the cautious stance.

in the home. When something happens, it is too late to plan. You have to think quickly but some semblance of a plan should be in place. In my case, at the moment the only child still at home is my pre-teen daughter, and visiting grandchildren – most in the diaper stage – often room with her. If I hear a strange noise from her room, a breaking window or an unfamiliar voice, I am not going to waste any time calling 911. I have run into a number of burglars as a peace officer and I can assure you, they are not people you want visiting your home unannounced. When it isn't a dream and you have a home invader, and perhaps a family member held hostage, a lot can happen before the cops come and set up a command post in the front yard.

Having a handgun on hand is a start and so is practicing several times a month. But you don't realize how difficult the situation can be. Forget Hollywood nonsense. Anyone with tactical sense would have blown away any number of actors during a typical cinematic room-clearing exercise. The main thing on their mind is not to get caught looking directly into the camera or tripping and spoiling the scene. Well, perhaps you could learn something from their fluid movement but little else.

While we may conduct dry-fire exercises in the home, there is no substitute for live-fire training on a range with structures approximating a dwelling. High-end trainers are able to construct real houses or "shoot houses" and repair them after they are shot up. But shooting clubs of all sizes are able to build constructs that give good training.

Moving inside a dwelling in pursuit of felons is never recommended except to save the lives of family members. If communication is broken with the outside world – and some burglars do cut telephone lines – then the situation becomes tense even for a single home defender who is in his own bedroom. An important first consideration is getting the handgun ready. Many of us keep a holstered handgun beside the bed at night. Safes and locks are fine but when we are in the home, we need a handgun reasonably ready. In the closet is not acceptable. I most often unholster my handgun and place both the handgun and the holster either between the mattress and box springs with the butt out or in the Diamond Sentry holster that accomplishes the same thing much, much more efficiently.

When awaking to a possible threat, first grasp the handgun and be certain that it is not in contact with or pointed at any part of your body. You may access the handgun while still lying in the bed. (A recent rash of burglaries in my hometown began with the first warning of the burglar's presence being his appearance at the foot of the bed. There were crowded beds in some areas until the fellow was caught. One of my friends slept with her nine-year-old daughter between her and her husband and their 28-inch-barreled sporting shotgun –the only firearm in the family – to one side. There was an active rapist in town at the same time.)

When you are standing with the handgun in hand you may have a light in the non-dominant hand. An important point essential to your survival is this: be certain you are awake. I have been blessed with vivid dreams, but I have never mistaken a dream with reality. I have arisen at one hour thinking it was another and so have you. In the first ten minutes of consciousness, none of us is at our sharpest. Be certain you are aware and capable of making the correct decisions.

It is important you have moved quietly up to this point. We are going to go past the often-repeated advice of crawling on the far side of the bed and calling 911. That is good common sense advice, but it won't work with children in the house. You must have practiced moving quickly or slowly, quietly, and with the proper stance in tactical movement. Stick close to the walls. Slide the feet rather than move your feet in long steps. If there are laundry or toys lying about, you may fall. A fall may result in a broken bone and will certainly alert an intruder.

It is a bad idea to cross your feet during this type of movement. You have to move quickly but take your time. Sometimes moving too quickly is a bad decision. As you move you may be on the lookout for what police trainers call target indicators. Target indicators are simply reflections, lights, or breaks in the usual outline of the wall or furniture. This indicates someone unauthorized is in the home. If that unauthorized person is Sissy's boyfriend, well, you can't just shoot him.

Remember, I am concentrating on true home defense with family members present. If you and your spouse are the only ones home the situation if different and yelling "I have a gun!" and waiting for the door to slam as the felon beats feet is certainly an option. But an occupied dwelling with family members present must be defended.

SLICING THE PIE

Slicing the pie works with large and small rooms and open spaces of all types. Remember, the felon in the room has a far less area of concern. He only has to watch the door. If you enter too soon the felon may grasp your handgun or he may bring a table or chair crashing down on you. Keep the handgun close in to the body. While the problems of fighting with a light are covered in another chapter, in room clearing you might keep the gun and light separated prior to recognizing the need to fire. If you lead with a light and give a momentary squirt, the felon may slash or strike at your light. But if he lands a blow he will not necessarily take the handgun out at the same time.

This homeowner is carefully moving parallel to the wall and close to the wall to avoid making a target indicator.

If you stand back from the opening and carefully "pie" the room, your chances of survival are much greater.

Take your time and attempt to scope out the situation – do not move too quickly.

Preparing to move is called staging. This is a finite moment when you get into the proper stance and grip the handgun and light properly. Then you begin to move. When you move from your own room you literally scoot on your feet quickly to the other side of the hall, presenting a difficult target. (Customize these recommendations for your own home.)

When approaching the next door, listen intently for sounds in the other room. Labored breathing, as that of someone in a struggle, or movement against furniture is important. Very carefully open the door or step toward an open doorway. Take a hard look at one slice of the room. Usually we attempt to look to the right on an inward opening door. We cover the sliver of territory and then slowly move to another, covering each area with our eyes and illuminating as needed. We will end up with a small section that is a blind section to us, usually to our left shoulder. We then stand back and carefully move into a position to observe this section before moving into the room. You have thus sliced the pie or covered the segmented sections of a room.

While in principle it is simple, in practice, you have to be cautious and move carefully on your feet. You need to take a dry run in your house and practice clearing each room. Rooms with a door in the corner of the room or middle of the room present different problems. Without training you will never realize what the different problems are. You are going to read this book, meet the author in the middle, and train yourself on room clearing. You have to crank the stress up and imagine you are in a race to save a family member – but you have to do it safely and well or you may be killed or injured and unable to protect the family member.

A burglar doesn't care what type of gun you have, and having a gun is important. The skill with which you wield the firearm is more important. At this point I am going to talk a little about the aftermath of a gunfight and also my opinion on instructors. It is best to learn from an instructor with police experience and one who has walked the mean streets. These fellows are not as few and far between as you may

This person is providing a target weighing well over 200 pounds. Even without sights, with a person silhouetted in the doorway in this manner, it would be hard to miss.

This resident is carefully eyeing the corner and "slicing the pie" before moving into the next room.

suppose. Not all have received international recognition but some have. The fellow who has attended lots of schools may be a good shot but he has not walked the walk. Knowing when to shoot is an important as knowing how to shoot. When you have been there you will avoid a shooting if at all possible.

A point that is not stressed enough is that a miss is not acceptable. We should not fire unless we are sure of a hit. This is not a harsh rule. Learning not to press the trigger unless you are lined up correctly is a skill worth any effort. An instructor who has looked over both ends of the gun barrel knows the "tyranny of the moment." No matter how clear cut the case, remember be certain you are right in firing. A hostile witness can be devastating to your case.

Peace officers involved in shootings under color of law find the experience gut-wrenching, even with union and legal support. According to my research, eighty percent of officers involved in shootings make a change in agencies soon after a shooting.

Your chances of being shot in a true gunfight, with both sides firing, are about 50-50. Most handgun wounds are survivable. Taking cover helps. If you shoot the adversary, do not leave cover. Be cautious. He may be a member of a team. Increasingly we are seeing "Bonnie and Clyde" teams, with one man and one woman.

You had better have your mind made up concerning whether you are able to pull the trigger on a woman. They are deadly as any male. Do not shoot the fellow after he is down. I have heard the expression "Better tried by twelve than carried by six." You may change your mind if you find yourself in the Crossbar Motel. If you have shot someone, call an ambulance immediately. Advise 911 operators of the general situation. Be concise. "I was attacked by a burglar. I shot him. Send an ambulance." If there are witnesses, be certain to get their names and addresses. Never move anything. A damaged crime scene is transparent to an investigator.

Remember, cops don't get armed-citizen calls. They get man-with-a-gun calls. Set the gun aside when you see the boys in blue. Control your emotions. Most officers will be sympathetic. Some have advised that you say nothing to the police. If you go that route, you will almost certainly be arrested. You may decline some questions but do not lie. If you lie, your motives and actions are suspect.

Do not put yourself in a situation in which you may make an inaccurate statement. I would never say I fired two, four, or six rounds because almost certainly you will be wrong. Another important piece of advice: after the shooting is over, check for injuries. I was once involved in an explosion and did not realize that I had received third degree burns. On two occasions I was struck by bullet fragments and the first was not noticed until blood leaked down my trouser leg. Be sure you have not been shot. As soon as possible, contact a reliable friend or family member and tell him of your situation.

There is a bit more to home defense than shooting. Be aware, be prepared.

THE STANCE DURING MOVEMENT

When moving in the home, it is not advisable to extend the arms in an isosceles stance. The Weaver is a proven stance that is more versatile than most think but can conflict with movement. Holding the handgun in front of the body with the arms extended may be tiring. The best stance or position I have found is to keep the handgun close to the body with the elbows bent. The handgun may be brought into action immediately but the line of vision is not obscured. The elbows-flexed position is faster into action than simply letting the arms hang in front of the body, but not nearly as much muscular effort is required as with an isosceles shooting stance.

A final tactical note: never lead into the next room with your handgun. Keep the handgun at low ready with the elbows bent as I described. High ready is popular in the cinema but less effective in real life. With the handgun in low ready position you have a good line of sight and you are able to instantly bring the handgun to eye level, ready to fire. If you lead with the firearm, a felon in the next room may be ready to grab the weapon. Be certain that you skirt corners when you move into the other room rather than hugging them. You stay close to the wall in linear movement, but when you are prepared to move into another room there should be considerable offset.

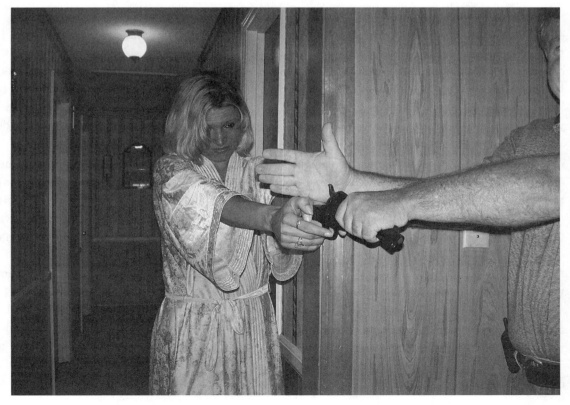

If you lead with the gun past a corner, this is what may happen.

15 Cover Up

The use of cover is among the most important tactical ideas that professional instructors will beat into your head. Those who use cover, live. If you have not got your man down or gotten to cover in the first three seconds, your battle may be over. Cover is quite simply the most precious thing you can have. Cover is anything that will stop a bullet. The best means of getting to cover is to be aware of your surroundings. As you walk down a street, casually but alertly examine the objects in your path such as vehicles and phone booths. Some offer little cover while others offer complete bullet-stopping protection even if the adversary has a high powered rifle. As a bonus, once you reach cover, you may be able to brace your handgun and return fire more accurately.

There is a grave difference between concealment and cover. Concealment may offer some protection if the adversary does not see you. A line of hedges qualifies as concealment. A plastic garbage can is only concealment, not cover. A metal trash bin is cover. Only objects that will stop a bullet are cover. A large tree is better than a longer line of hedges. A vehicle engine block is better than a car door.

When the subject of cover is introduced, most of us understand the value of cover but not how to successfully implement cover. For example, if you are caught flat-footed on the street and an assailant is approaching with a shotgun would you,

A) Run for nearby cover;

B) Draw and attempt to shoot him; or

C) Draw on the run for cover?

The author demonstrates the proper setback from the vehicle to avoid bullet splatter and ricochet and also to present a small target.

A) is close to being correct but C) is the answer. It would be foolish to draw against a drawn gun if there is an alternative. As for drawing on the run, in a given situation you need to either draw or run but not both. Drawing conflicts with movement (running) and movement conflicts with the draw. Once you are behind cover, you can then draw the handgun and respond with gunfire if appropriate. The assailant may take out his wrath on a vehicle, wall or whatever cover you have taken. You may be able to fire around cover or under cover in order to get a hit. The value of cover is dependent upon what type of armament your adversary is using. Most vehicle doors are proof against common pistol bullets if the bullet strikes support braces of the window track, but a high velocity 9mm can easily penetrate the outer skin of a vehicle door and continue into the vehicle. An engine block is proof against an elephant rifle, but the rear quarters of a vehicle are easily penetrated by handgun bullets.

I have dealt extensively with the subject of firearms versus vehicles in *SWAT Magazine, Police Magazine*, and *Voice of American Law Enforcement*. These tests are always enlightening and I like to perform a new series every few years with popular developments in ammunition tested against modern sheet metal. Vehicles play a part in as many as fifty percent of police gunfights. Bullet performance against vehicles is an important consideration for these agencies. For the personal defense shooter, vehicle penetration is far less important but we need to know what will happen when a bullet meets a vehicle. Here are a few rules that apply to vehicles:

WINDSHIELDS

When you must fire into a vehicle, the windshield can be resistant to handgun bullets. Shots fired from the front of the vehicle will be given a downward angle that is insignificant considering their short path. On the other hand, bullets fired from inside the vehicle through the windshield quickly find an upward angle. At as little as ten yards they may impact a foot above the point of aim. Glass shards can cover a vehicle and blow into your eyes when shots are fired into a vehicle or out of a vehicle. High-velocity, lightweight bullets such as the 90-grain 9mm and even 185-grain .45s shed their jacket in vehicle windshields and the bullet core will simply fall into the front seat. If the scenario involves felons in vehicles,

you would be wise to choose a law enforcement load such as the Hornady TAP, Winchester SXT, Federal HST, the Speer Gold Dot or Black Hills JHPs.

SIDE PANELS

Vehicle doors can be penetrated by most handgun bullets but if the track or window regulator is struck, even a .44 Magnum will be stopped. The most profitable point of aim is just above the center of the door to just below the center of the door.

REAR DOORS

The rear doors of most SUVs are very heavily constructed, with a heavy window lift and lock mechanism. In my testing, only the .357 Magnum with heavy loads and the .357 SIG would get *some* of the bullets into the passenger area when fired into an SUV's rear door. When firing into a vehicle, the need must be extreme. The bullet may bounce or ricochet and strike someone in the vehicle. The utmost caution should be observed.

IN THE HOME

In the home, most doors are hollow and offer little protection from gunfire. Drywall and studs offer some protection. Heavy furniture can be a lifesaver. The point is, cover may stop a bullet and mask your outline. Few of us can make an accurate estimate of the position of a body behind cover even if our handgun has sufficient power to penetrate the cover and take the felon out. By the same token, when behind a wall the attacker will not be able to gauge our position well. Sometimes, merely by taking cover we will force the foe to recognize they are in an untenable position.

Cover is a two-way street and all armed assailants are not ignorant of its value. We need to develop an ability to strike small targets. The adversary may take cover and leave only a foot or elbow in the open. By the same token, when firing from cover, do not leave any more of the body open to gunfire than you must. Firing over the top of cover is a bad idea if we can fire from the side. If you are behind cover you may just wait the adversary out. If he ventures behind our cover, it is his bad judgment.

If you are not a peace officer or soldier charged with apprehending criminals or terrorists, the risks you should take are much less. To find cover and stay there may be winning the battle, and doing so cheaply. If the threat persists, you must go with what you know.

Lee Berry is young and in good shape. He can compress his body behind cover and fire accurately. He would be a tough adversary, as he has proven in competition.

FIRING AROUND COVER

Firing from a kneeling braced position works well when from a covered position. Hopefully all of our cover will be strong-hand friendly but it might not be. Of special consideration is the fact that a right-handed shooter bracing against a wall to his right may find himself in the perfect situation for spent brass to bounce against the wall and then into the pistol's ejection port. I have had this happen in competition and, while quickly cleared, it is nothing we wish to repeat. At the range, firing too close to a wall blows soot and powder ash onto the shooter. By tilting the pistol slightly the spent case ejects farther from the wall and the case cannot bounce into the slide. This is a habit well worth developing.

Firing from a prone position around cover can be decidedly accurate. A rollover prone minimizes the target profile of the body and gives the shooter a solid platform. It is slow to roll out of if we need to make tactical movement, but when implemented it can be a good tactical move. When considering cover, three things must be understood. First, we wish to make our target area smaller. Second, we wish to place that target area behind something solid that will stop a bullet. Third, if we decide to return fire we must do so intelligently while exposing a minimum of our target area. The target area is our body. Having found myself on the wrong end of gunfire, I can tell you that cover is a precious thing that should be cultivated and, whenever possible, utilized.

One of the more difficult things to teach students is how to properly fire from cover or a barricade. A

This shooter is firing with the Kimber Defense Pistol from vehicle cover. Not ideal, but better than being naked.

constant mistake is crowding cover. If we are too close to the cover we take we run the risk of presenting an easy target and also of being on the receiving end of a ricochet. If you stand back just a little from cover you present a smaller target and you are able to fire more efficiency. Let's look at examples of the right and the wrong way.

If you are crowding cover you will draw the handgun and lean out to clear the barricade. You will bring the handgun to bear and engage targets. You can raise or lower the handgun to clear the barricade and you may have to move behind the barricade to adjust your firing position.

Try stepping back one yard back from the barricade and using it for cover. You will find that you are able to direct fire at the target and kneel or perform a reload without resorting to difficult movement while keeping your eye on the target. Likewise, if you are using a vehicle for cover it is best to be a yard or so behind the vehicle. Anyone attempting to rush the vehicle or sneak up on your firing position will probably assume you are crowding the vehicle. However, if you stand back a few feet and fire around the corner of a vehicle, you are much less susceptible to ricochet.

I once fired a .41 Magnum bullet into a heavy 1970s sedan. The bullet fully penetrated the vehicle door but struck a seat brace and flew out the roof of the vehicle and presumably kept going to Mars. The path of the Speer 200-grain JHP was remarkable. Bullet ricochet is unpredictable. A bullet that impacts the hood of a vehicle and bounces will bounce upwards. If you are standing close to the vehicle, chances are you will receive more than a bad headache. Standing back from cover is a first-line tactic that behooves every shooter to learn.

Be tactically aware of the cover available in your working environment. If the only cover you have is a street corner curb, take it. Cover may also be powerful psychologically. I once attended a class in which the instructor demonstrated a point by holding his hand in front of him as he drew. The student standing in front of him holding an unloaded firearm attempted to move into a position to fire around the instructor's hand. Logic should have told the student that the bullet would go through the hand, but even a hand held in front of the face deterred the student from firing for a second, and that was enough to make a valid point. When you are behind cover, you have reduced the opponent's tactical options. Even street thugs will realize this.

The subject of cover is a simple one but a subject that has been ignored far too often. Be prepared to stand and fight on your feet, but when cover is available, it's smart to take advantage of it.

Lee Berry demonstrates excellent form in firing from cover.

16 Female Defense Drills

A female acquaintance of mine recently became very interested in personal defense and concealed carry and enrolled in a crash course. I did not perceive a great deal of interest in handguns per se but more in tactics and the defensive lifestyle. She is a very good student who learns quickly. She wanted to obtain the right gear right now! She sees handguns as a tool or means to an end. Just the same, she desired a good handgun and wanted to make an appropriate choice.

The fellows at the gun shop she went to were probably well-meaning but they made a bad impression. "I am not handicapped," she said, "so why do I need a woman's gun?" All of her life she had been steered toward a woman's options – a woman's car and now a woman's gun! I sympathized with both sides. With the proper attitude there are pitfalls that may be avoided. It is not as if males make good choices every time they purchase a handgun. The typical scenario for most shooters is to purchase a handgun that is larger than they are able to comfortably carry and more powerful than they can control. The pistol is left at home, and eventually the shooter moves to a handgun that is smaller and more comfortable to carry. Perhaps steering a female shooter to a compact handgun in the first place is a good choice.

While both sexes are equally capable in marksmanship, there are differences in male and female physiques. On average, men are taller, broader, and heavier than women. Women have smaller hands but often have long fingers well suited to handgunning. The borrom line is that women must make discretionary choices. A female shooter must realistically evaluate her size and body shape just as a man must. There are thin males who cannot conceal a bulky Glock and women who carry the 1911. With differences in size and strength understood, let's put on our thinking caps and have a meeting of the minds.

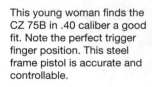

This young woman finds the CZ 75B in .40 caliber a good fit. Note the perfect trigger finger position. This steel frame pistol is accurate and controllable.

The first criteria for a woman's handgun must be reliability. Quality isn't cheap. I have tweaked and modified a few pistols into reliable specimens but the average shooter of either sex needs a reliable handgun from the beginning. Colt, Smith & Wesson, Ruger, Springfield, Kimber, Kahr, Beretta, SIG, CZ, Browning, Heckler & Koch and Taurus offer reliable handguns. A number of impressive handguns offer performance that outshines their price. But only reality-based decisions will be profitable for the shooter.

The question of semi-auto versus revolver comes up often. I recommend the snubnosed .38 Special revolver to all beginning shooters for concealed carry, regardless of their gender or statue. For home defense use, a four-inch-barreled .357 Magnum revolver that may be used with .38 Special ammunition is ideal. But some shooters advance more quickly than others and come to prefer the automatic.

As I have mentioned, in concealed carry the revolver's cylinder bulge may resemble a snake that has swallowed a possum. Careful wardrobe and holster selection is needed. But a compact automatic such as the Kel-Tec 9mm worn close to the body in an open-top holster is easier to conceal than a revolver.

The light automatic should probably be a double-action first shot or double-action-only because it will be carried snug to the form and in the beginning simplicity is important. I use single-action pistols but when the pistol is to be carried in deep concealment tight against the body, well, we are facing a different problem in handling.

Some short-slide semi-automatic pistols use heavy recoil springs in order to keep slide velocity and recoil controllable. These pistols can present some difficulty in racking the slide. There are techniques that are useful to allow all of use to use these pistols. The handgun is brought close to the body and the frame grasped tightly in the strong side hand. The weak hand grasps the slide on the cocking serrations – with the pistol as close to the body as possible – and racks the slide. If you can handle a vacuum-sealed jar, you can handle a pistol slide.

You cannot pick a pistol haphazardly and expect it to perform. Each pistol requires instruction, if not in a local class, then in the form of distance education. That means this book and others like it. A regular subscription to *Women and Guns* magazine is a good idea, too.

This shooter simply enjoys firing the Taurus .44 Magnum. For personal defense it is loaded with the Speer Gold Dot .44 Special. The result is a controllable, powerful home defense revolver.

Often a father, husband or boyfriend attempts firearms instruction. Sometimes it works well for all concerned but not always. If the male is concerned with his spouse, sister or daughter he should find good instruction. Husbands are seldom the best instructors. Often the gentle give-and-take inherent in a relationship suffers when one or the other becomes the instructor who is always right.

SIZE AND CALIBER

Size and caliber are related but not as much as they once were. I find that men tend to go looking for a good 9mm or .45 while females choose the handgun first and then inquire about caliber. Good-quality handguns weighing less than 25 oz. are available in .38 Special, 9mm Luger, .40 Smith & Wesson and even .357 Magnum. I am not comfortable with the lightweight Magnum revolvers below 28 oz. Few students survive with their nerves intact after firing a cylinder of Magnum cartridges in a five-shot revolver weighing less than 16 oz. I have been told my thumb joint is bony and not padded well. I am certain a mentally determined female shooter can use the .357 Magnum snubnose better than the author is able to. I am equally sure most of her practice should be done with the .38 Special cartridge.

For most female shooters, the concealable choice will be a compact 9mm or a snubnosed .38. I have my own ideas concerning effective calibers but I will not force these views on others in light of their own ability. A .380 automatic, as an example, is not worthless and there is considerable deterrent value in any handgun. But the handgun must be able to perform if the action proceeds past the deterrent stage. A light caliber is not necessarily a pistol devoid of recoil. Some of the light .380s exhibit considerable recoil. So do .38 snubs with serious loads.

Sharp edges are also a factor in controlling a handgun. I know cops who carried backup handguns they had never fired. I served under an executive who had his Sergeant – the author – evaluate and sight in the man's personal defense sidearm. While the range time and ammunition were enjoyable and I verified that the weapons were reliable, I am not certain I accomplished anything for the Chief. I certainly added little to his personal defense skills and nothing to his knowledge of the handgun's trigger and sights. But he was an ex-military man who told

me anyone should be able to get a gun off the rack and use it well. He was too busy to shoot for himself. Female shooters sometimes find themselves in the same situation and must avoid this thinking at all costs. Do your own shooting!

How well should you be able to use that handgun? Most defensive encounters take place at seven yards or less. The ability to quickly bring the pistol on target and make a center hit is important. A cluster of sixty rounds or so on the target after a training class is good, but perhaps we may not do as well if we run the same course with a snub .38 or compact 9mm. These handguns require intense concentration for good results. The one-shot qualifier is viable for such handguns. That is, draw and get a hit. Holster and try again. Just the same, competent shooters should be able to fire at least fifty rounds through their handguns comfortably.

Once the basic skills are in place and mastered, do not forget the one-shot qualifier and do not relax. A tip on learning to use the light handguns: once you have mastered a full-size handgun and developed confidence and skill the small guns are easier. It is far better to master a mid-sized handgun and then proceed to choosing a carry gun than to begin with the light handgun first. Female shooters will profit immensely from regular practice with a .22 caliber rimfire handgun. These handguns are relatively inexpensive but the ammunition is dirt cheap and it will build your defensive skills.

I think that if female shooters in particular and all shooters in general have a shortcoming, it is a lack of complete familiarity with the handgun. The controls and trigger action must be familiar to the shooter. The

The 1911 offers excellent hand fit for female shooters. This is a concealable RIA compact. Note the straight to the rear trigger compression.

fine art of trigger compression must be understood. The trigger break can be practiced with a triple-checked unloaded handgun. Women's hands may be smaller than males', but many women have long, slender fingers that are an advantage in trigger manipulation.

This partially offsets any hand-size problem. I think that the availability of comfortable, popular-sized handguns such as the Taurus 24/7 and the Kahr K40 are a great aid in outfitting shooters who have average; to small-sized hands. All that is required is that the user handle each pistol in the showcase and find a good hand fit. Other features such as high visibility sights and the finish may sway the final decision, but if you do not have hand fit you have nothing. If the handgun is too large for your hands you will never perform to your full potential.

On the other hand, do not jump to the micro-sized mini-automatic pistol. This includes the Glock 27 among others. I am not knocking these compact handguns but the light handguns are not best suited for general use and practice. If you choose a handgun that is uncomfortable to fire and difficult to use well, you will not practice often.

Choosing the action type is also important. Some of the double-action-only pistols are difficult to use well by a person of limited hand strength. The Taurus 24/7 is again one of the stars of the line up as far as hand fit and trigger action. This handgun is on my short list of the most versatile and effective handguns for all users.

Double-action and double-action-only handguns are well suited to the lifestyle of modern shooters. A truly smooth double-action-only handgun such as the Kel-Tec or Kahr compact handguns will fare well at the usual combat range. A smooth double-action press is an aid in preventing flinch, for example. There are several sizes of pistols – pocket, belt and holster gun being common descriptions. Holster guns are service pistols such as those carried by law officers. Holster guns are often carried on the belt under a light jacket. The pocket pistol is the lightest of handguns. We need to avoid extremes of size on either end of the spectrum, too large or too small, and choose a handgun in the middle ground. Only the woman who is interested can make the final decision. I think that the middle-of-the-road compacts such as the SIG P 229 or the Glock 23 are nearly ideal.

This is Izzie's first shot with a handgun. She has moved to the shotgun and even fired a few rounds from the .45 automatic. We predict she will become a good shot. There is nothing lacking in attitude and gumption.

The female shooter needs a reliable handgun that is as powerful as she can control and one that fits her hands well. These middle of the road handguns are good choices, and each is available in the hard-hitting .40 Smith & Wesson cartridge.

FEMALE-SPECIFIC DRILLS

I have studied the problem of assaults on females for nearly thirty years and have identified some of the tactics that assailants of all stripes and rapists in particular use when attacking female victim.

Criminals are most likely to grab a woman by the arm with both of their hands. This implies a confidence in their greater strength. Most often they are stronger and heavier than their victim. The first impulse of the victim is to jerk the arm away. This is seldom successful. The thug may have a considerable weight advantage and you are not going to tug him off balance. You cannot win. Even if you are armed, if the assailant has grabbed your gun hand and you are off balance, you have little chance with the weak hand unless you have practiced the weak-hand draw diligently.

The proper technique is to use the assailant's own force against him. Step backward, forcing the attacker to apply more pressure to pull your arm. Whether you move him or not, it is a natural reaction for him to pull harder. Before he actually pulls you off balance, move forward rapidly into his line of force, driving your hand into his body as hard as possible. The thug has braced for a pull against him and by driving forward aggressively and instantly, you may be able to force him off balance. If you are able to combine a strike with your nails to his eyes with the free hand or a strike with your feet, you have an excellent chance of working free and surviving. An important component of this drill is to grasp the trapped hand with the free hand as you strike and pull the trapped hand up and free.

The second most common method of attack is a rearward-originating attack. The felon may be prepared for a struggle but not prepared for you to go limp and immediately fall to the ground with all your weight. Even a muscular thug will find the sudden tug of your body weight slamming to the floor difficult to support. As you fall, reach behind your back in a wide

This young woman enjoys the SIG P229 .40. However, she has proven she has the ability to get the most out of any handgun. Some of the ability seems a natural high coordination but some is good instruction. She is the strong link in the equation, not the handgun.

sweep and grab the lowest part of his body. The ankles are preferred. Pull forward with all of your might. He should lose his feet and the fall may be hard enough to injure him temporarily. Then get away!

Good personal defense skills build confidence and allow you to remain calm during a critical incident. If the above-described tactics work and you are able to free yourself, you should immediately draw your weapon and retreat, even run. If the attack is resumed, go with what you know and use deadly force. If you are unarmed, run for your life to your vehicle or into a crowd or the nearest business in a well-lighted area. None is a sure thing, but if you are unarmed your options are limited.

As for specific firearms drills, female shooters should practice the same drills and tactics as anyone else interested in personal defense. However, I have discovered that female shooters in particular excel at the Applegate drill for some reason. Colonel Rex Applegate was an accomplished trainer of vast experience in Army Special Operations and crowd control as well as weapons. The Applegate drill, or Applegate point as it is sometimes called, borrows from his wartime experience with British trainers. This drill is covered in the section on close range combat.

Female shooters are well advised to keep the handgun close at hand when home alone, even if this means moving the handgun from the bedroom to the kitchen during the day. Too often an unauthorized person has gained entry to the home and attacked a defenseless woman who could have saved herself had she been armed. The practice of stashing an inexpensive handgun or two around the homestead could be a lifesaver.

FEMALE-SPECIFIC GEAR

Women have high waists and low ribs. This combination can lead to a holster that jams into the ribcage if a holster designed for the typical male build is used. When the holster has a high rise and little drop, most female shooters simply will not be able to use this combination well. It is my contention that all shooters have benefited from the addition of female-specific holsters in the product line because they are now able to choose from a variety of holsters with a wide choice of drop and draw angle.

The leader in service gear for female shooters used to be Gould and Goodrich. Their innovative Lady Paddle or Lady Gripper was among the first female-specific duty holsters. The drop of a female-specific holster is well suited to the female shape. The curve of a woman's hips moves the holster in the wrong direction otherwise. The first female-specific holsters used a hardened leather wedge to move the holster in the proper direction. Today this wedge is often a design component of the holster.

Full-force hands-on training is essential for a well-developed personal defense program.

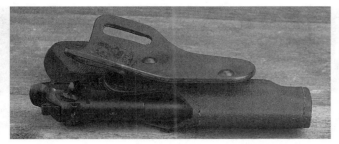

The Wilson Combat company offers first-class leather gear specifically designed with the proper offset for female shooters.

There are a number of makers offering good female-specific holsters. Chris Cunningham grew tired of wearing men's holsters and designed her own. These holsters are now available to the public. Jim Murnak of Fist, Inc., offers a special line called the Lady Fist. These are good choices for serious female shooters. Remember the requirements of a good holster are the same for male and female but female-specific holsters have a different cant and offset that allow a rapid draw and good concealment.

All new shooters find the weight of a handgun uncomfortable at first but once the acclimation period is over, they find the pistol comforting but still not comfortable. You simply acclimate. I am not enthusiastic about concealed carry handbags but then I admit some are very well made and designed. Women often carry in handbags and men have the briefcase. It sure beats having no weapon at all but carefully consider the draw from a handbag and keep the purse close at hand.

A defensive skill that should be mastered by females is the knife. A book on fighting with a knife is something I have seriously considered but the fact is if you are able to box, you can fight with a knife. I recently presented my stepdaughter, Jessie, with a P'Kal from Spyderco and a companion trainer. She is getting pretty smart with the knife and it goes where a gun cannot go. Few felons would like to venture into a female's slashing defensive circle.

At this point I will address a fallacy concerning armed resistance to felons and especially resistance to rapists. There have been ill-advised officials who have recommended to women not to resist as they may be killed if they offer a fight. In my experience and after studying hundreds of cases, I feel the opposite is true. Those who resist often escape and live. The criminal element chooses women as victims because they are perceived as easy victims. Nothing makes me happier than when a victim gives the thug a well-deserved surprise.

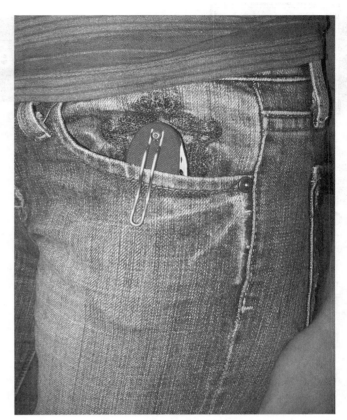

When practicing with a Spyderco training knife, safety is foremost while speed is learned.

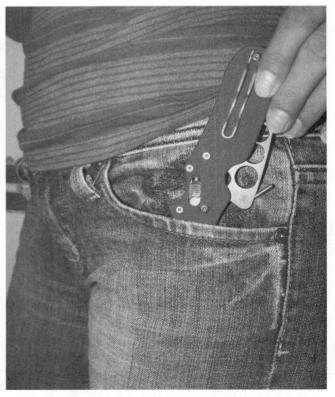

Anyone would be a fool to walk into the slashing defensive circle of this young lady. She is pretty quick drawing her Spyderco and practices with this training knife often.

17 Animal Defense

Animal homicides are relatively rare but this is not a comfort if you are one of the five hundred or so humans killed by animals each year in America. This figure excludes snake and insect bites. I get around a dozen queries of all types for every query on animal attacks but when an attack of this type is in the news, the ratio is reversed. Most of the critical dog-attack victims are children or older people. But peace officers have been severely injured by animals as well.

Let's look at the proven reality of the situation. First, wild animals. All animals must have a certain comfort zone. This may range from one hundred yards to a half mile, depending upon the animal. This is why hunters must be excellent stalkers and very patient to have any degree of success in the wild. The woods are full of creatures that you do not see when hiking. If you startle the beast he may be dangerous. By the same token, a sick or injured animal reduced to raiding human camps for food can be quite dangerous.

The most dangerous animals are probably the big cats. Bears are certainly deadly but they are so big they are often spotted before they come close in for the attack. If you do not have a handgun, it doesn't matter much if he is spotted. You are still helpless. On the other hand, I am aware of a bear killed with a log and another with an axe. Big cats have recently been invading human territory and attacking joggers and bikers. One victim reported being dragged one hundred yards by her hair. She survived but was terribly injured. And that is the real story in animal attacks. While few are actually killed by animals, many are scarred or crippled.

This is a good result in rapid fire with Black Hills 9mm +P loads. This rapid fire volley should do the business.

The range is a bit long and unrealistic in this range drill, but it could happen. Rapid fire with a powerful handgun will be a lifesaver.

When hiking or camping in country that may have a dangerous animal population, the obvious first line of defense is a Magnum revolver. There have been discussions concerning the penetration ability of the .38 Super and 9mm NATO and various other automatic pistol calibers but that is playing with your life. The .357 Magnum and the .44 Magnum have done the business and the users have survived. The .44-40 has served and so has the .45 Colt, but in standard revolvers the last two really need to be loaded with heavy handloads using hard-cast bullets. A .357 Magnum with a four-inch barrel is a fine choice. With a 180-grain hard-cast bullet such as the Buffalo Bore, the .357 will serve. The .44 Magnum with Black Hills, 300-grain JHP is a fine choice.

The reason I am adamant about the revolver is my study of successful animal defense. In the majority of cases the attack occurred so quickly the defender had time only to jam his revolver into the animal's body and press the trigger. In this type of shooting, a semi-automatic pistol would jam. It is patently flawed logic to expect anything else. If all you

have is a semi-automatic, practice situational awareness and hope for the best. If you have some warning and can make an accurate shot, the semi-automatic may serve. Once you are bowled over you are at a disadvantage with any automatic.

For a semi-automatic for the outdoors, the 10mm automatic comes to mind as comparable to the .357 Magnum. Cor-Bon's heavyweight hunting loads would be the choice. But the revolver is the best choice. In September of 2007 a woman defended herself against pit bulls but her pistol jammed. In another incident a peace officer rolling on the ground with a dog failed to disengage the safety of his off-duty pistol quickly enough to shoot the dog. He survived but things could have gone better.

If you are hunting or fishing in Alaska and wish to have a hogleg on the hip suitable for stopping a grizzly bear there are few choices. The .44 Magnum with one of the 320-grain Cor-Bon Penetrator loads is just about all any of us could expect to master. But there are numerous lightweight .44 Magnums and the short barrel steel-frame Ruger Alaskan. The

`This is a custom revolver from BCR—Bowen Custom Revolvers. If you really need a .500 caliber handgun in your travels this is the place to begin looking.

At short range, you have got to keep your head about you and pump rounds into the charging beast!

Alaskan is a .454 Casull handgun. I have used one hundred rounds of Cor-Bon over the past six months evaluating this handgun. Never in my life have my hands trembled from blast and shock after a shooting session. A sturdy death grip is required and even then the piece rises over my head. But for those in real need this is the champ.

The .44 Magnum with penetrator loads is viable option but for an experienced handgunner comfortable with the big bore Magnums, the .454 offers a great deal of gee-whiz and real power. In .45 Colt, the Buck ammo 260-grain 'Woodshed' bullet is controllable and well worth consideration.

My main concern in animal defense is in dealing with a feral dog or a dangerous dog that is running loose. I investigated a number of dog bites during my time as a peace officer. The force of the attack and the manner of injury is horrific. Mixed breed dogs are most likely to bite and the Chow registers the most bites among thoroughbreds. But pit bulls are among the most deadly of animals. The fact is a 35-lb. dog may bite but the potential for death is far

less. A grown man or woman in good physical condition can fight off a Chow or similar-sized dog and even kill them with a strong kick. A 100-lb. animal is a different story.

Dog attacks come quickly, with the animal sometimes seeming to fly and bound off the ground. Dogs can be very hard to put down with pistol fire. I am aware of a case in which an officer was forced to fire at a large bulldog. Two 9mm rounds into the dog's shoulder expanded to about one inch in less than three inches of hard muscle and bone. The officer was bitten and suffered months of recovery. The dog was stopped with a shotgun slug. In another case an officer fired a dozen 147-grain 9mms into a dog before he released the child that was clomped in his jaws.

I had a similar experience with a bad dog and a 9mm, finally firing a round into the relatively thin and narrow skull. This was a difficult target. In fairness I once fired two rounds of .45 into a drug dealer's guard dog on the attack. The first round had no affect at all. The load was a highly recommended 200-grain JHP that was the darling of the popular

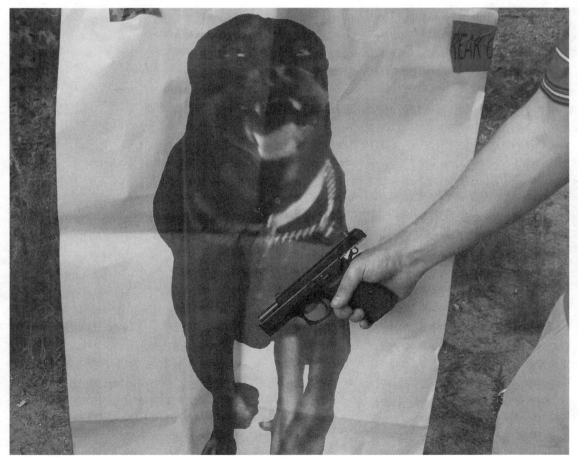

This is the ideal aiming point, just above the collar, in order to produce a shot that angles to vital organs. Study the anatomy of the most likely threat.

press at the time. The first round overexpanded and underpenetrated. But when using the .357 Magnum in a similar situation, no second shot was required and the results were immediate.

The problem lies in the speed of the attack and the fact that we often do not aim for the place that will do the most good. After learning to fire correctly at the K-zone of man sized targets, we must understand that this tactic does not transfer to dogs. When the dog is charging we tend to fire at center mass. Center-mass hits on the animal are not very effective from a forward perspective. Since he is on four legs, not two, his center is not obvious from the front. Our aim is deflected downward and the bullets will simply rake the lower body and continue on to the earth. Shots to the side are often similarly

ineffective. Remember, a dog takes as much killing as a man, but an animal is much less susceptible to shock. They have no physiological aspects of defeat because they do not know they have been shot.

When a dog is on the charge, the proper aiming point is just above the collar or at the base of the neck if there is no collar. With this aiming point the bullets should travel into the heart and lung area. Remember, the dog is lower in relation to us and the shots may be traveling through non-vital tissue. He may die but only after he has taken out your knee cap. Clearly a cartridge and load with adequate penetration are essential.

When practicing animal defense drills, I draw and fire as quickly and as accurately as possible. I make extensive use of the Law Enforcement Incorporated

An aggressive stance, confidence in your skill at arms, and a compact .45 may all combine to save your life in the face of an attack by a vicious animal.

targets specifically designed for this problem. Animal defense is a tough problem. An animal does not know he is in danger of deadly force and he may not notice being shot. Only a rapidly placed hit with a major caliber is a sure thing.

The question of the big cats comes up often. In the western states there have been a number of horrific incidents. But the potential for cougar attack exists in the south and north as well. Recently a friend of mine in South Carolina reported a cougar sighting. A conscientious hunter, he had downed a deer and watched from the stand as it fell. He carefully marked the spot mentally and climbed down the tree stand to field dress the animal. He walked the hundred yards or so and as he neared the animal it appeared to be moving. This was not the case. As he walked closer a panther leapt from the back of the deer and ran away. My friend was so startled he could not have reacted if the beast had attacked. He now carries a pistol when hunting, for close range use. A scope-mounted rifle is not ideal to stem a cougar attack at point-blank range.

The rules in cougar defense are similar to those in bear defense but cougars are not as hard to kill. The .357 is ideal but the big, slow .44s and .45s will do the business. An acquaintance of mine took a cougar from a tree with a .22 Magnum revolver with a single shot. The CCI Speer JHP performed well. While I do not doubt his word, hunting and fighting are different things. A treed cougar can be taken cleanly with a single shot. A cougar you are in a fight with just may take a lot of killing. I recommend a

heavy loaded revolver of at least .38 Special for this chore. If you have warning, it is best to take careful aim. If he is on top of you, by pressing the revolver against the animal's body the gas of powder burning amplifies the power of any cartridge but I hope not to find myself in that situation. In a pinch the gun you have on hand will be used, if it is a .32 automatic or a 10mm Glock. Marksmanship and a cool head will carry the day.

Postscript

As I finish this chapter an off-duty peace officer was attacked by two dogs that he was forced to shoot and kill. In another incident a hunter wounded a bear and the hunter's companions followed the bear into the bush. A conscientious hunter does not allow a wounded animal – especially one that may prove dangerous – to escape. The bear had been wounded with a .338 Magnum rifle. One of the men was armed with a .45 automatic. He fired a shot at close range that struck the bear in the noggin. The bear charged. I understand the shot was nearly between the eyes. As the man was bowled over, he fired three more times into the bear with little effect. The gun jammed, reportably due to shooter error and an ejected magazine. Another person fired a .44 Magnum into the bear's midsection with little effect. The man ran closer and fired a .44 into the bear's cranium just behind the ear, dropping him. Let's see: one .338 Magnum, two .44 Magnum bullets and four .45s. I could go on with examples but the facts are clear. If you contemplate going into areas where animal attack is a possibility, animal defense tactics should be practiced often.

Competition and Combat

There is a certain controversy among trainers and competitors. Some folks are trainers and some are sport shooters, and some are both and peace officers as well. This latter three-in-one mix often has the best overall outlook. The author has been a trainer, competitor and peace officer, and I understand the differences well. The great difference between competition and combat is that combat is unpredictable and final. You cannot call a mulligan and try again. In competition, the course dictates the number of shots fired and your movement. In combat, the adversary dictates your response. If you do fire, the effect on the target dictates the need to fire again. In competition you may fire two to five rounds at each target but none at all during a real confrontation. The adversary may flee upon being shot, return fire, drop his pistol, or do the Watusi. The threat is more than a target and the course of fire is unpredictable.

Competition is good in that trigger control, slight alignment, multiple shots at moving targets and general rapid manipulation of the firearm are requisites. Can competition be preparation for combat? It depends upon the individual's drive and the competition involved. Competition can introduce a certain level of stress to the shooting process. I have heard trainers state that competition helps young cops in building stress fighting skills in preparation for the day we hope will not come. This is OK as far as it goes, but stress inoculation comes from dealing with street people and in control situations, in my opinion. Dealing with the bad guys and street people on a daily basis affords many opportunities for stress control and developing situational awareness. Those who have been to lots of schools and have not walked the walk on the street with a badge have no idea of the process. For them competition is the substitute.

Competition can be physically demanding. When bullseye shooting was the only game in town many years ago, competition was very difficult but not exciting and contained little that would be an aid in

This young man is polishing his skills at the draw and producing a quick center hit.

combat. As one oldtimer put it, "I was well prepared for a duel at twenty paces and little else." Just the same, an important part of police training was once bullseye shooting.

Any sport requires practice and self-discipline. Competition is a great proving ground for both equipment and strategy. The absurd doesn't prosper for long. Claims of microsecond draw times are exposed when modern time measuring devices are involved. Competition supports performance, not lackadaisical attitudes. An important difference between competition and personal defense is the difference between tactics and simply shooting. Tactics are life-saving maneuvers. Tactical movement may be accomplished without the addition of gunfire. Competition reinforces shooting skills. The trigger press, grip, stance and sight picture are important. This book is primarily concerned with personal defense but I am enthusiastic concerning the future of the shooting sports and find them an exercise well worth our support and praise. These sports have merit outside of the personal defense field.

In life, we have differing natural domains. Should personal defense trainers stay in their domain and discourage competition? Are there bad habits that can be picked up playing "games"? My answer is there is nothing to lose and much to gain. I think some of the drills that are incorporated into sport shooting can be taken out of context.

These people are a group of intelligent, thoughtful individuals who plan a course related to real life. The author has a lot of faith in their scenarios.

Sometimes a little honest competition is a good thing. Setting up obstacles and promoting tactical movement are a great aid in building the tactical mindset and also in promoting safe gun handling.

Standing in the open and addressing a string of adversaries would get you shot and killed in real life. But address the problem in a shooting match for what it is: five different targets and five different problems. It would be boring if we stood off against only one target squared to us on a range. In a match, stand on your hind legs and do the best you can. The point is, you are evaluating a problem and attempting to solve it. You are not a gladiator but an interested student. As you progress, you will learn self-confidence and build skill. You will learn the skills needed to master a handgun and to move quickly and surely.

A considerable advantage is the application of core gun handling skills and gun safety. Safety is more important to beginners than anything else and safety is always stressed at pistol matches. Accuracy and speed will become second nature. If you need help, you will be able to get it at a match. Don't be shy. We all started somewhere!

Pistol competition is good. It can build core skills that will be an aid in handgun shooting.

IDPA

The International Defensive Pistol Association (IDPA) is the best thing to come along in many years for defensive shooters. IDPA competition stresses the use of practical gear including full-power service ammunition and holsters suited to concealed carry. As of this writing, an equipment race has not taken over the sport but a race to hone skills is evident. Before IDPA there was really no place to compete with street gear. The common service handguns simply could not compete alongside a "race gun" costing several thousands of dollars. As a bonus, the problems to be solved are often practical problems based on real life incidents.

IDPA's governing body states several goals. These include the following:

- The promotion of safe and proficient use of guns and equipment.
- Providing a level playing field for all competitors.
- Providing separate divisions for equipment and classification for shooters.
- Providing shooters with practical and realistic courses of fire that simulate a potentially life threatening situation.
- Offering a practical shooting sport that is responsive to shooters and sponsors with unprecedented stability of equipment rules.
- Offering a practical shooting sport that allows competitors to concentrate on development of shooting skills and fellowship with other like-minded shooters.

All who may legally own a handgun are welcome. IDPA includes members of diverse races and religions as well as many women. As for the problems to be solved, IDPA matches run from three to twenty yards and often require tactical movement, a very good thing. Equipment is not very expensive. A 9mm or .38 or larger handgun is all that is required. There are different categories for semi-automatics and revolvers. There are categories for double-action, double-action-only, and single-action semi-automatics as well as standard and snubnosed revolvers. I recommend IDPA without reservation.

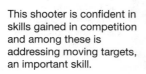
This shooter is confident in skills gained in competition and among these is addressing moving targets, an important skill.

19 | Keeping the Edge

No one is born with proficiency in combat or with skill at arms. It must be learned. You can serve in the military or as a peace officer and receive good training. You may attend Gabriel Suarez's highly respected schools or the Rangemaster in Memphis, Tennessee. But the fact remains that you must practice to maintain proficiency.

Personal defense skills are perishable. There are many issues in training. Some folks can no more perform with an audience than I could sing at Carnegie Hall. Others are limited financially or physically. I certainly want each and every one of these brothers and sisters to have a fighting chance in personal defense. That is one reason I wrote this book.

It may seem that self-training is a plausible alternative to more formalized instruction. But is it?

Before you can answer, first you must understand the difference between shooting and fighting. I have trained quite a few young people in open-hand disciplines. They are not shooters and some may never be shooters. On the other hand I see shooters at the range on a regular basis that do a credible job in hitting the bullseye. But they are not training for fighting.

Some will take all of the time in the world to fire. They stand erect facing a stationary target, shake their arms, wring their hands, take a few deep breaths and draw the pistol. They leisurely line up on the target, align the sights, and execute a perfect trigger press. They may believe that the one to two seconds involved is pretty fast. Some buy the right books and videos. Others purchase the wrong ones. (God help the ones who use television as a guide.)

Here's a tip: purchase training videos and books from qualified instructors who have been involved in police training. The author who has attended lots of schools but not walked the streets himself is missing many important pieces of information that are difficult to pick up in any other way. A number of writers are good at spelling out legal concerns and public mores but personal defense is too important to leave to those who have no street experience. I think many of you realize that professionals often

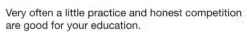

Very often a little practice and honest competition are good for your education.

The author is practicing a tactical load with his personal Kel-Tec PF9. Practice makes perfect and perfect practice is important!

LAPD's SWAT team relies upon the Kimber .45, Winchester ammunition, and lots of practice.

receive less training than they should. As a result, many soldiers and peace officers seek training on their own time and pay with their own dime. Some become very good at what they do. Others have good interpersonal and open-hand skills but neglect the handgun. There must be a balance, and that is what we will discuss.

I think that if you have purchased this book, you realize it is not for entertainment value. This book is not literature; it is technical writing. I hope we both agree that if you own a handgun and hope to use it well, some training is needed. I have often commented on the growth of a shooter compared to the growth of a martial artist. As my daughter has just won her green belt in karate, I understand the need for mileposts in training. I am of the opinion that handgun training progresses more slowly than some other disciplines.

If you're like most of us, you begin at a certain hopeless point. When my first week of training was finished, I would have been about as well off with a slingshot as a handgun. But within a few weeks I was a credible shot and in a few months a very good shot. I owe this growth to my grandfather, Wilburn Robert Williams. Later as a peace officer, I concentrated on personal defense skills. I progressed quickly and reached a plateau that demanded constant practice to maintain. My increase in proficiency was gradual. I would not say karate is easier, but handgunning requires more equipment and cannot be practiced with live ammunition in the home. You may do a good workout in the basement without a dojo, but a lack of a firing range is daunting. Some of us have long drives to a proper range.

There are many questions on skill building but I am of the opinion that it all must coalesce together. Muscle memory is fine in shooting and driving a stick shift vehicle, but you may do it the wrong way time and again. You will learn the basics in a pyramid fashion. You learn the grip, you learn sight picture, and you learn trigger compression and each must work together. Each skill does not necessarily build at the same rate. Once you get the basics reasonably committed to muscle memory you will begin more complex skills. This includes tactical presentation, speed shooting, firing on the move and firing at moving targets. Advanced gun handling skills such as quickly reloading and clearing malfunctions must be covered.

These men are checking results with their identical 1911 Kimber .45s. They know how important regular practice is.

When you have engaged in training, you must practice to keep the skill you have acquired sharp. Sure, you never forget how to ride a bike but you will not be steady if you do not ride often. Understand also that the quantity of ammunition expended is not necessarily an indication of the quality of practice. As an active police officer in my twenties I often fired five hundred rounds of ammunition in a single week. Not as heavy a practice schedule as that of a competitor working toward the Bianchi Cup, but about ten times more than most officers expend. A friend practices and when he gets the drill right he no longer wastes ammunition, as he puts it, but moves on to another drill. He is a fine shot with his CZ pistols and perhaps he is on to something.

The problem with practicing on your own is self-correction. Rather than going to the range and littering the landscape with spent brass we must learn as we train. An instructor can demonstrate the skills needed – and I firmly believe that mirror-image training and demonstration is best – and he or she will also work to correct the mistakes and shortcomings the student exhibits. Even if you take a friend to the range, it may be a case of the blind leading the blind. What if you shoot together and do not pay attention to the other's shooting? Do you take correction well? Do you like competition between friends? Having a program is necessary if you continue to execute only

Cover is vital and so is practicing quickly moving around cover, firing to the rear if you are flanked, and firing with one hand.

the drills you are good at. Frankly I practice the drills I am good at fairly often. I compare new handguns and test and evaluate them using proven drills on a pretty mundane combat course. This is a good means of comparing handguns but not very inspiring.

Confidence is good. It is good to be competent in standard drills in the beginning. Progression takes many weeks. But stopping and enjoying mediocrity is a potentially fatal flaw. Like the green belt in karate who is awed by how well a certain throw or jab works, some shooters will become caught up in the same old drill and become a one-trick pony.

We have to push ourselves. The motivation to excel must come from within. The motivation to survive a critical incident is external. The perpetrator attacks and we respond in the best way we know how. The motivation is not difficult to work up. On the other hand the motivation to train must be internal. We are creating something where there was nothing. We are working up proficiency for personal defense but on the other hand we are also working up these skills for their own sake. Discipline and motivation must be there. Without these two traits, you will not excel with the combat handgun.

A RECOMMENDED WEEKLY PRACTICE SCHEDULE

- Speed rock: Execute once.
- One hand shoulder point at five yards: Execute once.
- Two hand shoulder point at seven yards: Execute once
- Draw and fire at a target at seven yards and achieve a center hit in no more than 1.5 seconds.
- Draw and fire six rounds at a seven yard target as quickly as accurate fire allows.
- Fire for a head shot in a failure to stop drill at seven yards.
- Fire from the barricade position at a twenty-five yard target.

Fire five rounds in each exercise, then reshoot the drills you did not ace on the score (all in the X ring). That will take care of your box of Winchester ammo for the week. Within six months or so you will be a pretty decent shot.

There are other considerations. The budget and crushing work schedule have played against me in the past. I have worked eighteen months at a stretch with exactly one weekend day off during the entire period, and survived, although my combat skills may not have been where I wanted them to be. But you must continue to build skill as you progress as a shooter. I am going to outline a practice regimen that is well suited to most shooters but one that will not overly stress anyone. If you are able to stick to this practice schedule you are on the way to real combat ability.

COMBATING FLINCH

If you cannot defeat flinch, you will never progress. Anyone who does not flinch now has flinched in the past or will flinch in the future. Flinch is an involuntary muscle contraction in anticipation of muzzle blast. The hand moves and the trigger finger jerks and we have missed the shot. Flinch affects the most hardened shooter. No matter who you are or what your skill level, flinch is a mountain you must climb.

Flinch exists in many forms. An illustration is children who flinch from the needle before a shot is actually administered in the doctor's officer. They will cry before the needle touches their skin. Flinch is detrimental to accuracy, and overcoming flinch is like defeating any other fear or bad habit.

Trigger control is more important to marksmanship than sight alignment or the sight picture or

This young lady is the wife of a JAG officer and a good shot in her own right. She is practicing with the SIG P229. Note the spent case in the air and the pistol back on target.

When it come to skill building, quality of practice is vital. This is the Kimber SIS, a first-class 1911 that demands a skilled operator.

even a proper grip. When your hands spasm and jerk the handgun, accuracy is lost. As an example, most of us have a good mental picture of the sights and slide in full recoil. If you cannot see the sights in recoil, you are probably closing your eyes in flinch. Flinch affects not only the hands but also the arms and eyes and even the shoulders may flinch. I think that while recoil is one factor in flinch, muzzle blast is probably a greater problem. We have all been started by a Fourth of July firecracker. While we like to think small bores and non-magnum calibers are less offensive, sometimes flinch knows no bounds.

Shooters can flinch with practically any handgun. I have even seen actors demonstrate acute flinch with blank-firing cinema guns! There have been many good shooters who have found their nerves frayed when they attempt to move to big-bore hand cannons. The blast in front of your face is much more than a firecracker. The force of gas is not an explosion but rather a controlled pressure as powder burns in the barrel. But the sound effect is the same. I am certain flinch is more a product of muzzle blast than recoil and this proved out during one of the photographic sessions for this book. My assistant was taking photographs and when I touched off a particularly loud pistol, my assistant jerked the camera to an extent the photo showed only the upper part of a tree – and she was wearing good hearing protection!

There is an absolute need to wear both hearing protection and glasses when firing any firearm. In my youth a few trainers who are now thankfully retired insisted that peace officers sometimes fire

This is the best illustration of flinch I could find. Izzie did just fine after initial acclimation and now enjoys the Defender .45. But one first shot was an eye shutter, not an eye opener.

a few rounds without hearing protection in order to prepare them for combat. The requirement goes against the facts of auditory exclusion. During a gun battle most participants report the sound of their pistol as a mere pop and not at all distracting. During a gun battle you will have more on your mind than the muzzle report. On the other hand there have been incidents of officers trained on the .357 Magnum with .38 Special wadcutters startled by the muzzle blast of a full power Magnum cartridge when fired for real.

My advice is to keep the hearing protection on at all times when practicing. My personal battery of hearing protection muffs includes All Pro units that are ideal for trainers. They muffle shots well but the electronic component acts as an amplifier for normal conversation. Muzzle blast is greatly muffled but the main difference is the sharpness of the crack upon firing.

If you have developed flinch or other bad shooting habits, it is time to return to the .22-caliber handgun for remedial training. The basics of trigger control sight picture and sight alignment are best learned with a rimfire pistol. There is little recoil and no sharp blast a few inches from your nose.

If you prefer to practice solely with the centerfire handgun, then you may choose to load light loads for remedial work. The .38 Special wadcutter works well in the .357 Magnum. 147-grain target loads are fine in the 9mm and the Black Hills 200-grain SWC or 230 gr. RNL in .45 ACP works well. But just the same, nothing works better than a good .22 caliber pistol for remedial training.

Among the causes of flinch is holding the handgun too tightly. The correct grip is a firm handshake. Take the pistol in hand and grasp the pistol until your hands tremble. Then back off and you have the correct grip. Often a very small or very powerful handgun requires a tighter grasp that is difficult to sustain in training. Once again, the .22 will bring you back up to speed with an absence of muzzle blast and recoil.

Ignoring flinch is difficult but it can be learned. Fire the .22 until you are completely comfortable with the rimfire. Whether your flinch is recoil or muzzle-blast sensitive, the .22 will quickly teach your muscles that there is nothing to fear. The greatest tool in eliminating flinch is to develop a good stance and grip and concentrate on sight picture and sight alignment along with trigger press. The surprise break trigger press must be cultivated. If you do not know when the pistol will go off, you will not know when to flinch.

When working to eliminate flinch, use dry fire as a training resource. This will train your hands and body into the proper technique without the hindrance of muzzle blast. Another technique is to perform a blind test administered by a shooting partner. A revolver can be loaded with one empty chamber in the cylinder and a semi-automatic can be loaded with an STI Pro dummy cartridge in the magazine. You will be firing and there will be a click. If you are suffering from flinch you will jerk the pistol and push it forward. After a few episodes of this drill you will need to steel your nerves and defeat flinch.

When fighting flinch, most of your shooting should be at a minimal distance to build confidence. Seven to ten yards distance is ideal. You should be able to fire an offhand group of two to four inches offhand at this distance on demand. Practice the surprise break and hold the pistol properly. Fighting flinch is really just the application of proper shooting technique.

Part Three:
Long Guns

20 The Rifle

When looking at the rifle, you need to consider all of the advantages of the type. The rifle is not simply a large and heavy handgun. Taking a rifle to a gunfight is like taking a chainsaw to a knife fight. The rifle has advantages in close-quarters combat as well as the obvious advantage of long range effectiveness.

They say you learn from mistakes but you also learn from success. The rifle has been a success story when adopted and deployed by domestic police and civilians. Rifles have been widely adopted and extensively used by large and small police agencies and we are able to learn from these experiences. Many of these agencies combined an antiquated and ineffectual shooting program with modern rifles. Nevertheless, depending upon how many cylinders they were running on that day, officers learned to shoot the rifle and use it well. Some agencies have patrol rifle training programs in place that would rival those of a federal agency.

As for peace officer's rifles, they have been a diverse group until very recently. The Washington State Patrol was ahead of the times, issuing a Winchester Model 94 .30-30 rifle to each trooper for many years. The Los Angeles Police Department had the same type on hand for about fifty years. The FBI once issued Remington 760 slide action rifles in .308 caliber. The 760 would still be an efficient problem solver, especially in rural areas. The slide action 760 offered the same handling as the efficient Remington 870 shotgun.

Today the AR-15 rifle is virtually universal among police agencies. The popularity of the AR-15, America's "Black Rifle," and the .223 cartridge are undeniable. Officers with military experience naturally appreciate the AR-15 and are familiar with its handling. Another plus is the effectiveness of the cartridge. The .223 Remington/5.56mm cartridge is a very effective antipersonnel round. Also, fears of overpenetration of rifle cartridges have been put to rest with the .223. It is practically ideal for police and urban use. The .223 offers good penetration against vehicles and light cover and especially against bulletproof vests. But intensive testing with ballistic gelatin and against common barriers such as wall board and sheet rock shows that the .223 is less likely to overpenetrate than the common 9mm and .40 caliber police cartridges.

A great advantage of a rifle is the ability to shut down a deadly felon with a minimum of gunfire. In many incidents in the past, offenders have been the recipient of numerous pistol rounds with little effect. They have returned fire, endangering peace officers and the public. Officers and civilians have been wounded during such actions. More often than not a single well-placed rifle round will do the business and end the threat's rampage.

This is a Rock River Arms carbine. This is a rifle that leaves nothing to be desired.

An incident in California particularly underscores the effectiveness of the carbine. A person with a large edged weapon went on a rampage on a crowded street. A cop with a carbine shut him down with a single shot. While it is unfortunate that the assailant lost his life, the possibility of great carnage was ended with the application of a single, well-placed bullet.

The rifle has much greater accuracy potential than the handgun. The rifle handles quickly and offers greater repeatability for accurate shots due to the rifle's three-point lockup: the rifle is held at three points (by the forend, by the grip, and at the cheek). Cheek weld, forend grip and the firing hand control the rifle. While long range accuracy is fine, the power increase alone makes deploying a rifle for home defense worthwhile. When we compare a full-power rifle cartridge to the handgun, the "weak .38" and "strong .45" are more alike than they differ.

A rifle cartridge of modest power has more energy than a handgun cartridge. We go to great lengths to maximize handgun cartridges whereas we often must find a way to limit the penetration of rifle cartridge. There is no shortage of power or energy. A good long gun in trained hands is an advantage in nearly every situation.

It is true that the handgun seems superior for close-quarters battle, but just the same a rifle can be handled in surprisingly close quarters. When you fight inside a bus or airplane, the long gun has certain advantages: the situation is more linear, more strung out, and with more movement. While civilians will seldom face this situation, a felon going berserk in a crowded workplace is certainly a difficult problem. If proper tactical doctrine is followed, a carbine – a short-barreled rifle – is quite manageable inside a dwelling. If you place a handgun at full extension with both hands and then hold a 16-inch carbine in the proper hold extended and ready, there is little difference in your profile. The distance of the muzzle from the eye is similar when using a short carbine, although of course one-hand fire and other considerations are different.

There are occasionally shooters who simply never advance with the handgun. Those not willing to practice monthly would do well to adopt a rifle for home defense. It is easier to bring a mediocre shooter up to speed quickly with a long gun. Those who are diligent in training would also be wise to adopt a

The Bushmaster carbon frame .223 is especially popular with female shooters. It is light and reliable and does not kick badly.

long gun for home defense. If you live in a rural area where predators and large animals are a real concern, a versatile rifle would be a real boon. The rifle is an indispensable all-around tool for many of us.

The practical aspects of the long gun must be understood. Unfortunately, some localities within the United States limit handgun ownership or make such ownership difficult. The rifle is almost always less difficult to purchase, possess, transport and keep ready than a handgun. This is perhaps more true when traveling. Rifle ammunition is often available in bulk at reasonable prices, which is a considerable aid in practice.

The AR-15 rifle is now the most common rifle deployed by police agencies. As a result there has been considerable development of the type, giving us a broad choice for personal defense shooters. You are not fighting a war, but neither do have administrators limiting your choice. Your only limits are skill and personal finance. I think weight is less of a concern because we are not engaging in a campaign or running six miles with the rifle.

There are other action types that are viable for home defense. The single shot, bolt action, lever action, slide action and semi-automatic rifles other than the AR-15 have merit. The lever action is appealing on many levels but I personally lean toward the semi-automatic. I believe the slide action Remington is also a fine choice, in either .223 or .308. A theoretical advantage of the slide action rifle is that the firing hand never leaves the stock and trigger. The weak hand operates the action while the firing grip is broken by the lever action shooter. But limited choice among slide action rifles makes the type less popular.

Most American shooters are familiar with the lever action rifle, a great advantage. I won't discount the single shot but we are putting all of our eggs in one basket with the single shot. A repeater makes more sense. Safety features are important but true safety lies between the ears. The repeater will be kept at home at the ready, chamber empty, in most situations.

There are significant differences between handling and reliability among the various types. For those who deploy a certain action type in the shotgun perhaps it makes sense to adopt the same type of rifle. You can take this only so far as there is only one lever-action shotgun currently available, and it isn't well-distributed. Any number of farm boys and hunters have gotten along quite well with a slide action shotgun and lever action rifle for decades. My friends in police agencies note there is some difficulty in training recruits to use pump action shotguns after they have acclimated to the semi-automatic pistol. Fewer and fewer recruits have any prior experience with firearms. Rookies fire the pump and forget to cock it for a subsequent shot. As a result, numerous agencies have moved to the semi-automatic carbine and either adopted semi-automatic shotguns or eliminated the shotgun altogether. Let's look at the action types one by one.

Lever Action Rifles

The lever action requires some skill in manipulation but with practice – and only with practice does any skill increase – a lever action rifle can be manipulated quickly and an accurate cadence of fire can be kept up. Remember *The Rifleman* and *Bounty Hunter*? I grew up watching these westerns and my father owned a nice, short lever action rifle. Yes, you can get pretty smart with a lever action rifle. In a number of jurisdictions in our northern states and perhaps a few on the "left coast," handgun permits have been very difficult to obtain unless you were well heeled, politically well connected or a member of the mob. It's usually much easier to purchase a lever action rifle, at least in terms of legal requirements.

The lever action rifle is such a part of America that is has figured into quite a few actions and has

not fired its last shot by any means. I am aware of an attempted murder in which a felon suspected of killing a peace officer's wife and wounding the officer pulled up at a business and opened fire from his vehicle. The man under fire moved quickly, grabbing a Winchester Model 94 .30-30 rifle as he made a hasty exit from the line of fire. He quickly cranked a round into the chamber of his rifle and fired into the vehicle where this known murderer was seated. He fired several rounds and the .30-caliber jacketed softpoint bullets did the business even after penetrating a car door.

This is one of the author's dream rifles. The Winchester Trapper in .44 Magnum is very hard to find and demands a premium when found. This one belongs to gospel singer Paul Jordan.

The lever action rifle is available in a host of hunting calibers including the .30-30 Winchester, .35 Remington, and .45-70 Springfield as well as pistol calibers including the .32-20, .357 Magnum, .44-40, .44 Magnum and .45 Colt. As a rule, the pistol caliber carbines have more leverage in the action and are very quick to manipulate. The longer action of the .30-caliber rifles are more difficult to quickly manipulate but with practice a rifleman can chamber the cartridge and keep up a steady cadence of fire.

A slight disadvantage is that the lever action rifle is difficult to operate from prone position. We should practice firing the lever action from different stances and also rapid manipulation. We all like to think we will solve a problem with the first shot but it doesn't always play out that way.

The pistol caliber carbines from Rossi are particularly good choices among lever action rifles. The Rossi is a modern clone of the Winchester Model 92 rifle and a good one. Marlin offers pistol caliber carbines based upon the Model 1894 with certain improvements that are reminiscent of the Model 336 Marlin. Winchester rifles are widely available on the used market in .30-30. The Winchester Trapper, a 16-inch-barreled carbine in .44 Magnum caliber, is a real jewel but out of production and difficult to locate.

The pistol caliber carbine is very handy and could give us an edge when facing multiple threats. Lever action rifles are usually very reliable, providing the operator is careful not to short-cycle the action (i.e., not fully operate the lever). I have seen tie-ups in lever action rifles. Some were the result of well-worn rifles and in other cases sloppy handling was the culprit. If the cartridge case jumps the magazine and misses the lifting bar, you have a jam that is difficult to clear without disassembly. I have experienced such a tie-up with a Winchester .30-30.

An advantage of the lever action is its exposed hammer. A considerable argument can be made for the safety and speed of operation of an exposed hammer.

Bolt Action Rifles

Bolt action rifles are the most accurate action type but probably the least well suited to personal defense. They are usable in prone fire and often are supplied with a good trigger. Bolt action rifles are well suited to tactical use by trained operators making precision shots. This is not something the civilian defensive shooter will be called on to do.

There are a few bolt action military rifles that can be pressed into service simply because they are the only rifle on hand. The various Mauser rifles including the Spanish and Argentine carbines might serve, assuming ammunition is available.

A great advantage of the Mauser bolt action is the controlled feed extractor. When the bolt is pulled fully to the rear, the claw extractor captures a cartridge from the magazine. The claw snaps over the cartridge rim and controls the feed through every step. Conversely, modern bolt rifles are often push-feed types. The bolt simply pushes the cartridge from the magazine and into the chamber. If the rifle is canted in the least manner, the cartridge may fall out of the rifle or tie up. A dedicated tactical bolt action rifle should have a controlled feed design. (The modern Kimber is one example of a modern controlled feed action.)

There are a number of short .308 caliber bolt action rifles that are suitable as ranch rifles and for specialized use in the American West, but only a single shot rifle is less suitable in my mind than the bolt action for personal defense.

Slide Action

The only slide action rifle suitable for personal defense is the Remington in .223 and .308 caliber. The .308 in particular is impressively light and handy. There are various reproductions of the Colt Lightning but with very little in the way of feedback so far, I cannot comment on them. The original Colt was rather fragile and was not especially popular. Various out-of-production pump action rifles, both foreign and domestic, are best relegated to the curiosity file. If you favor the slide action shotgun ,you do not necessarily have to use a slide action rifle. After all I prefer the pump shotgun but the AR-15 rifle figures heavily in my defense plan.

The Remington is a fine rifle with many good features. Some feel the pump has greater leverage than the fulcrum type action of the lever gun. Speed is superior but either may be fired about as quickly accurately as the other.

Semi-Automatic Rifles

Some call them automatics but I have always thought that shooters know what we are speaking of when we mention semi-automatic. This simply means the rifle is an autoloader – it loads itself. A single pull of the trigger fires the rifle and then it loads another round from the magazine and you are ready to go. A fully-automatic weapon fires as long as the trigger is depressed – in other words, a machine-gun. While it is possible to own fully-automatic rifles in most states, there is little to be accomplished with a full-automatic that cannot be done as well with accurate rapid semi-automatic rifle fire.

Conventional sporting rifles such as the Browning BAR and the Remington 742 are not well-suited to personal defense. If kept perfectly maintained and lubricated they are fine for hunting, but other types are better suited to personal defense.

When considering which rifle, you must critically evaluate reliability above all else. Reliability cannot be ascertained over the bench but must be learned over the long haul. We are able to take advantage of long police and military experience and choose rifles of proven reliability. These include the rifles offered by Armalite, Bushmaster, Colt, Rock River Arms and Smith & Wesson. Other than the AR-15 types, Armalite offers the competing AR-180, a good rifle that suits some better than the AR-15. There are also the Ruger Mini-14, the Saiga and the AK-47. Each fills a niche and one or the other should fit your personal needs. But do not purchase what is sexy or trendy, but what works.

A good friend of the author is a retired military officer. He is very familiar with the AR-15/M16 and M4 rifles. When the time came to choose a rifle, he chose a synthetic stocked Ruger Mini-14. He simply preferred a rifle that was more "sporting" in appearance. The FN FAL and M1A1 may be worth considering depending upon your situation. If your personal defense rifle is also a hunting rifle – and many are – then a .308 looks good. I prefer the dedicated .223 caliber defense rifle but there are other choices.

There is nothing wrong with a full-size AR -15 type rifle. The carrying handle variants are rugged, reliable and accurate.

When I first became a peace officer, the .30-caliber M1 carbine was very much in evidence. It was used by the NYPD and proved its worth in many shootouts. You are well armed with a good reliable .30 carbine. Cor-Bon has recently introduced a 100-grain DPX loading for the M1 carbine that maximizes the caliber. This load breaks just over 2,000 fps from the 18-inch carbine barrel. This is a considerable improvement over the military ball loading. Auto-Ordnance has recently introduced a neat little .30 caliber carbine that should prove a fine home defender.

My personal first choice is the .223-caliber AR-15 with 16-inch barrel. This is a combination that is light enough, easy to hit with, and reliable. Shooting is a learned process, not instinctive, but human engineering helps. On the move, firing quickly, the AR-15 carbine is a fast hitter that is also capable of making hits on man-sized targets well past 200 yards (although the effectiveness of the cartridge fades rapidly past 100 yards). The extended range may not mean anything in home defense, but if you find yourself in a Katrina situation with gunmen on the roof, the power, accuracy and versatility of a good rifle are appreciated. Large hulking hominids – and alligators – can take a lot of shooting and the AR-15 lets you deliver the shots in good order. The extended range of the AR-15, coupled with stopping power and the ability to penetrate light armor, makes for a great choice.

Black Hills V-Max loads make the most of .308 rifle accuracy. If you choose a rifle in this caliber you have many advantages including penetration and gilt edged accuracy.

Whatever else you do, acquire plenty of magazines and the Magpul loader!

This is a tricked out AK-47 with quite a few parts from Command Arms Accessories and an EOTech sight. The AK-47 can work well in trained hands.

The AK-47

An alternative to the AR15 is the Russian AK-47. The AK-47 is widely used in America and many experienced tactical shooters, both police and military, have the greatest respect for the AK-type rifle. It was the first successful assault weapon and remains the most widely produced. The AK-47 has been in constant production since 1947. The rifle's sights and accuracy are not impressive but the piece is very reliable. The AK is intended for short-range battle and it is not as accurate as the AR-15 or the Mini-14.

And while reliable, it is not infallible. Anyone who believes otherwise has not been to the same classes I have. I have seen the AK-47 capture spent cases in the bolt and also seen AK-type rifles with headspace problems. That being said, I am of the opinion the AK-47 will survive with the least maintenance of any modern assault weapon. The ergonomics of the rifle compare well to practically any other rifle and in its day it was the rifle to beat. The rifle comes to the shoulder quickly and is well balanced. The handguard heats up quickly in prolonged firing but this is of little concern except in practice sessions.

There is a profound difference between qualification and learning to fight with a rifle. You can learn to fight well with the AK-47. A significant drawback is the position of the safety. Fitted to the right side of the receiver, it requires much practice to accomplish a modicum of speed as we will discuss in a few pages.

Unfortunately many AK-47 rifles have been supplied with a horrible folding stock or plastic add-ons that do not do the business. Some debate the quality of AK-47 rifles produced in various parts of the world but most are comparable in reliability and accuracy. With a quality loading such as Winchester's 7.62 x 39mm JSP, a tight AK-47 might do three inches at 100 yards for a three-shot group but four to eight inches is more likely for most rifles. The ultimate AK-47 rifle for those who prefer the type and the cartridge is the Krebs custom rifle. Krebs offers an improved safety and even a speed-feed option. These are world-class rifles that are not cheap but are very well regarded.

A drawback to the AK-47 – and this may be a personal quirk – is its association with our adversaries in the war on terror. I am not certain I want to be the man running around with an AK-47 in a truly desperate situation.

Ruger Mini-14

The Ruger Mini-14 is either a more powerful M1 carbine or a downsized M-14 rifle, depending on your perspective. The Mini-14 has been used extensively by American police forces, South American military

This is a combat light attachment from Command Arms Accessories. The AK-47 rivals the AR-15 in number of available combat accessories.

Quite a few shooters find the Ruger Mini-14 an excellent all-around rifle. The Mini-14 is reliable and accurate enough for most uses inside 100 yards.

units, and especially by American sportsmen. The AR-15 may exhibit superior ergonomics on paper but there are many shooters who are not comfortable with the black rifle's handling. I grew up on the Remington Speedmaster .22 and the Mini-14 isn't a big step from that classic rifle.

The Ruger has figured into quite a few hostage rescue operations and has made a good name for itself. Like any quality rifle it must be cleaned and lubricated. Spare magazines are pricier than those of the AR-15, but recently I tried an affordable Pro Mag and it worked just fine. The Mini-14 is less accurate on average than the AR-15. Three inches at 100 yards is a good standard for the Mini-14. Some who have used the rifle operationally may be surprised at this pedestrian accuracy. At typical engagement ranges for police marksmen, the rifle will put every bullet in the same hole. Two inches at 50 yards is more than adequate for most situations.

I am very enthusiastic about this rifle. It is affordable, reliable, and not offensive in appearance, which can be important. The similar Ruger Mini-30 chambers the 7.62x39 AK-47 cartridge but in my experience its accuracy is problematical and magazines a real problem. The Mini-14 is a good rifle that has given quite a number of Americans a good rifle at a fair price.

SKS

The humble SKS has figured into quite a few shootings in my experience. Usually the adversary goes down in a volley of fire. In practically every case the rifle was purchased for recreation but pressed into self-defense service. The rifle is robust and reliable enough, as are most Soviet designs. The rifle holds ten rounds in a box magazine and can be charged with stripper clips from the top or loaded one round at a time. It can be cocked and gotten into action quickly.

The SKS is sometimes more accurate than the average AK-47, if that matters. SKS rifles were once a good buy but they are increasingly more expensive, making the Saiga or Mini-14 more attractive. With the Cor-Bon 125-grain urban load, 7.62x39 they certainly could be effective. My main warning is that many are old rifles with much wear. Ergonomics are not as good as the Mini-14 but for those on a budget, the SKS will serve.

Saiga Rifle

The Saiga is based upon the AK-47 rifle but with a sporting stock and superior controls. The internal action has been beefed up in certain regards to handle the powerful .308 Winchester cartridge. AK-47 magazines will not fit the 7.62 x 39mm variant. The rifle is available in .223, 7.62 x 39mm and .308 Winchester (the latter also known as the 7.62 NATO). I have little experience with the type but found the 16-inch-barreled .308 a very handy and well-balanced carbine. Handling was good and recoil subdued. I was able to fire the carbine at a maximum of fifty yards. Accuracy seemed good, at least on the level with the AK-47 and perhaps a bit better. Black Hills 168-grain match loads fed perfectly and gave good results. There were no excess pressure signs.

This short shooting session left me with a favorable impression of the Saiga. With its lineage it simply should be a good performer.

Pistol Caliber Carbines

Pistol caliber lever action rifles chamber re-volver cartridges including the .44-40 Winchester and .44 Magnum. These make good short-range rifle cartridges. Semi-automatic carbines are also chambered for pistol cartridges. Most are in 9mm but a few are available in .40 and .45 caliber. These carbines are light, handy and compact. While there are usually semi-automatic versions of popular machineguns, our most practical pistol caliber carbines are civilian designs. They cannot be expected to be as rugged as military rifles, but they are also less expensive. As a peace officer, I preferred the rifle-caliber carbine. But after an open-minded evaluation of several of the better pistol caliber carbines I find there is a place for these firearms in personal defense. They deliver pistol power but deliver this power much more accurately. Accuracy can make up for power while the reverse is seldom true. Recoil is light enough that a slightly-built female or teen can handle the carbines if need be. For a truck gun there is much merit in the concept. The carbine's long barrel will provide more velocity with a given load than a handgun, but the real advantage is in accuracy and handling.

A mediocre pistol shot can do wonders with the carbine. As a bonus there are two affordable carbines available. ....
The Hi-Point carbine can be obtained for around two hundred dollars. The magazine capacity is limited – nine rounds in 9mm – but that should be enough to settle the issue. After all, all rounds may be fired into a single ragged hole at ten yards. The Hi-Point carbine is remarkable easy to use well, has

The Saiga rifle is an improved AK-47. According to the author, the rifle is reliable and more accurate than standard AK rifles.

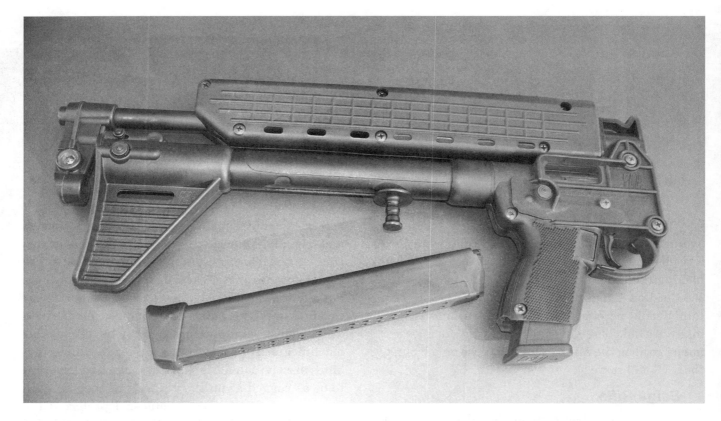

The Kel-Tec 9mm carbine is a light and credible semi-automatic carbine (shown here in folded position with magazine removed). The rifle folds down into action and the cocking lever is under the stock. Be certain to keep your hands away when the piece is firing.

good sights, and feeds hollowpoints well. This is a straight blowback rather than a gas-operated action and the .40 caliber version has more recoil than expected, but remains controllable with a minimum of practice. I recommend the larger caliber but in the case of the pistol caliber carbines the price of practice ammunition and the wide availability of 9mm ammunition makes one lean toward the 9mm. The 9mm +P will approach .357 Magnum ballistics when fired from the 16-inch carbine barrel.

The Kel-Tec 9mm carbine is a foldable, stowable little wonder. An excellent all-around light carbine, the Kel-Tec accepts Glock 17 magazines including the 33-round extended version. A neat trick is that the Kel-Tec retains its balance with the extended magazine. It's a friendly carbine that proved enjoyable to all who fired it. Recoil is light and the trigger and sights are well designed. I have quite a few handguns and rifles costing well over a thousand dollars but many of my friends and acquaintances agree that the Kel-Tec is as well suited to personal defense as anything they have seen! The rifle is easy to get into action, light, easy to handle even with one hand, and it is easy enough to fire a moderately powerful handgun cartridge into the target with a high expectation of accuracy.

As an experiment I compared the Kel-Tec to one of my favorite FM High Power 9mm pistols. I began with the firearm in hand and ran courses of fire that varied from 7, 10, 15 and 25 yards. There is no handgun I can use better but the Kel-Tec carbine walked away from the pistol in all courses. The Kel-Tec digested my personal handloads and a number of Black Hills offerings in 115-, 124- and 147-grain weights without a single failure to feed, chamber, fire or eject. So, a rather inexpensive carbine proved its worth against a professional's long-serving High Power. That is food for thought.

Rifles are challenging and effective firearms. I recommend obtaining the best quality rifle you can afford and practicing diligently. A good rifle is indispensable if you live in a rural area or if predators or large dangerous animals are part of the threat profile. A good rifle encourages practice and pride of ownership and can be an incentive to excel.

As I finish this chapter, I have learned that a single area in San Francisco has suffered eight takeover robberies in one month. A good pistol caliber carbine might be one answer to such a threat.

Handling the Rifle

When you decide to use a long gun for personal defense, you are making a wise decision. A good AR-15, AK-47 or FN-FAL would give you at least a fighting chance in a tight pinch. Marksmanship is one thing and very important. But handling is another subject. The rifle is the most formidable of firearms in the hands of a trained shooter.

Whichever rifle you choose, you must learn to use it to your best advantage. You may be limited to a bolt action rifle or you may have a state of the art Armalite rifle. You must learn to clean, lubricate and service it. Learning to field strip the rifle for routine checks is important. Perhaps the most important point is to find a combination of sights that works for you and to stick with it. You will be all but married to the rifle.

Let's look at the best means of handling each type of rifle.

Lever Action Operation

I have lost count of the times I have seen actors grasp the bottom of the lever of the lever action rifle rather than properly inserting their fingers into the lever ring. I mean, how hard is it to get it right? How obvious does the lever ring have to be? To manipu-

The author is quickly working the lever action rifle. His hand is in the proper location in the ring lever and he is looking through the see-through mount to the iron sights.

late the rifle, keep your trigger finger separated and three fingers go into the ring. The thumb controls the hammer. The thumb is never in any danger of being hit by the bolt because the hand comes away from the stock as you smartly work the lever.

The lever throw must be complete, with a full travel for the lever and a smart lock back. To lower the hammer once the piece is cocked, simply take control of the hammer with your thumb and then gently press the trigger. Keep the muzzle pointed straight down as you perform this action. To load the lever action, some practice is required in learning the proper angle to press cartridges into the magazine. The lever action should be manipulated without moving the rifle from the shoulder.

Bolt Action Operation

The bolt action cannot be topped off with cartridges without stopping the firing sequence, so you will be fighting with the gun load.

To properly manipulate the bolt, begin in the high ready position with your eyes on the sights and the hand on the butt stock near the trigger. Swiftly move the hand to the bolt. Do not close your fingers on the bolt but rather use the open hand to take control of the bolt handle and move the bolt handle up and back, bringing the bolt back to the rear in full travel. With the hand still open, shift the hand position to press the bolt forward and lock the bolt down. Move the hand to the firing position and you are ready. Repeat for subsequent shots.

The Mini-14 is very controllable in rapid fire, as you can see. There are two cases in the air from a double tap.

Slide Action Rifle Operation

The Remington slide action rifle features sturdy action rails and the rifle is smooth in operation. Anyone who can use the pump action shotgun quickly can use the slide action rifle well. Press the bolt release and then rack the action fully to the rear, then bring the forend to the front. You are ready to fire. When you fire, allow recoil to aid in quickly and aggressively racking the action.

Semi-automatic Rifle Operation

I adhere to "lesson learned" training. Those who have been there and done it know the advantages of the AR-15 and also the steps needed to keep the rifle working. The AR works just fine but needs plenty of lubrication. The bolt should be sopping with oil when engaged in training. It takes a lot of ammunition to master a rifle or to refresh perishable skills. AR shooters tend to get into high round counts.

For best reliability you need to change the AR's extractor every 10,000 rounds or when the extractor is no longer sharp to the touch. The extractor spring canbe changed every 5,000 rounds for best reliability. Check the extractor insert pin under magnification for cracks on a regular basis. In high round count rifles it is good to check the gas rings. To do so, place the bolt in the carrier without the bolt pin. If the bolt falls out as you press it home, you need a new gas ring. Also, check the buffer spring often. The buffer spring is long-lived but you are playing with reliability and perhaps your life if you allow the spring to go past 10,000 rounds.

A problem I have seen a half dozen times is an improperly staked gas key. This is bad news and leads to tie-ups and even damaged rifles. I have seen most of these in kit guns or parts guns. Brownells offers quality replacement parts. Gun show parts may be another matter; some are good but know what you are looking for. If you build a parts gun for personal defense, be certain the parts are properly staked. Only a quality rifle with quality parts is worth owning. Another recommendation: anything that is screwed on needs LocTite!

When the rifle has been proven in high level testing, you know you have a reliable rifle. Whatever the rifle, you need to know how to clear a malfunction. Malfunctions seldom occur with a well-maintained rifle but no machine is immune from a tie-up. A short cycle with an AR-15 rifle is often solved with a varia-

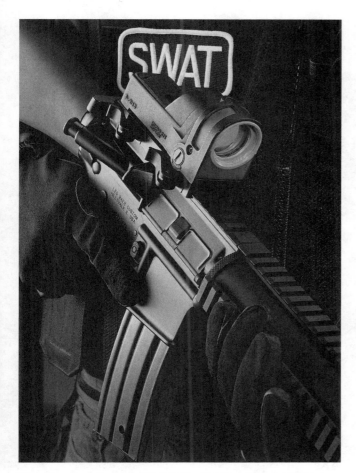

This a Les Baer Custom .223 AR-15 with Meprolight sight. This is first class kit all of the way. But practice is demanded. This rifle is in the low ready position..

The 200 Yard Zero

Those using the AR-15 will do well to adopt the 200 yard zero. There is some discussion on the proper sighting for the AR-15. Some feel that a defensive rifle should be sighted in for fifteen to twenty-five yards. Let's run over this. The AR-15 has approximately a 2.6 inch sight offset or the height of the sights above the bore. If you use a conventional zero for 100 yards the rifle may fire several inches low at home defense range. You must understand the exact point of aim and point of impact at close range. But for most of us most of the time the 200 yard zero works the best.

Let's look at the calculations, obtained using the Bushmaster rifle and the 60 grain JSP from Black Hills.

Range	Offset
200 yards	0
125 yards	2.5 inches high
100 yards	2.0 inches high
50 yards	0
25 yards	1.25 inches below the point of aim

We could expend more ammunition but this illustration proves the point. Once you have the zero, paint your sight's adjusting marks with white paint. If they move or are knocked out of alignment you will be able to quickly restore zero.

Magazine Changes

The AR-15 rifle is the fastest of all assault weapons to handle and use well, and magazine changes are no exception. Press the magazine release with the forefinger and as the magazine falls, move the weak side hand to the magazine pouch (if you do not have one on your body, the speed load is pointless) and grasp a spare magazine. Move the magazine to the rifle and angle it into the magazine well. Snap the magazine into place and move the hand to the bolt release. You are back in action.

I stress tactical movement and marksmanship foremost. Tactical loads are far less important than making the first shot count. Just the same, I can easily see situations in which a tactical reload might be required. A takeover robbery or a civil upheaval may get pretty ugly. If you are going to perform a reload, you need to carry spare ammunition or have a pouch near the rifle's ready position.

tion of the tap-tack-bang. The magazine is tapped, the forward assist struck, and the rifle tilted on its side to the right. In order to clear a failure to extract, the magazine is dropped and the bolt is racked forcefully three times.

A useful drill in checking for a loaded chamber takes a sure hand but is not particularly difficult. The butt is tucked into the shoulder as the right hand grasps the front of the magazine well and the right hand thumb feels for a cartridge as the weak hand retracts the bolt. This chamber check should be quick and effortless with practice.

When firing the AR-15 and practicing tactical maneuver, I like to keep accessories light. Some time ago I was practicing tactical movement in a dimly-lighted room with an AR with a muzzle-mounted light. Actually, the light was mounted slightly in offset to the barrel. The light made a terrible shadow as the barrel was to one side of the light. As for the AR-15 and hard use, the best advice I can give is to pay attention to hard wear items and replace them as necessary.

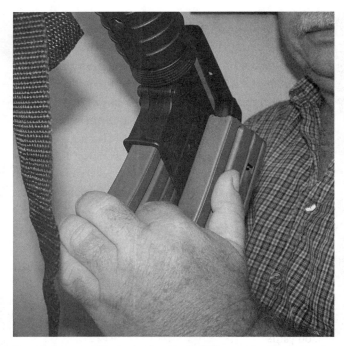

The AR-15 is among the fastest of all rifles to reload. But practice must be undertaken to achieve real speed and smoothness.

I don't like bracketing two magazines together. For me, the balance of the rifle is adversely affected. I also think that pressure on the magazine can affect function and finally that the bracketed-together magazines are more likely to snag and disrupt handling. The load in the magazine will save your life but just the same a speed load may be indicated. I think that practice is worthwhile because rapid action drills build familiarity with the rifle and rifle manipulation. Let's go over the tactical load. I have adopted the Magpul device for use in speed loading. The Magpul is too inexpensive and too handy to ignore.

First, grasp the spare magazine by the Magpul. The little finger works just fine; the other fingers will stabilize the magazine. Draw the spare magazine and rotate it so that the spare is parallel with the magazine that remains in the rifle. Grip both magazines at one time in the support hand and pull the partially empty magazine away from the rifle as you activate the magazine release with the strong hand.

The next maneuver is not as complicated as it first seems. Grasp both magazines in a kind of U pattern and quickly insert the new magazine making certain that it catches. You may either leave the original magazine dangling on the finger or you may insert it in a magazine pouch. The Magpul allows you to pull magazines from a carrier quickly and also protects the magazine if dropped. You will drop a few magazines in practice.

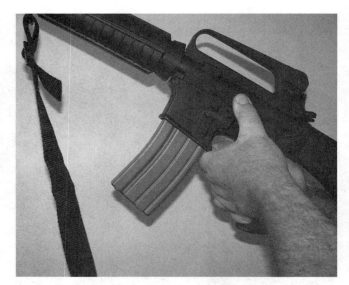

The bolt release of the AR-15 is well positioned for rapid reloads.

AK-47 Drills

The AK 47 is rugged and reliable. The most common AK failure seems to be a failure to extract. This may be related to surplus ammunition of varying quality. I have used cases of Wolf Ammunition with good results but I have seen failures to extract with practically every brand of ammunition in different AKs.

Maintenance is important. Accuracy must be stressed with the AK-47. It should be noted that I have seen a number of shootings with the .30-30 in rural districts over the years and of course there is no shortage of reports of the .30-30's effect on game. The effect of the .30-30 is often immediate. On game the cartridge is decisive inside 100 yards. While often compared to the .30-30, the 7.62 x 39mm cartridge has not exhibited the performance of the .30-30 Win-

Lee Berry is sweeping off the safety of his personal AK-47 in a rapid action drill.

When moving quickly to disengage the AK-47 safety, do not sweep the hand back on the grip and fire the rifle until you really mean to!

chester. Multiple hits are a rule. One of my friends was hit five times in the stomach and abdominal region with the AK-47 and survived. Good JSP loads or the Cor Bon JHP are a must for personal defense.

The rifle has no bolt lock and does not tell you when it is empty. The AR-15 locks open and you have a dead trigger. The AK-47 snaps on an empty chamber. The safety is only a dust cover that is a bit difficult to operate. The safety is best manipulated from a high ready position. You move to the safety and take it off forcefully snapping it down.

You then move the hand quickly back to the ready position. Be certain not to press the trigger as you move quickly. Always keep the trigger finger straight and do not move the finger to the trigger until you fire.

Changing magazines is not difficult but doing so quickly is a challenge. An advantage is that the AK-47 magazines are rugged. I have seen a quick-change executed in which the spare magazine hammered the magazine release and then knocked the empty magazine from the rifle. I cannot recommend this technique as you may spring the magazine catch and render it unusable but the operator performed the drill quickly. Most of us will activate the magazine release, rock the magazine out, and then rock a new magazine in. Clearance drills with the AK-47 are complicated by the magazine release. When you encounter a short cycle with the AK or a failure to feed rock the magazine in the magazine well in order to fully seat the

magazine then rack the bolt with the rifle tilted to the right side. If you have to remove the magazine to clear a malfunction you must have plenty of practice or plenty of time. A failure to extract and a double feed will require removal of the magazine.

The AK-47 has a narrow rear sight that takes time to acclimate to. Most variants feature wings that protect the front sight. At one time or the other almost every student confuses one of the wings with the front post, resulting in a wild shot. This most often occurs in rapid fire. Meprolight offers a replacement sight with self luminous inserts that works just fine.

Using The Sling

Slings are an important addition even to a rifle that is kept at home ready rather than carried in the field. Most slings are carrying straps. You sling the rifle on the shoulder and it is not in your hands when you need it. You should always use a sling that allows a hasty off-hand rest to be taken. The support arm is passed through the sling and the sling tightened up to give excellent support. Any rifle that can be used past 25 yards will benefit from even a hasty rest. Basically the hasty rest gives the user support in lieu of a barricade to fire from.

The tactical sling is another matter. The tactical sling carries the rifle on the chest or muzzle down on the strong side arm. The tactical sling allows the user to quickly bring the rifle into action with a minimum of lost motion.

The old time leather sling is OK but a tactical rifle needs a good tactical sling. You may need the rifle for mobile defense, around the campsite, or when guarding a section of a large property. Tactical slings are sometimes called loop slings and when properly worn the webbing goes over the right shoulder. This supports the weight of the rifle. The attachment points are near the muzzle and the rear of the buttstock rather than under the stock as with conventional slings. The rifle is suspended just under the right shoulder. With a natural movement, the rifle is brought into action quickly. This type of sling offers considerable speed while keeping the rifle out of the way during maneuvers. I have used the GRSC snap sling with excellent results. Available from Dillon Precision, this sling offers a versatile array of hooks including a quick release hook. The GRSC is my favorite and I have adopted this sling on my most highly developed rifles.

In this illustration, Jessica is steadying the .45-70 rifle for an accurate shot at moderate range. A good sling and the skill to use it properly are a great aid to marksmanship.

Firing the Rifle from Cover

Just because you have a rifle, do not neglect cover. In fact search out cover because you have a rifle. When you are firmly behind cover, your chances of survival have gone up considerably. The ratio of cover and distance must be considered. If you are caught in the open and the opponent is thirty yards away and cover is also twenty yards away, you will probably be shot before you are able to get to cover. Time, proximity and availability are watchwords for cover.

It is always the best to fire around, not over, cover. When firing the rifle from behind cover, it is important not to hyperextend the rifle muzzle. Firing from behind cover with only the very muzzle of the rifle exposed is ideal. If we extend the rifle muzzle too much we are taking a chance on the muzzle being struck by gunfire. A real danger is that the rifle and the shooter will be struck by ricochet. Keep the shoulder against cover, remain a few feet back from the edge of cover, and do not expose any more of the rifle muzzle than necessary.

Movement with the Rifle

When moving with the rifle, there are three ready positions. These are high ready, low ready and indoor ready. They may be called something else by different trainers but these descriptions suit our needs. In high ready the rifle is snugged into the shoulder.

The eyes are on the sights. In low ready, the rifle is lowered but ready to instantly return to high ready.

In indoor ready, the muzzle of the rifle is in front of our body pointed toward the floor. The high ready position is used when we are ready for instant action.

When moving through a dwelling or building, low ready is preferred. This is because there is a danger of leading around a corner with the muzzle of the rifle and an adversary grasping the muzzle and pulling the rifle away from you. Once an assailant has his hands on the rifle, he has some leverage and it is difficult to retain control of the firearm. There are techniques for dealing with this situation. In the first, the defender immediately puts the greatest effort into reversing the situation by exerting force on the buttstock into the down position while using a fulcrum action to bring the muzzle up and toward the defender. The buttstock continues upwards and butt strokes the adversary across the chin or face. This is a technique that works.

Another technique is more lethal but is certainly worth considering. After all, if the adversary gains control of the weapon you are probably going to be on the receiving end or either blunt trauma or hot steel and lead. In the second technique the muzzle of the long gun is immediately pressed forcefully toward the adversary. As soon as the muzzle is pointed in his direction, the trigger is pressed.

While you may have an advantage in deploying a long gun, never forget that the length of the long gun gives an adversary an advantage in a gun grab attempt. Always remain vigilant and control your weapon.

22 Carbine Marksmanship

Civilian shooters can be lifesavers in a critical incident. During the Charles Whitman/Texas Tower incident of 1966, often termed the birthing cry of modern special teams, aid by civilians helped save the day. The police chief at the time commented that personal initiative from his officers avoided an even greater tragedy. Once the crazed shooter began receiving incoming fire, the killing stopped.

I am often asked what makes a good rifle marksman. As a police trainer, I felt that a qualified combat marksman should be good in trigger and sight work and also in deployment and manipulation. He should be able to stand in a shooting position and strike a man sized target at 100 yards on demand. He should be able to do the same from a braced position at 125 yards. You have to have a good practice schedule and find a good range that allows off-hand shooting. Structured training produces results. Bench rest shooting simply does not allow growth as a shooter. Dry-fire practice with a triple checked unloaded rifle is the beginning. If you cannot control muscle tremors during dry-fire, live fire will certainly be a challenge. The same technique used in finding the perfect firing grip for the handgun is used. Grip the rifle until your hands tremble then back off.

The AR-15 in action: a considerable fireball springs from the muzzle as the rifle cycles. The shooter's eyes are on the target through the ATN scope.

The author is quickly addressing a target with the AR-15 held fast and sure in a positive grip.

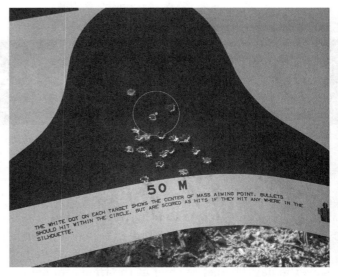

This is a rapid-fire group with the AR-15. Not bad at all and the type of shooting that saves lives.

The all-around marksman must be familiar with the various shooting positions. During all movement, the shooter must retain control of the weapon. When you move into the firing position, you must practice proper cheek weld and keep the stock hard into the shoulder. The three shooting positions most profitable for the home defense marksman are standing kneeling and prone. The prone position may seem out of place in personal defense but if you are able to quickly slide to the floor or take cover behind a vehicle or a wall prone may offer an excellent low profile position with a high likelihood of accuracy. The prone position is pretty static, however, and you may need practice in quickly breaking out of the prone position.

I have followed the advice of my early mentors, including combat veterans of World War II, Korea and Vietnam. These men advised to literally melt around the rifle and to hold it firmly into the shoulder. The important thing is to be prepared. If you have sparred with the same partner in the dojo for years you are prepared for anything he will do from the twelve angles of attack. But you need a new sparring partner and a new

range program to avoid becoming a one-trick pony. It is very important to practice all gunhandling skills but I feel that if time is limited you may not exercise very often in reloading the carbine. After all the carbine holds more rounds than the shotgun or handgun and will carry you through the night just fine with the gunload. Most battles are over before the bolt locks back on the last round. If you have time, fine, but otherwise work on marksmanship until you are very comfortable with the rifle.

When practicing offhand fire, the rifle is held with the weak hand on the forend in a combat rather than target shooting grip. The hand does not lie under the forend and support the rifle with this weak

This shooter is practicing the proper stance and trigger press with the Springfield M1A1 .308 caliber rifle. Both rifle and shooter are giving a good showing.

grip. Weight bias is toward the front as the non dominant foot is to the forefront and the shooter rocked forward to control the rifle and the recoil generated in firing. When you are at ready but not firing, standing with the knees flexed is comfortable for long periods and is ideal for waiting and listening in the home.

When it comes to live fire, the most common deficit is that the student will not achieve good cheek weld. The steps to good cheek weld are simple. Move the butt of the rifle into the shoulder. Then you have a fulcrum for bringing the rifle up and the sights to the eye. We need to get on the sights and get good shot placement quickly. An inconsistent cheek weld will result in poor accuracy.

Trigger control is very important. Poor trigger control may result in missed shots at ridiculously short range. The trigger must be pressed straight to the rear with smooth motion. The long sight radius, good sights and excellent accuracy of the rifle do not excuse the shooter from learning proper trigger compressing. Next, you must learn to use the sights well. The first thing is getting on target quickly and this means achieving a quick sight picture. There are different techniques for the different types of sights. When bringing the sights to bear if the rifle has an optical sight, take a quick bead on the top of the scope or the top adjustment turret. Line up roughly on target then go to the scope and center the reticule on the threat. For open sights of the AK-47 type you find the front post first and then bring the front post into alignment with the rear sight.

This is a brass bread front sight in a .44 Magnum Winchester rifle. This is ideal sighting equipment for down and dirty close-range work. This rifle belongs to gospel singer Paul Jordan.

The aperture or peep sight is preferred for most uses in personal defense. When using the aperture sight, you first look through the aperture and then you focus on the front sight. The open rear sight has the effect of centering the front sight on the target and giving you a quick and efficient sight picture. You have got to execute the sight picture quickly and smoothly. If you think too long you will have a problem.

Red dot sights have changed the face of combat shooting and are in active use with the military with excellent results. There are a number of types available that have given excellent results. I feel that the Bushnell Holosight or the EOTech version have proven themselves to my satisfaction and are excellent choices. Another sight that my trusted friends have used comes from Meprolight. The Meprolight has enjoyed considerable use by government agencies and remains a favorite of professionals.

The rules are different when using the Holosight. The speed available with the red dot sight can be a significant improvement for some shooters. Red dot sights have the advantage

The EOTech red dot scope has proven itself time and again in police and military usage. At present this is the recommended red dot scope.

Lee Berry demonstrates the proper technique with an EOTech sight. Both eyes are open, looking through the scope. All that matters next are trigger press and sight alignment.

of placing all focus on one plane. Rather than focusing the eye on a rear sight, front sight and target, you simply focus on the red dot. The red dot is also called a reflex sight. The red dot utilizes reflective or refractive optics with no magnification. There is no reticle, only the red dot.

The red dot is free of parallax. The red dot may be seen at practically any distance from the eye and good hits made with a less than perfect lineup. Shooting with both eyes open is preferred. The advantage is less evident at longer ranges and more care must be taken in aiming and to avoid lateral offset. A final caution: keep your powder dry and your batteries fresh.

I stress bringing the rifle to the shoulder as quickly as possible and beginning to acquire the sight picture as soon as the rifle clears the plane between the threat and the eye. If the adversary is fully exposed, you have a great advantage. Bring the rifle on target and fire when the sights are on the centerline

of the body. If you wait for a better hit, you may be too late if the opponent is firing at you. Bring the rifle to bear and compress the trigger and you will get a hit. Naturally the longer the range, the more time you must expend in aiming. The longer the distance, the finer the sight picture must be.

With a handgun I have always practiced double taps. When I bring the rifle on target at close range I do the same thing. I bring the rifle up and on target and quickly fire two shots. The need for precision fire increases inversely proportionally to the distance involved. The advantages of the rifle are power and accuracy, and the proper combination is a winning combination on all counts. But quickly firing the rifle at moderate range is also important.

A number of drills can show you just how fast the rifle can be on target. I think that one disadvantage students have is a tendency to fire the second shot too quickly. They fire the first shot and then fire again before the front sight is pulled back into the rear sight or before the red dot is back on target. This results in a high shot. Accustom yourself to getting on target and making a hit quickly but also bringing the front sight back into agreement with the rear

This soldier is practicing off the bench with the Bushmaster carbine to confirm the zero with his ATN scope. This rifle and scope make a fine all-around combination.

sight before you fire the second shot. This is especially important to the home defender who must account for every shot.

Combat shooting is sometimes deliberate shooting. The rifle gives a trained shooter every advantage. When addressing a small target, the rifle is a great advantage compared to a handgun. When holding the rifle firmly in place, we often place the hand close to the magazine well of AR-15 type rifles for greater control in close-quarters battle. This is a good technique that aids in quickly swinging the rifle. But we must also concentrate on marksmanship at longer range. I grew up shooting a rifle with my hand forward near the end of the forend. This works for me and seems to give better accuracy, es-

pecially when coupled with a good sling. But I use the alternative gripping the forend closer to the magazine when moving quickly at moderate range. Without a doubt there is room for both techniques. We should be able to quickly acquire a sight picture and address small targets such as a foot or elbow protruding from cover. A handgun stuck around a corner is another target that might be addressed by a rifleman.

A final technique for down-and-dirty close-range battle just might save the day. This is a form of the Applegate point in some ways but the technique has been around a long time and may have been used as long as firearms have been around. The tactic involves firing with only the front sight as an aiming point. There are times when it may be profitable to use only the front sight. This includes when darkness makes using the rear sight impossible or when the distance is so close you may not be able to fully shoulder the long gun. At close range, seven yards or so, you simply lower the rifle and place the front sight on the opponent's belt buckle. The shots will be directed into the body.

With practice on the range, you will understand the approximate point of impact at ranges from three to fifteen yards. If you are forced to fire in dim light at a target at greater than conversational distance, using the front sight only is better than using no sight at all and just may carry the day.

The bottom line is that we must practice. Practice, training, and most of all careful thought and application of the trigger press, sight picture and follow-through. Skill will carry the day. There are no shortcuts to proficiency.

Lee Berry is demonstrating the proper technique with the AK-47 and red dot sight. Both eyes are open and he is looking directly through the sight.

The Shotgun

There are many misconceptions about the shotgun. By its nature, the shotgun is all-encompassing rather than a precision instrument. There is no other firearm as effective at close range and no firearm more likely to strike and incapacitate the adversary at moderate range.

As its name implies, the shotgun launches a charge of shot rather than a single projectile, although it may also be used with solid projectiles. Small shot such as 7-½ size (the higher the size number, the smaller the shot) is used to engage flying birds. Slightly larger shot is used to take squirrel and rabbit. Progressively larger shot sizes are used for larger game up to deer. Deer is the largest game practical for use with shot and the shot intended for use with deer is, not surprisingly, called buckshot. Shot is not intended to produce a hit with every pellet but rather to produce a veritable cloud of shot that will find a small animal and strike it a few times in order to produce edible table fare. As the game

The intricacies of the shotgun must be carefully explained for a novice to understand the nuances of loading and unloading. While there are simpler shotguns, the pump shotgun is the recommended action type.

Here is the great appeal of the shotgun. A single press of the trigger equals a storm of hits on the target.

becomes larger, there is a need for a greater concentration of shot. It is preferable that all of the balls in a buckshot load strike the animal in order to bring it down.

When it comes to personal defense the object is to land the shot centered in the adversary. A hit or two may produce damage but we really need a high concentration of buckshot for immediate incapacitation. Another difference between the shotgun and rifle is that the shotgun is aimed largely by feel. The great difference in shotgunning and rifle marksmanship is that the shotgun is often aimed where the game will be. The swing is most important in shotgunning. A personal defense shooter isn't a hunter, but if we learn the swing and develop the ability to strike a moving target then we will maximize the shotgun's effectiveness. While we wish to center the charge to maximize the effect of the shotgun, the fit and feel of the shotgun are also important in combat shooting. The handling qualities of the shotgun are important.

When it comes to the personal defense shotgun, part of our education is dispelling myths. You can miss with the shotgun at ridiculously close range. Shotguns cannot scatter shot the length of a vehicle and are not always instantly effective. When the myths are eliminated, what remains is an effective

This young woman has mastered the shotgun and is a good stance to execute a solid hit.

This is a humble but workmanlike shotgun. The single shot Rossi is inexpensive by design but can be a lifesaver.

firearm. The shotgun is at its best defending a static location such as a home, ranch or campsite. The shotgun is able to deploy a wide variety of loads, making the versatility of the type appealing. The shotgun must be learned and learned well for maximum potential. Often the shotgun is underutilized for a variety of reasons including a fear of recoil.

When you choose a personal defense shotgun, you really need a short handy shotgun with a barrel length of 18 to 20 inches. This barrel length is shorter than the nominal 28-inch length of most sporting guns. When navigating a hallway or deploying from a tent or truck, the 18-inch tube looks good. The legal minimum overall length for the firearm is 27 inches with the shortest allowable barrel being 18 inches. A

The double barrel shotgun is still an effective choice with more than a little intimidation factor.

short-barreled shotgun handles quickly and points well.

Shotguns have a certain degree of choke in the barrel to control the shot pattern. Choke is simply a barrel restriction that tightens the pattern or produces a more cohesive pattern. Chokes are most often categorized as open, modified and full choke. A bird hunter may wish to use an open choke. The fellow who hunts deer with buckshot may wish to own one of the new "super full" chokes. Personal defense shotguns usually have an open choke. This is fine for use inside a dwelling or at relatively close range but limits versatility. The FN Herstal SLP shotgun is an exception. This is one of the few modern combat shotguns supplied with a set of choke tubes. For home defense, choke matters little. The shotgun charge will be tightly compressed at home defense range.

There are a number of accessories available that may look good for police or military use, when the possibility of a protracted engagement is more real. For the home defense shotgun, I think keeping it simple makes the most sense. I might use a slip-on or leather lace-on shell carrier on the buttstock if the home defense shotgun is a single shot or a double barrel, but that is about the limit of my modifications. The shotgun thrives on simplicity. Gadgets and gimmicks are poor choices. These devices add weight and offset the balance of the shotgun. On the other hand if the shotgun is more than a backup but your primary do-everything, go-everywhere defensive firearm, then a modest custom upgrade is another matter. I think the addition of peep sights or a quality red dot sight are within the bounds of reason.

The exact choice of a home defense shotgun is personal but some criteria aren't debatable. The shotgun must be completely reliable. Feel and balance are important attributes. There are several types of shotguns to choose from. These include the single shot, double barrel, slide or pump action, and semi-automatic. (Single shots are sometimes called single barrel shotguns and doubles are called side by sides or over/unders.) A single shot shotgun is an

Double barrel shotguns feature excellent balance. Since the shotgun is fired mostly by feel, the double is a contender for the most effective of shotguns.

effective shotgun in the right hands but you are putting your eggs in just one basket. An exposed hammer shotgun is handy, simple, and in the case of the modern Rossi with transfer bar ignition, safe in operation. It is not well known but in South America, quite a few military bases are guarded by soldiers with a single shot shotgun. The theory is the shotgun must be feared but if guerillas overpower the soldier and take the single shot firearm they haven't gotten much. A short, light double barrel is also a fine choice. The Bounty Hunter line of Russian-produced double barrel shotguns have given good service in cowboy action matches and seem to be good shotguns. The choke is practically nonexistent in my personal example, but that is fine for home defense. The double barrel has only two shots but they handle very well and shots may be delivered quickly and with a high degree of confidence in a hit.

Sporting type semi-automatic shotguns are problematical. If well maintained and consistently lubricated, a semi-automatic may be as reliable as a pump action shotgun but a dirty semi-automatic will never be as reliable as a dirty pump. Plus, some semi-automatics must be used with full-power shells at all times to operate the action. Some will not function with the various reduced recoil buckshot and slug loads intended for personal defense. This is a real drawback. If you wish to own a good automatic shotgun for personal defense at present, you need either to obtain a FN Herstal SLP or have a sporting

shotgun shortened and fitted with proper sights, and there is no guarantee of success.

For most of us most of the time the slide action shotgun is by far the best choice. I have access to practically any shotgun but the only shotgun I own more than one example of is the Remington 870. I also own a Winchester 1300 and I have used the FN Herstal TPS, basically a highly modified 1300, with good results. The Remington 870 is an ideal choice. The 870 has good features but it also has a great track record. Other choices include the used rack at the pawnshop where you may find a good Ithaca or even a used High Standard shotgun. You may spend a modest amount having the barrel shortened and you will have a fine personal defense shotgun. But in the end I think the money invested in a new 870 is well spent. If you have a slightly built spouse you might consider the youth model in 20 gauge. I don't think honest wear and long use will wear out an 870. Abuse might, but then no one abuses equipment more than cops and 870 shotguns keep on plugging year after year.

When I was young and into pointless competitions, I sometimes proved I could chuck out more rounds with the slide action shotgun than a shooter could with the semi-automatic. More often than not I won the contest by a nose. On one occasion I was using a low-bid shotgun issued to an agency and sheared an action pin. I have never seen this occur with the Remington. The Remington's twin operat-

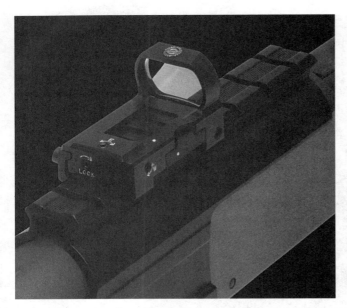

The Meprolight sight has given good service and can add up to rapid efficiency when mounted on a shotgun.

ing rails ensure smoothness. Its well-placed controls make using the shotgun efficient. Learn the position of the safety and bolt release and how to load and unload the Remington and you will be in fine shape.

Among the neatest Remington shotguns I own is the youth model 870 20 gauge. This is a light and lively shotgun that handles quickly and smoothly. It is not as powerful as the 12 gauge and I would not choose it for police service or for defense against large animals. But in a personal defense situation in

the home the Remington 20 gauge pump is capable of putting a lot of lead in the air quickly. My example features a rib and bead front sight.

This brings us to a general discussion of shotgun sights. Some are of the opinion that anything other than a simple front bread slows the shooter down. Since the shotgun is most often used in reactive fire at a few feet, this is a credible argument. The bead is remarkably fast. Most of the riot guns used by police agencies during the previous century were bead sighted. The buck special is a popular variation with rifle sights. There are areas deemed too crowded for rifle use and game departments have allowed the buck special. These shotguns often have rifled barrels. While a slug gun may be effective past 100 yards the maximum range is far less than that of a rifle. If you envision using the rifle past 25 yards you need good sights. The Remington 870 Police Magnum with rifle sights is ideal. It isn't difficult to sight the shotgun properly for 25 yard use with slugs.

There are any number of operators who strongly prefer the slug to buckshot for a number of reasons. My own research indicates that a 12 gauge slug is more consistently effective than buckshot. The decision to use slugs or buckshot must be made depending upon the threat level. The likelihood of overpenetration is less with buckshot, another important consideration.

This shotgun is fitted with an AR-15 stock and EOTech red dot sight. Note the heat guard on the barrel. The heat guard may not be necessary in personal defense but certainly is an aid in dissipating heat during long training sessions.

The Ideal Shotgun

While other shotguns are viable for personal defense, the ideal personal defense shotgun remains a pump action 12 gauge shotgun with iron sights. The versatility and effectiveness of the type in trained hands is excellent. The shotgun requires considerable practice to master. Learning to deal with recoil is important and for this reason I recommend light loads for practice. Of course you will have to familiarize yourself with the recoil of full power loads at some point but in the beginning light loads such as number 7-½ shot are recommended. Winchester loads are available in bulk at a good price during hunting season at many retailers. The pattern is such that birdshot makes a reasonable substitute for buckshot for practice. You must pattern the shotgun with shot loads as well. The pattern may be a little high or a little low in relation to the bead but you must learn the relationship between the pattern and the bead's position on the target.

You will discover that buckshot gives up at a certain range and the pattern is no longer dense enough to produce a telling strike on the target. A fact that has been proven is that buckshot performs differently in individual shotguns. You also need to qualify the slug load and its point of aim and point of impact as well. Slug load selection varies considerably from buckshot selection. For example, I most often use Winchester's Winlite reduced recoil buck, a #00 (double ought) load that carries 9 pellets when qualifying students with 12 gauge shotguns. With the slug there are also reduced recoil slugs but the best accuracy I have obtained has been with the Winchester Supreme full power slug. Effect of buckshot loads is good at short range and sometimes the pattern is denser than with full power loads. But when range testing various reduced recoil slug loads I discovered a considerable difference in performance between reduced recoil slugs and full power slugs. There is a considerable difference in recoil and the reduced recoil slugs offer less punishment.

A decrease in recoil of perhaps twenty-five percent is realized with both buckshot and slugs in their reduced energy form. Both exhibit acceptable penetration or pattern. But full-power slugs have often stayed in the body and expanded considerably, with a flattening of the nose and even a shredding of pieces of the slug in the body. Reduced recoil slugs do not mushroom in my testing. Another problem is increased drop at longer range. I remind the reader that a long gun may be used at 50 yards or more in a desperate situation against predators or an active shooter.

As an experiment I took my Winchester 1300 with rifled barrel and a stock Remington 870 to the range with a variety of slug loads. At fifty yards, the holdover needed to produce a center hit was significant. I held on the neck to produce a center chest hit with reduced recoil loads. Full power loads were another matter, often striking to the point of aim. With the Winchester Supreme loading groups of three to five inches at fifty yards were fired offhand. This is a good result considering the Winchester 1300 is a utilitarian shotgun. However, at 100 yards I could not get on the paper in off-hand fire. The reason was discovered when I fired a few shots into the berm. The shotgun was recoiling while the slug was still in the barrel and I was firing high. I resorted to firing for the belt buckle region to produce center

These are nine #OO buck pellets from a Winchester Winlite buckshot 12 gauge shell. They will do the business!

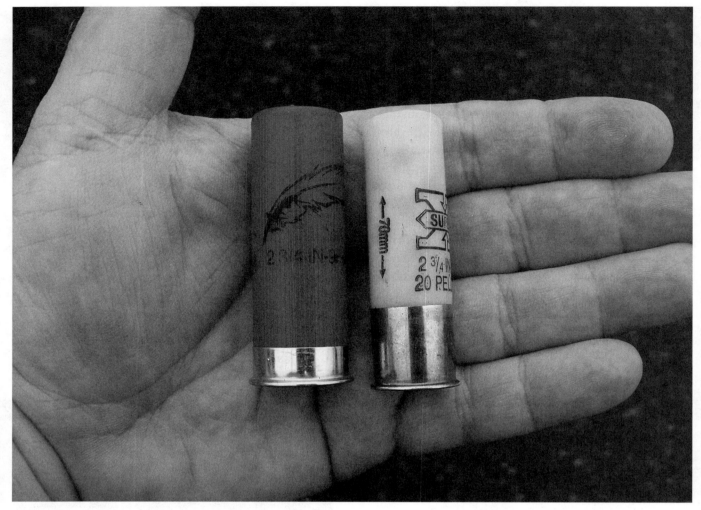

The 12 gauge shell is larger than the 20 gauge but the 20 gauge is adequate for personal defense situations in the home. The 20 gauge has the advantage of light recoil for the occasional shooter.

hits. Conversely with low power slugs I held center chest for a hit in the abdomen. I have to admit the recoil of full power slugs took their toll in an extended range session. A shotgunner using slugs at long range must be well-versed in application. At moderate range, slugs present little difficulty in sighting in.

Gauges

There are two shotgun gauges I recommend for personal defense. These are the 20 gauge and the 12 gauge, with the 20 gauge very much the understudy. The .410 is useful in indoctrinating youngsters into shooting shotguns but not for personal defense. As soon as the youth is able, he or she should move to a 20 gauge. The .410 shotgun's meager pattern is a hindrance to learning wingshooting. The 28 gauge is in a similar category. The 20 is a reasonable choice with the 20 pellet load of #3 buckshot. The 20 gauge is far less versatile against large animals and at long range but for the recoil shy or physically limited, the 20 gauge is a lifesaver of the first order. The 16 gauge is between the 20 gauge and the 12 gauge and just fine for personal defense with suitable loads if you have one on hand. The 16 gauge and its shells are far less common and the 12 gauge is more effective. The 12 gauge is the most powerful and can throw the heaviest shot with the densest pattern, and 12 gauge shells are universally available.

When choosing a combat shotgun, pay attention to conventional reasoning and choose wisely. While "classic" is an overused term, some firearms are classics and have become so because they are impeccable performers.

As we discussed in the previous chapter, there is good gear waiting for the strong men and women who can handle it. The shotgun strikes me as a very personal answer to home defense, the ideal firearm for a working man or woman defending the family. Training with the shotgun can be grueling but the results are very rewarding. The following instructions, especially those concerning the stance and firing position, may apply to all types of shotguns but we will concentrate on the pump shotgun.

I will repeat that birdshot is best suited for initial training. The proven technique begins with learning a solid stance. When taking up the shotgun, place the butt firmly into the hollow of the shoulder. Lean forward with the shoulder forward of the hips. The non-dominant side leg is cast forward. The impression of leaning into recoil is correct. Even when kneeling the basic elements of this stance remain intact.

With the rifle cheekweld is important. The shotgun is fired largely based on feel. That is why I prefer the standard shotgun stock for general use rather than a folding stock or carbine type stock. The pistol grip shotgun especially is to be avoided as it is useless past seven yards. (This means a shotgun with only a pistol grip, not the well-designed shotgun stocks that

Lee Berry is working at full speed with a Remington pump. Note shell in ejection port.

convert the shotgun to an AR-15-type pistol grip and folding stock.) I understand the commonality with a carbine and the reason some might like to add a carbine-like stock to the shotgun. If you own both the AR-15 and the shotgun and prefer to carefully aim the shotgun rather than operate by feel, then make your choice. My personal plain old 870 is just fine for who it is for.

If you significantly alter the handling qualities of the shotgun, understand the consequences. If the need exists to launch flash-bang grenades through a window, then you probably need a rifle stock and rifle sights. The shotgun is a wonderful all-around weapons system for police. For myself, the fit and feel of the double barrel and slide action shotgun are just fine. My shotgun is for personal defense and animal control but also for the occasional taking of large game. When learning the shotgun, go with what you know and choose the shotgun carefully, then jump into training. Training is more important than the exact firearms choice.

This is high ready. While a good position for a quick shot, high ready is not comfortable for extended periods.

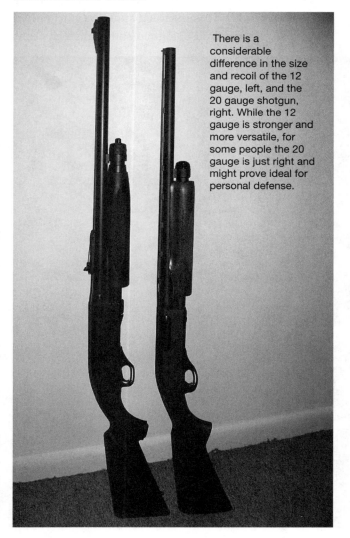

There is a considerable difference in the size and recoil of the 12 gauge, left, and the 20 gauge shotgun, right. While the 12 gauge is stronger and more versatile, for some people the 20 gauge is just right and might prove ideal for personal defense.

Ready Positions

The shotgun can be used with three ready positions. These are:

High Ready: The shotgun is held into the shoulder with the muzzle forward and the eyes on the sights. This position cannot be maintained comfortably for long periods.

Low Ready: Low ready is assumed with both hands on the shotgun and the muzzle held in a lowered position. This is a comfortable position for long periods.

Indoor Ready: In indoor ready the shotgun is held with the muzzle near the ground but away from the feet. Indoor ready is an excellent position for searching and moving indoors.

You must practice all three positions and quickly moving to high ready from the other two positions and also quickly moving into a firing position.

The shotgun must be aimed as precisely as a rifle at short range. The shot pattern has not yet spread and will strike en masse at short range. The greatest

This is low ready. This is the single most useful ready position, in the author's opinion.

This is indoor ready. The indoor ready position is useful in home defense. Care must be taken the shotgun never points toward the user's feet.

advantage of the shotgun is evident at twelve to fifteen yards. At this range the shot has spread and the cone of shot is likely to strike a moving target if the shooter swings properly. The different ranges are often referred to as A, B and C range. A range is about seven yards. The shotgun must be carefully aimed. B range is the range at which the greatest advantage is evident, and may be ten to twenty yards. Past twenty yards the pattern has spread to the point it is not effective, with only a few of the buckshot balls landing on target. C range is slug range, twenty yards and farther.

When you begin practice, bring the bead of the shotgun on the target and center the bead on the X ring. Static shooting is just fine in the beginning but then we progress to moving targets. It is important to understand swing. In the firing position, the support arm moves the shotgun as you track the target with the front sight or bead. At moderate range you do not have to lead; you simply place the front bead on the far side of the target in their direction of travel. As you swing, keep the front post on the target

and press the trigger. It is vital that you do not stop the swing as the shot breaks but keep the bead on the target and continue swinging in follow-through. With the shotgun, follow-through is more than continuing to retain the sight picture and your grip on the firearm. Follow-through also encompasses continuing the swing.

Swing and move with the target and do not stop the swing as you break the shot. Keep the front post on the leading edge of the target and you will not miss. I have tested this technique on tactical resetting targets and targets as simple as old tires rolled down a hill. (Not to mention a youth spent bird hunting.) It works.

The shotgun packs plenty of power but it is not infallible. You may need a backup shot. You should practice quickly cycling the shotgun and giving the target a second quick shot. It is important that you bring the front sight out of recoil and completely back on the target before you trigger another shot. I am aware of a number of felons who have taken buckshot or slug hits and remained mobile. One was engaged by a shopkeeper who had wisely loaded his shotgun with a combination of buck and ball, i.e., buckshot followed by a slug. The felon took a hit from buckshot that had been partially stopped by machinery. The slug hit and spun him down, but he survived.

Take this to heart and practice often with moving targets and then transition to slugs at C range. It is a good idea to keep the repeater downloaded by one shell. That is three shells instead of four in the Remington 870. With a lace-on shell carrier loaded with slugs, you are ready to instantly transition to slugs. In fact, if you have maintained the original stock and forend of your shotgun you must may discover that you are able to fire the piece largely by feel even with slugs and connect rather quickly on moving targets.

When you are moving, keep the muzzle of the shotgun down. You are thinking a second ahead and you are preparing to address a threat. The pump gun should have the magazine loaded and the chamber empty except when you are ready for engagement. There is no firing pin block on the shotgun and the safety locks the trigger only. Over the years there have been a number of unfortunate incidents involving police shotguns.

Shotguns from the major makers have fired when dropped or bumped. Semi-automatics do not differ significantly in this regard. About 50 percent of the time, pump shotguns that are cocked will fire if struck hard enough or dropped from chest height. There are two ways of keeping the piece at ready while the chamber is empty. You may keep the piece cocked and the magazine loaded or uncocked. When uncocked, the bolt is not locked and the piece may cock itself as you pick it up. Bad news.

As I have mentioned, the racking of the slide can have a pronounced psychological effect. The portent is certainly lethal. The steps in making the shotgun ready for action should be practiced often at the range:

- Activate slide release.
- Rack action.
- Release safety.
- Fire.

Perform these actions the same each time. An intuitive assessment of ability is easier with students than when addressing personal development, but as we progress in training we will begin to be proficient in handling the shotgun. You will rack the slide when moving to a high risk danger assessment.

In order to control the shotgun, it is vital to lean into it and maintain control of the action and recoil at all times.

Confidence is vital. You must know your shotgun and your ability. You are moving forward with the shotgun in order to dominate a home defense situation. Accuracy, power and speed are important and while the shotgun has power and speed in the hands of a skilled operator, accuracy remains most important.

Combat Load

The combat load is simply the action of topping the shotgun's magazine while in action. The gun hand holds the shotgun while the weak hand grasps a shell and feeds a shell into the magazine. It is a good idea to practice such loading with every range trip and to practice transition from buckshot to slugs.

There is an alternative used to stoke an empty shotgun. When the shotgun runs empty, you can simply drop a shell in the chamber and close the action. I find this type of load clumsy compared to the combat load. You can simply load the magazine and rack the action to load the chamber. You must constantly train to avoid an illusion of security and the combat load is an important tactic. During a critical incident, events unfold in seconds. There is little time

Lee Berry has paused to replenish the magazine of his Remington pump. He will be up and running in a heartbeat or two.

to recover from a failure to fire or a failure to stop. Manipulation is very important.

Combat Drill

The following drill answers a lot of needs in combat shooting. I fire five rounds at each distance and often incorporate at least one combat load. A good cadence of fire is to fire two rounds, combat load, and fire two more. Alternating slugs is another good drill. During this training you will get a good idea of the pattern of your shotgun. After practicing with birdshot you must pattern the shotgun with the combat load.

- Five shots at 7 yards at center mass.
- Five shots at 15 yards at center mass.
- Five shots at 25 yards at center mass with slugs.

Semi-Automatic Shotgun Drills

There are advantages to the semi-automatic shotgun. While I have on occasion fired against the semi-automatic using the pump with good results, a modern timer such as the Competition Electronics version shows that the intervals between shots are less with the semi-automatic. Intervals between shots are .5 to .9 seconds with the pump and .5 to .7 with the semi-automatic. The latter may be the better performer when firing from a barricade.

Certainly a good semi-automatic shotgun is credible as long as it is completely reliable with the service load. But you must immerse yourself in the type and be certain you have mastered it. For example, some models make the combat load difficult.

You must press the bolt release in order to top off the magazine while the bolt is down. The semi-automatic shotgun locks open on the last shot and you should practice quickly dropping a shell in the chamber. Unlike the pump action, this is a good maneuver to practice. Otherwise you may have to drop the bolt, press the bolt release, and only then top the magazine off and next rack the bolt to chamber a round. Dropping a shell in the chamber then dropping the bolt makes more sense.

Unloading the Shotgun

You are completely familiar with the shotgun only when you have mastered unloading the type and making it safe. With the single shot break top you need only press the release, either a lever or a plunger type, to open the chamber and tilt the barrel. Some have automatic ejectors but most will require you to pluck the shell out. If you practice quick reloading you should be aware of this. The double barrel is little different. But those using the repeaters have sometimes picked up a terrible habit in unloading the shotgun. They will work the action vigorously and work each shell through the action. This is terribly unsafe and makes the author wish to run from the range each time he sees this safety breech.

The proper means of unloading a slide action shotgun or a semi-automatic is to turn the piece upside down and carefully keep the muzzle angled down in a safe direction. There are release bars under the bolt that keep the shell in the magazine prior to the shell being loaded into the chamber. To manually release these bars squeeze each bar simultaneously and capture the shell that pops out in the hand. You will have to squeeze the bar, capture a shell, and squeeze the bar again. When you have unloaded the magazine, either thumb the bolt release in the slide action and clear the chamber or rack the bolt in the case of the semi-automatic.

This is a double feed, perhaps caused by a short stroke. It can be cleared, but quick action is demanded if you have this problem during a fight.

Clearing a Short Cycle

A short cycle occurs when the action of a slide action shotgun is not worked properly through its cycle, that is, when the slide is not racked fully to the rear and then fully forward. I have found that some recruits will fire one or two rounds before short cycling. Some never short cycle. I am aware of a short cycle during a critical incident that resulted in the death of an officer. By keeping the shotgun firmly into the shoulder and manipulating the shotgun smoothly and aggressively, short cycles will be eliminated. When they occur, they are very difficult to clear.

The short cycle occurs when you have fired a shell and you are racking the slide to the rear. You do not complete the cycle to the rear and shuck the bolt forward. You have a partial feed of a fresh shell and a nice tie-up. The only answer I have seen that works is to forcefully slam the butt of the shotgun against the ground as you hold the piece by the forend. This forces the bolt to the rear and ejects the spent shell. Then ram the forend forward and this will load the shotgun. You may damage the action bars, but chances are you will get a live shell into the chamber.

Another short cycle we encountered when working up the book is when two live shells jump the magazine and try to load simultaneously. My cohort Lee Berry quickly ran his thumb into the chamber and pressed the shell farthest to the rear forward. The second shell was forced back into the magazine and the other, into the chamber. This is an expedient that works well.

25 Quickly Getting a Long Gun into Action

We have covered marksmanship and tactical drills with the long gun. Now we will cover getting the long gun into operation.

A difference in the wounds generated by an accidental shooting with the long gun as compared to the handgun is that the handgun most often produces self-inflicted wounds. A negligent discharge with a long gun most often injures someone other than the person holding the gun. Long gun discharges have struck fellow team members or family members. Peace officers have killed one another and innocent persons by allowing the long gun to discharge by mistake. The cardinal rule is to keep the finger off the trigger. Another rule is to stay away from the muzzle and never allow it to cover anything you are not willing to destroy.

The great scout Kit Carson described an accident in which a man grabbed a rifle by the muzzle. As he removed the rifle from a wagon, the hammer caught and the rifle discharged. Carson assisted in amputating the man's shattered arm. Due to the length of the long gun, it seems convenient to lean the rifle against a tree, post or wall. Even with a chamber empty or triple-checked unloaded firearm, this is a bad idea.

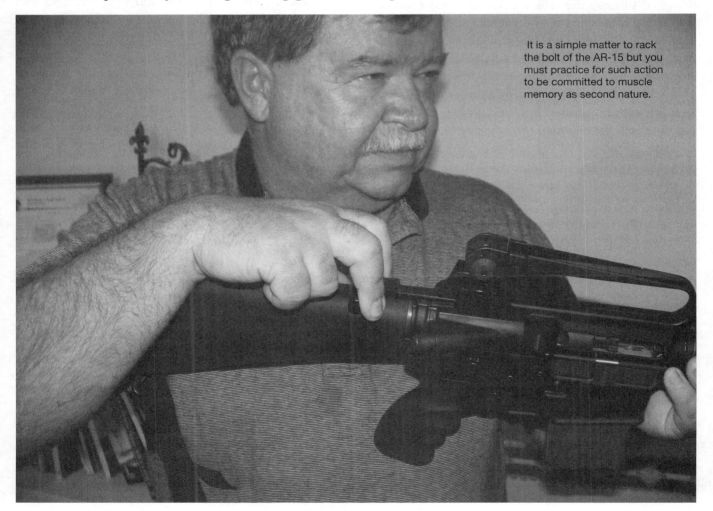

It is a simple matter to rack the bolt of the AR-15 but you must practice for such action to be committed to muscle memory as second nature.

This is a Rossi single shot. The transfer far safety makes keeping the chamber loaded attractive, but care must be taken in doing so. The large, accessible hammer is a good safety feature.

This young woman is practicing quickly manipulating the slide action Remington shotgun. Fire, rack, fire. After a time, the cadence is second nature.

Never pick the long gun up from the muzzle. Never allow the firearm to point over your shoulder at a person behind you. I understand gun safes are designed to keep the rifle muzzle up. Just exercise the same, utmost care when removing a long gun from storage. Stoop if need be and move the long gun from the safe with the strong-side hand on the butt stock and the support hand on the forend. I control and balance the long gun in this manner and always keep the muzzle pointed in a safe direction. I immediately check the chamber on removing the gun from the safe.

Keep your finger well clear of the trigger and control the long gun's movement. When the long gun is kept at ready for defensive use, you must give some thought into how accessible the long gun should be. I recommend keeping the long gun horizontal beside the bed. You can simply pick it up off the floor with none of the danger inherent in bracing a long gun on the wall. Some will keep the long gun locked during the day and only bring it out at

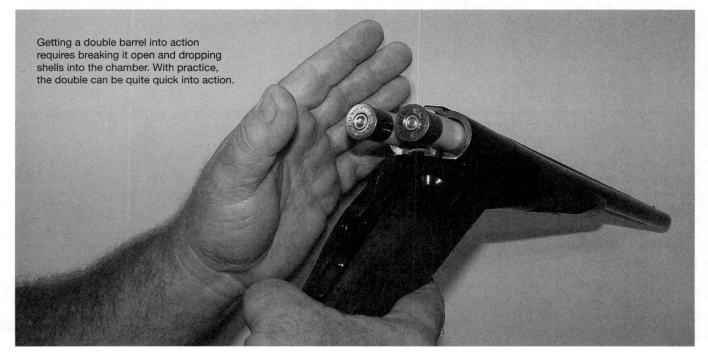

Getting a double barrel into action requires breaking it open and dropping shells into the chamber. With practice, the double can be quite quick into action.

When cocking a semi-automatic rifle, it is important to bring the bolt fully to the rear. . .

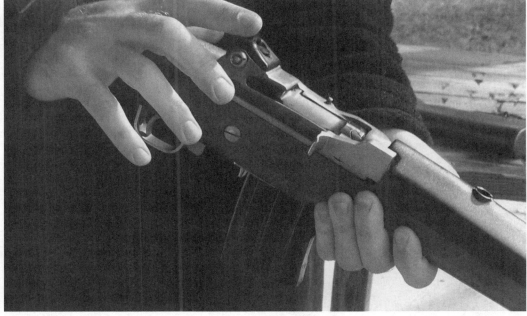

. . .and let it fly forward. This ensures proper feeding.

night. There is no time clock for assaults and take-over robberies in particular seem to occur as often in the daytime. If you are at home, it is a good time to have the long gun at ready. When accessing the long gun, cradle it in your arms and then decide if the time is ripe to load the chamber. I have stressed that the long gun should be kept chamber empty. A single shotgun or double barrel shotgun can be kept with the action broken open and chamber loaded for safety. In this condition the long arm can be made ready in an instant.

Lever action and slide action long guns are easily made ready. (When you consider the time involved to make the long gun ready, sometimes the .38 under the pillow looks good!) The user must be absolutely familiar with the action of the long gun.

The Kel-Tec carbine is easily secreted behind a light truck seat. The chamber should never be loaded when the carbine is kept in such a manner.

We have discussed the indoor ready position for indoor searches. At this time we are listening for scraping noises and calls for help from our family as we prepare to address a situation. When it is time to get the long gun into action we should use one deft stroke to make the piece ready.

When the rifle is held at chest height, the AK-47, Mini-14 or FN Herstal SLP all can be made ready with a quick rack of the bolt. With the AR-15, the rifle may be butted into the shoulder as the firing hand grasps the cocking lever and quickly cycles the action. The action must be worked sharply. It is important that the bolt be brought fully to the rear and allowed to snap forward forcefully (or worked forcefully, in the case of a manually-operated repeater). Some feel that this action may alert an invader to your presence. This may be true, but we will usually give a verbal warning before we fire. The racking of a bolt may simply underscore our intentions.

When cocking the action, be certain that you keep your finger off of the trigger. Once the long gun is up and ready, you are prepared to meet the threat. Be certain of the position of the safety.

I could discuss every safety type but the important point is that you are familiar with the type used on your personal long gun. There are few if any as quick and positive as the AR-15. The AK is a challenge. We may debate the cross bolt or sliding shotgun safety but either is quick in action if the operator is skilled. The bottom line: be certain the safety is under your control at all times. There are times when you will cock the piece and then place it on safe during movement but remain instantly ready to fire.

If you are not careful in properly making the rifle ready, you will have a double feed or short cycle. Rack the bolt aggressively and allow the cartridge to slide forward under bolt momentum.

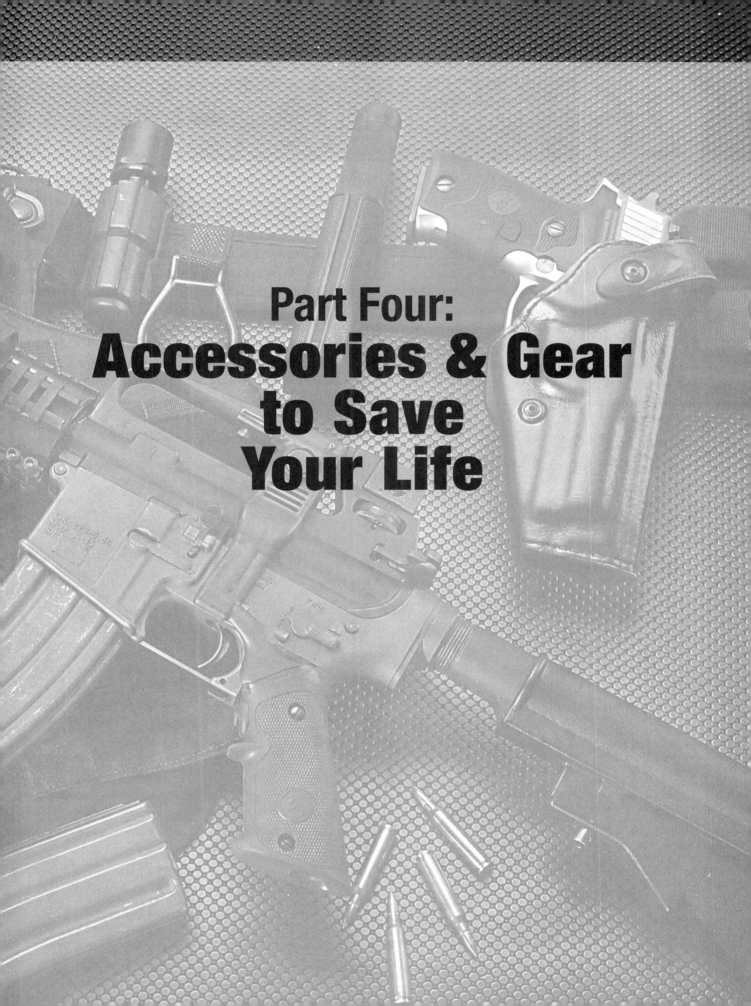

Part Four:
Accessories & Gear to Save Your Life

26

Practice Tools

Among the first questions I am asked by students is, what type of gear do I need?

A handy and sturdy Blackhawk! gear bag is indispensable. I have several on hand and my son, the military intelligence office, rates them highly as well, with one kept at the ready for alarms and excursions. For the instructor who needs to keep several types of handguns and ammunition on hand, Bagmaster produces a well-designed bag with compartments and pockets that work just fine. I have seen shooters arrive at the range with a cardboard box and this just does not work out.

Recently I have used an LA Gear Force Multiplier bag that is tall and relatively flat. It well fits my needs for solo trips. Don't go cheap. A flea market bag will not do to carry expensive gear and you can build up a lot of gear in a short time. A service pistol or two and hearing protection, shooting glasses, targets and ammunition may stress a bag considerably more than a jogging suit and tennis shoes. Just the same, we do not have to go the route of the tactical hypochondriac and bring along sixteen magazines, two spare handguns and a case of ammunition on every trip to the range. You are training for personal

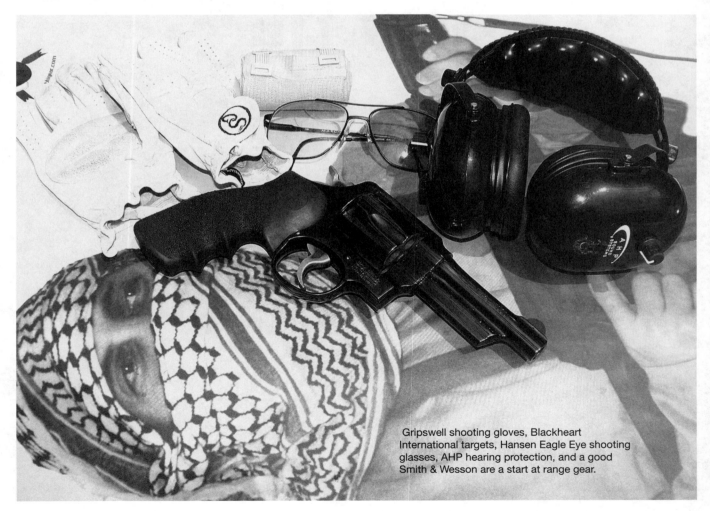

Gripswell shooting gloves, Blackheart International targets, Hansen Eagle Eye shooting glasses, AHP hearing protection, and a good Smith & Wesson are a start at range gear.

defense, not a SWAT expedition.

Here is a short list that will fill the need for most concealed carry qualification classes and other adventures.

- A quality handgun.
- Spare magazines or speedloaders.
- A good holster and magazine carrier or speed loader carrier.
- A sufficient supply of ammunition.
- Targets.
- Target tape or staples for the target stand.
- Shooting glasses.
- Hearing protection.
- Clothing and water supply appropriate for the weather.

I strongly recommend sticking with one handgun when learning. Most of us gravitate to two handguns after we gain experience, carrying a lighter handgun depending upon the season, but when building skills common sense dictates we stick with one handgun type.

Be certain the ammunition and the holster are suitable before attending a class or an impromptu shooting session. I have seen students arrive at class with an untried holster that fit the handgun but which was too tight to use because it had not been broken in. This results in an unusable holster and disappointment.

The ammunition should be proven feed reliable in your handgun. Full metal jacketed or lead round nose ammunition is just fine for practice. Speer Lawman, Black Hills blue box, Winchester USA and Fiocchi are among the brands I trust and use on a daily basis. When training, a good supply of challenging targets is also necessary. I use bullseye targets only when sighting the pistol in. Once I am certain the sights are regulated properly, I use combat style targets for practice. While bullseye targets are fine for marksmanship training once the pistol is sighted, in we learn more from firing at targets at known and unknown ranges. I have pistols I have never fired for a group and probably never well. But they are properly sighted for my use.

Targets

For combat practice, the black silhouette target used by most police agencies, the B27, works fine. A disadvantage that may be solved by mental discipline is the tendency of students to fire at paper targets and look over the sights to see if they have hit the target. That is bad news and must be avoided. Some trainers use plain buff targets that represent an outline and this is fine as far as it goes. Personally I like to use lifelike photographic quality targets. I have made extensive use of Law Enforcement Incor-

This is among the author's favorite targets, from Law Enforcement Targets, Inc.

This is a hostage rescue target from Law Enforcement Targets, Inc. In the author's opinion, this is the premier supplier for credible training targets.

porated products for a decade or more. This company offers a diverse selection that makes training more interesting.

Some of the targets imply the student needs to make a decision. Others, such as the obviously pregnant woman with a gun, are thought-provoking and well worth your consideration. I especially appreciate the various hostage rescue targets. These targets represent a challenging problem. When a rookie hits the wrong guy or has not considered what may be behind his target, these targets are worth their weight in gold for education. Another personal favorite of mine is the charging dog used by the Federal Bureau of Investigation. This target is especially difficult and outlines a real problem. Animal homicides are fairly rare with perhaps five hundred people killed by animals each year (excluding insect, spider and snake bites). But many more are mauled and badly

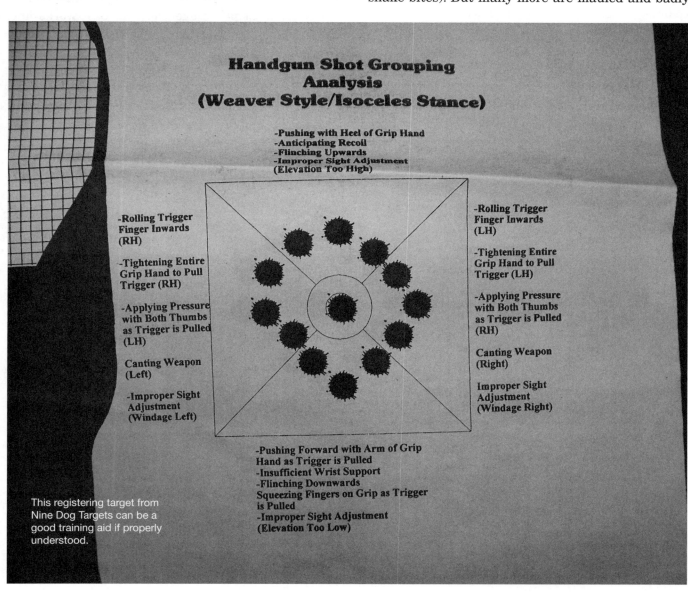

Handgun Shot Grouping Analysis (Weaver Style/Isoceles Stance)

-Pushing with Heel of Grip Hand
-Anticipating Recoil
-Flinching Upwards
-Improper Sight Adjustment
(Elevation Too High)

-Rolling Trigger Finger Inwards (RH)

-Tightening Entire Grip Hand to Pull Trigger (RH)

-Applying Pressure with Both Thumbs as Trigger is Pulled (LH)

Canting Weapon (Left)

-Improper Sight Adjustment (Windage Left)

-Rolling Trigger Finger Inwards (LH)

-Tightening Entire Grip Hand to Pull Trigger (LH)

-Applying Pressure with Both Thumbs as Trigger is Pulled (RH)

Canting Weapon (Right)

Improper Sight Adjustment (Windage Right)

-Pushing Forward with Arm of Grip Hand as Trigger is Pulled
-Insufficient Wrist Support
-Flinching Downwards
Squeezing Fingers on Grip as Trigger is Pulled
-Improper Sight Adjustment (Elevation Too Low)

This registering target from Nine Dog Targets can be a good training aid if properly understood.

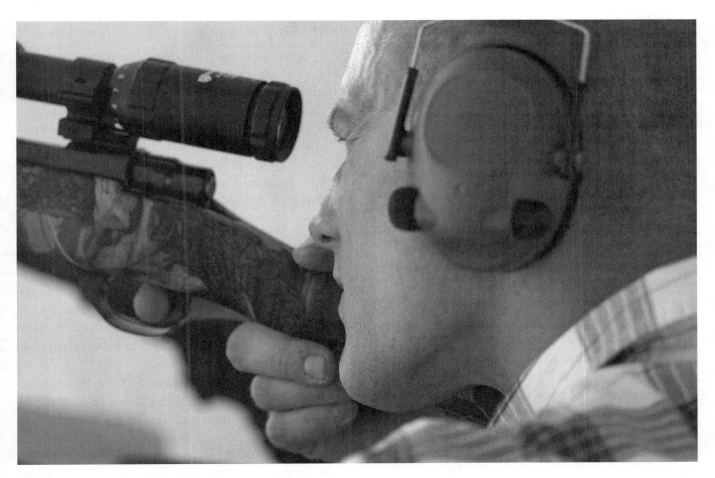

bitten. An animal defense target is an essential part of training.

Reaction targets are also a good training aid. They supply something we all long for: instant gratification. If you strike the target you have feedback at the speed of sound. If you miss, you try again. If you hit the gong on the side, it spins in a predictable fashion. There is instant feedback on marksmanship and an indicator of a solid center hit or a hit that is off-center. I like steel reaction targets because they offer good tools for skill building exercises. If you strike the middle of the target, the results are predictable. The target is swept back and out of the way. You can gauge your marksmanship rather easily. There is a good correlation to a flesh and blood target. If you hit the center of the target you just may be successful but if the target is struck off center it will have some effect but perhaps not the effect desired. A steel target gives dynamic feedback. If we miss a steel target with an audience present, the results may be embarrassing, but on the street a miss is more than embarrassing.

At one time only well-equipped clubs had steel targets available. Fixed steel gongs are relatively in-

expensive and available to all. There are important safety considerations to be addressed. Ricochet must be limited. Steel targets are designed so that they angle the bullet into the ground. This is not difficult to set up properly. The steel target is angled to the rear slightly. The bullet pushes the gong backwards and the projectile is directed toward the earth. Just the same, steel clad and steel core bullets must never be used against steel reaction targets. The danger of ricochet is too great.

I have conducted experiments with several types of bullets and steel targets. As long as standard jacketed or lead ammunition is used, steel targets are perfectly safe. At five to ten yards some platter is possible from jacket material but this is not a real danger as long as standard loads are used. For extreme close range training, frangible bullets – those that disintegrate on hitting a hard target – are available. I have found the Winchester frangible loads especially suitable to high-volume training with the 9mm pistol. Frangibles are intended to give peace officers real safety when training at close range with steel reaction targets and vehicles used as range props. I have seen training films in which operators shot steel targets at point-blank range with no splatter, only powdered dust falling at the base of the targets. Frangible ammunition is like lead sawdust. Sinters of metal are glued together to form a bullet. Naturally they have little cohesion and when they strike a steel target they become dust.

A word of caution: never use frangible loads for service. I have unloaded frangible rounds from the pistol chamber and broken their noses off in the chamber. The base was still in the cartridge while the chunk in the chamber fell out when I cleared the pistol. It did not obstruct the barrel but obviously could have. Frangible ammunition is an important resource but best relegated to training. Be certain to double-check any chamber cleared of frangible ammunition.

Steel reaction targets are now available to fit every budget. Do All Traps offers an excellent steel reaction target for set up on the range that may be carried in your vehicle trunk. Some of the targets are available for .22 rimfire use, while others are suitable for centerfire rifles. These targets are excellent trainers. A maker of steel reaction targets that I have used with excellent results is Mike Gibson Manufacturing. I have used several variations but my favorite remains the "Popper." This is a spring loaded target shaped much like a bowling pin. When the target is struck properly it is shot down but the spring returns it to the original position. A good hand with a .45 automatic may keep the Gibson resetting target moving without completely resetting, but few indeed will be able to keep it rolling with every shot. The Gibson steel resetting target is a fine resource for interested shooters and it is not expensive. Instead of taking out a line of steels targets at a range you fire at this target and wait for it to reset. It you wait for the reset instead of trying to beat the target, you are firing at a decent cadence and hitting at a rate you should not be ashamed of. There are shooters who keep the Gibson target rocking with a good 1911.

For inexpensive practice, the .22 Long Rifle cartridge is a godsend. The cartridge is accurate and in extreme cases has been a lifesaver.

The .22

Some may state the .22 rimfire is the greatest of training tools. I agree. The cartridge and the handguns that chamber the .22 are first class trainers. Often when a shooter has problems with a centerfire in managing the trigger or recoil ,a return to the .22 for a few practice sessions will quickly isolate the problem and help in clear up the problem. There is nothing like a good .22 for practice. Flash blast and recoil are practically eliminated, at least in offensive quantity. This allows concentration on marksmanship. Trigger compression is accomplished without recoil and blast introduced flinch into the picture. Quite a few shooters flinch upon firing as a result of muzzle blast. Some flinch due to recoil but the smart money is on muzzle blast as the primary cause of flinch. I recently went through 4,000 rounds of .22 caliber ammunition as a training exercise. I am more than certain the experiment sharpened the skills of all involved.

Over two billion rounds of .22 Long Rifle ammunition are produced in America in one year. Well over ninety percent of this quantity is the 40-grain high velocity loading. The .22 Short is a specialty cartridge that is shorter and less powerful but also more expensive than the .22 Long Rifle. The .22 Long is obsolete. The .22 CB cap as manufactured by CCI Speer is a special low-report, low-velocity cartridge with much merit. I often use CB caps to introduce young shooters to the handgun. While not a powerful handgun cartridge, the CB cap must be respected. I have taken pests out of the picture with the CB cap and it is more powerful than most air rifles. As an expedient I once took out a 50-lb. animal with the CB with a single shot. The area was fairly crowded but I had a good backstop in the form of a high grassy knoll behind the animal. The animal leaped up, spun around in a complete circle and collapsed, dead. The handgun used was a four-inch-barreled Smith & Wesson and the distance was thirty yards. Accuracy is often excellent with the CB cap to twenty-five yards or so but drop becomes severe at this range. The CB cap and other standard velocity loadings will not function in semi-automatic pistols; they will fire but must be manually fed into and removed from the chamber.

By far the most common .22 caliber loading is the .22 Long Rifle 40-grain high velocity version. Velocity is usually around 900 to 1,000 fps from a four-inch barrel. It is equally well-suited to revolvers and semi-automatic pistols. While marksmanship may be learned with any of the action types, if personal defense practice is the goal, then the practice handgun should be of the same general type as the personal defense handgun. I have used the Taurus double-action .22 revolver with good results. At one time I owned several High Standard Sentinel revolvers that I enjoyed but age has taken its toll. These handguns are getting rather long in the tooth and sometimes fail to fire. The new Ruger, Smith and Wesson, or Taurus revolvers are a good bet.

In automatic pistols there are small handguns that are fun guns but not as reliable as I would like. The Walther PPK, Walther P-22, and Bersa small frame automatics are a credible choice. The best all-around choices for practice handguns are the Ruger Standard Model and the Browning Buck Mark. The

Ruger is proven and available in many incarnations. The Ruger is so good, so affordable and so easily modified that there is little reason to choose any other type of semi-automatic pistol in .22 caliber. I have sometimes thought I use the Browning Buck Mark simply to be different and this may be true. It's a good pistol that has introduced many new shooters to marksmanship.

I have used practically every type of .22 caliber handgun and ammunition available. In my youth there was dirty and inaccurate ammunition sometimes on sale, but today it seems .22 rimfire loads are held to a higher standard. I have used cases of Winchester Wildcat with several generations of the Dynapoint thrown in for good measure. You don't really need hypervelocity slugs such as the Stinger for practice but CCI's Mini

For meaningful practice, nothing works quite like a good quality .22 caliber conversion unit. Most are surprisingly accurate.

Mag is never a bad choice. While I recommend a larger handgun for personal defense, if the only handgun you are able to afford is a .22, it can serve in good hands. I am aware of a case in a southern state in which a woman saved her life and that of her husband with a .22 caliber Ruger and in the process took two thugs out for good. In Greenville, South Carolina, a retired minister was stabbed during a home invasion but shot and killed his attacker in a flurry of fire. It took a reported seven rounds to do the business but the .22 got the job done.

A wonderful option for those who are serious about self-defense training is a good .22 caliber conversion unit. These are available for the Beretta, Colt 1911 and others, the Browning High Power, and a number of long guns, all from Jonathan Arthur Ciener. Factory units for the CZ 75 are available from CZ, and EAA has factory conversion units available for most of the Witness pistols. FMAP of Argentina offers an excellent conversion for the Browning High Power that differs considerably from the others and works quite well. Kimber offers a first-class conversion for their pistols. Other conversions may not work well with the Kimber, as the Kimber is very reliable but manufactured with the greatest tolerable specs to produce a tight, accurate handgun.

I have tested a number of conversion units for the Glock but none so far have proven reliable, which is unfortunate. If Ciener introduces a Glock conversion, that will be the smart money. With a .22 conversion in place you have a good trainer and even

Smith & Wesson
Model 586 airgun

a passing fair hunting pistol for small game. A .22 caliber conversion unit usually consists of an aluminum slide, steel rimfire barrel, a special recoil spring and a dedicated .22 caliber magazine. The conversion converts the pistol to blowback operation. The aluminum slide is light enough to operate in this manner.

I have seen criticism of the accuracy of conversions but in my experience these units are as accurate as most service pistols and occasionally will prove exceptionally accurate. The accuracy demonstrated is often tied to the frame that is used. Frequent cleaning and lubrication are needed for reliability but overall I have been impressed with the conversions. As long as I lubricate the conversion every one to two hundred rounds and keep it reasonably clean, it works just fine. I own several conversions for the 1911 and the High Power. These units have given excellent results and are an important part of my training sessions. The FM unit differs in that it is all steel with a bolt that is cocked from the rear. This bolt recoils from the steel slide of the conversion (the slide is really a receiver). The bolt reciprocates on firing. These conversions make good sense but a quality .22 caliber semi-automatic pistol is never a bad choice.

Airguns

A good training resource is airguns. Airguns are often regarded as primarily for youngsters but a number of first-quality airguns are realistic enough to give good training time. An advantage is that new shooters do not fear the airgun but it gives them a feel for the general idea of firearms. Airguns vary in price and the better types are not inexpensive. A range may be constructed practically anywhere and restrictions on airgun sales are practically nonexistent – although some localities restrict their use outdoors.

Good shooting with an airgun requires trigger control and proper sight alignment. And while hearing protection is not an absolute requirement, shooting glasses are. And why not require hearing protection just to get into the groove? At an early age my sons were required to trek along with Dad with a wooden training rifle and never, ever cover each other or anyone else with the muzzle. After they learned safety, they were introduced to airguns. Safety and good shooting are often a part and parcel of airgun use.

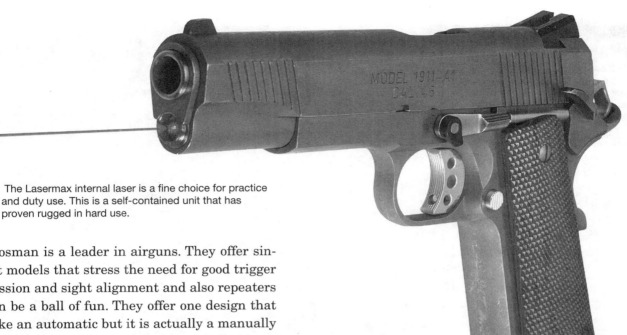

The Lasermax internal laser is a fine choice for practice and duty use. This is a self-contained unit that has proven rugged in hard use.

Crosman is a leader in airguns. They offer single shot models that stress the need for good trigger compression and sight alignment and also repeaters that can be a ball of fun. They offer one design that looks like an automatic but it is actually a manually operated revolver. My favorite airgun of all time is the remarkable Model 586 Smith & Wesson, a lookalike of the Smith & Wesson Magnum revolver. This neat airgun offers both single-action and double-action trigger action, adjustable sights, interchangeable barrel lengths, and excellent accuracy. I have consistently popped pinecones well past thirty feet with this air pistol.

A special automatic version of the Walther PPK not only features semi-automatic operation, but the slide even cycles as the piece is fired! This is a neat little airgun that makes a credible companion to the real steel Walther. Airguns are a training resource that should never be overlooked.

My family and I have used airguns extensively for well over twenty-five years and continue to do so.

This Crimson Trace equipped 1911 is very useful in learning trigger control.

These training aids have paid off more than once in the growth of shooting skills and the introduction of shooters into handgunning who might have otherwise not have done so.

Laser Grips

Much has been written concerning the efficiency of laser grips for peace officers and armed civilians. I agree on principle although I am not as enthusiastic about battery-operated devices as some are. But the laser, particularly Crimson Trace Lasergrips, is among the finest training resources we have. By activating the laser and attempting to hit a target on the wall we can observe every wobble and jerk in our trigger press (with a Triple-checked unloaded handgun and a good backstop only!). If we do not press the trigger properly, the red laser will be all over the wall, bouncing like a boy scout with ants in his pants.

The laser sight offers a good opportunity for training: press, and observe the light. This goes against the conventional wisdom of concentrating on the sights and letting the target blur, but in this case I think that the experience is worthwhile. In short order, playing beat-the-dot leads to greater trigger discipline.

It is not realized by most shooters that laser sights demand maintenance. The batteries are one

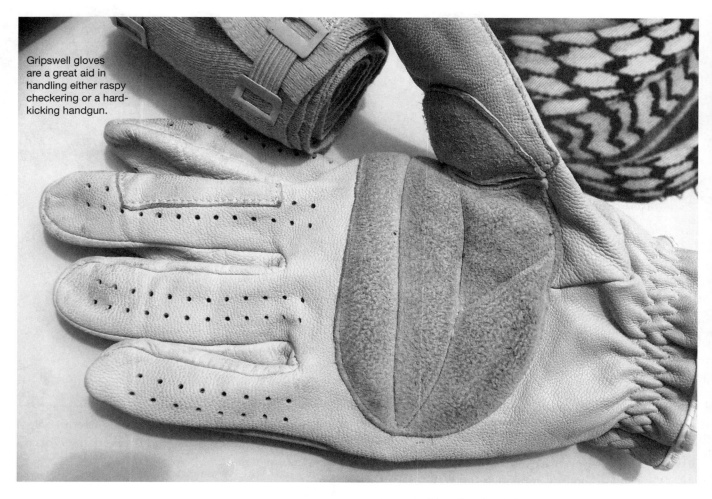

Gripswell gloves are a great aid in handling either raspy checkering or a hard-kicking handgun.

concern but the focal lens should be cleaned every time the pistol is cleaned. Tiny swabs are supplied with the laser grips by Crimson Trace. Be certain to keep solvent away from the lens. The Crimson Trace Lasergrip enjoys an excellent reputation and this is a resource I use often.

Pro Tech Ears

These hearing protectors are a good resource for the shooting and a great resource for the trainer. Modern baffle technology allows the protectors to muffle gunshots while at the same time allowing a greater range of hearing on the range. We are all familiar with the awkward pantomime of moving the hearing protectors over our ears and raising one side or the other to listen to instruction. With the Pro Tech ears in place, you can simply leave the muffs on for the duration of the range trip. While batteries may occasionally need to be changed, these are a fine addition, especially for a person training others to use the handguns. Good hearing protection is a must and the Pro Tech ears are first-class.

27

Life-saving Accessories: Holsters, Magazines and More

The firearm is just one part of an important package. The operator is the most important but quality gear goes a long way toward saving your skin. An editor once remarked that he would allow another person to choose his sidearm, given a high quality piece, and he would be happy to choose his own holster and ammunition. There is some truth to this. I have developed a genuine faith in the 1911 and as much affection as one can have for an inanimate object.

A generation ago some favored the Single Action Army or the N frame Smith & Wesson. The Browning High Power has always had intelligent adherents. Some choose a cartridge such as the .44 Special and then find the ideal handgun to wrap it around. The AR-15 rifle is practically universal and the AK-47 formidable. There are shooters who have mastered the SIG, Benelli and AUG who would be formidable opponents. Ruger rifles and handguns often show up on the winning side in personal defense situations. What is good, affordable and available will be used.

But the firearm itself is only half the battle.

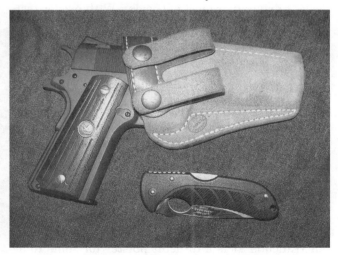

The Milt Sparks Summer Special inside the waistband holster features a combination of a strong spine, reinforced holstering welt, built-in sight track, and double belt loops. This is the standard by which all others are judged and a leading choice in a concealment holster.

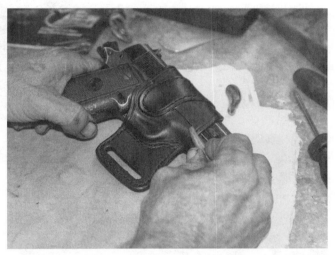

A skilled artisan at DeSantis holsters turns out a custom quality holster. It takes years to build this type of skill.

Holsters

The first rule is to conceal the handgun. This means discreet carry. We cannot allow bulges or telltale signs of carry. Even off-duty peace officers should be interested in going about their day as discreetly as possible. Sometimes surprise is an important factor in armed response. Unfortunately, many wish to be armed but do not wish to make concessions in their wardrobe. Purchasing trousers an inch or two larger in the waistband is necessary for successful carry of a handgun in an inside-the-waistband holster. Wearing a heavy belt is absolutely required for successful positioning of a handgun of any size. A quality holster on a poor-quality belt is a wasted effort.

The handgun must be retained securely in exactly the same place day in and day out. There are a number of trick holsters that offer concealment under the shirt, in ankle carry, and various covert forms. Among the most successful under the shirt or tuckable holsters is the Crossbreed, a hybrid holster manufactured from a combination of soft comfortable leather and rigid Kydex. These holsters should be carefully chosen as they are a personal investment.

Right: These holsters are from GDS, a relatively new maker. The special revolver holster is ideal for use with hammerless .38 snubs.

Below: In this illustration. our family member is wearing the Summer Special outside of her pants to demonstrate how the holster is worn. If the holster were much longer, it would pinch when we sit, so we do not desire a closed bottom holster. This is an ideal holster for concealed carry.

This is a Ted Blocker crossdraw for the Glock M37. The Blocker designs – and there are many – are well thought out and useful for concealed carry. Some are very versatile and others are more specialized depending upon the user's wishes. The tanning is very good, a mark of this company for decades.

The Mitch Rosen Workman is another good choice for under the shirt carry. While tuckables work well, most of us can use the IWB most of the time. Let's look at the different types of holsters and attempt to determine what we really need.

Crossdraw

The crossdraw places the handgun on the weak side, with the butt of the handgun moved forward toward the strong side muzzle downward. (An exception is the special purpose-driven holster from KN Null. The Vampire holds the revolver parallel to the belt line.) The crossdraw is the most accessible of all holsters from a seated position or when driving. It is ideal for concealed carry if the user is behind a desk or driving for most of the day. With proper technique with the weak side facing a threat, the crossdraw can be brilliantly fast into action. Sweaters and pullovers work well with the crossdraw; blazers and sport coats, perhaps not as well.

Inside the Waistband

Perhaps the most misunderstood type is the inside-the-waistband (IWB) holster. The IWB is a versatile holster that is among the most applicable to the need for concealed carry. The IWB allows the deployment of a serious handgun under relatively light covering garments. But the IWB is not without tradeoffs. It is a difficult holster for some to acclimate to. But no other holster offers the concealed carry advantages of the IWB. A standard belt holster needs a longer covering garment to conceal a handgun carried in a high ride belt holster. The IWB rides inside the pants. This allows the holster and gun combination to be covered with a relatively short covering garment. Another advantage is that there is very little offset from the body. The IWB hugs the body. This may be a disadvantage on the draw, but then everything is a tradeoff. When drawing from an IWB holster the hand must pull the handgun away from the body slightly in order to execute a rapid draw. Considering the advantages inherent in concealment, this is a minor consideration.

A well designed IWB holster features a welt at the top of the holster that prevents the holster from collapsing once it is drawn. The Milt Sparks Summer Special is a good example of an IWB and in fact the one example of a concealment holster that is the standard by which all others are judged. A sight track, holstering welt and strong spine are hallmarks of the Summer Special.

Some discretion must be used in choosing an IWB and handgun combination. Depending on your body type, a full length 1911 may pinch your buttocks when you sit down with the IWB. A Commander or an Officer's Model may be a better choice. This simply another consideration of the IWB and the IWB carry mode. A holster and gun combination need not be comfortable but should be comforting.

When deploying an IWB holster, adhere to certain rules. Be careful your shirt does not roll up over

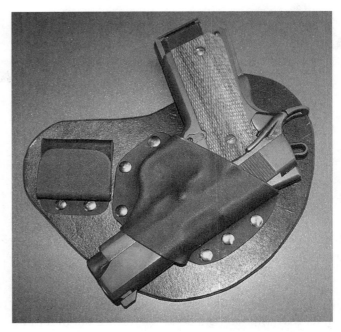

This is the Crossbreed, a type known as the Tuckable. It is designed to be worn with the shirt tucked in. It is comfortable and conceals well, largely due to an intelligent blend of Kydex and supple leather.

the holster during movement. Considerable effort is needed to master the IWB draw. (Master the range holster first.) The firing hand runs under the covering garment and moves the garment, be it jacket or shirt, away. The strong side hand then draws the handgun. In some cases the support hand may be used to clear the covering garment up and away from the handgun during the draw. The IWB holster solves most of the problems of civilian concealed carry. I like it very much but the holster demands practice and acclimation.

Shoulder Holsters

The shoulder holster is a good holster for those who can tolerate the constriction across the chest some of us feel. The shoulder holster has some of the drawbacks and advantages of the crossdraw. The main advantage is that the weight of the handgun and the spare magazines is well distributed. The Westwood Landing holster has become a favorite, one of the more affordable but high-quality holsters to emerge during the past few years. A line from Passport Sports offers excellent all-around durability at a decent price. Some users can tolerate fabric far better than stiffer leather, and the Passport Sports holsters have a wide shoulder support strap that distributes weight well. It is wise to try the used bin at the gun store or pawnshop for a type you may

This IWB offers excellent concealment by virtue of offset belt clips. It is quite flat and comfortable. From Sideguard Holsters.

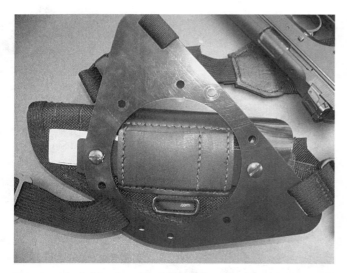

This shoulder holster from West Woods Landing has excellent features. This is among the top choices in the field today.

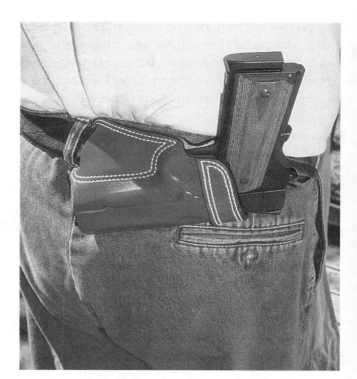

This is a Master's small of the back holster. For those who cannot tolerate an inside the waistband holster, the small of the back offers good concealment with a light covering garment.

like. Give the strong side, crossdraw or shoulder holster an honest try. Next, purchase the highest quality holster of the type that suits you. Like all of us, you may go through a number of holsters before steeling on a certain type. You will probably end up with several types for different situations.

Strong-Side

The strong-side holster allows a natural motion to the hip to draw the handgun. There should always be a good reason to move to any other type of holster. The strong-side holster is quite simply a classic concealment holster and the most efficient. However, strong-side carry is not always possible depending on the weather and the outer garments we are wearing. In the strong-side draw, we shoot the elbow to the rear and the hand moves under the pistol and scoops it out of the holster. The strong side holster is available in various renditions in kydex, leather and fabric and in many levels of quality. Milt Sparks

makes excellent designs. New makers who offer promising designs are Graham Gunleather, Raven Concealment, and Nighthawk Custom.

Choices

The choices in angle and rake are many and may be daunting to the most practice gun carrier. Certain types of holsters work well with difference angle. The size of the body is always a consideration. Let's look at a few definitions:

Drop

The length of drop below the belt line for the individual holster. Some holsters are high-ride and some are low-ride. A person with a more pronounced middle age spread would do well to choose a holster with greater drop. Otherwise the holster will be suspended at the point of their greatest spread. A straight up and down carry will be uncomfortable for persons with this build. A longer drop is a specialty of a number of concealment holsters. Simply put, lowering the handgun allows the butt to be more concealed with certain builds as the handle is not as likely to protrude or hit the ribs; however, a longer covering garment will be needed to conceal the handgun. Those who have a thinner physique may be best served with the more traditional high ride holster with a pronounced rear rake for concealed carry.

If you need an ankle holster, you need a very good one. This is an example from Gould and Goodrich. It laces into the bootstraps, but this is not necessary for day to day use with regular shoes.

DeSantis is among our largest holster makers but the quality seems custom. This is a thumbreak for the large frame Smith & Wesson. This holster offers good retention and is comfortable when carrying a heavy revolver for long periods of time.

Cant or Rake

This is the angle of the muzzle in the holster. Canting to point the muzzle to the rear is considered a rear rake; pointed to the front, a forward rake. The rear rake is ideal for concealment. Only an unusually tall individual world consider rear rake. Most crossdraw holsters are a neutral rake.

Offset

Some holsters have a pronounced offset from the body. Others hug the body. The GSS by KN Null, for example, hugs the body and offers excellent concealment. This is a pancake type that follows the bodyline closely. This is limited offset for maximum concealment. The Speed Scabbard type holster from the same maker has a more pronounced shank and offset and brilliant speed. For some body types, the difference is quite noticeable. Whichever you choose, you have decades behind the development of a Null holster.

A rule in angle and cant is the greater the angle of the cant, the greater the distance to the rear the holster must be in order for the draw to be comfort-able. There are many considerations but also many holsters available to suit every need. A word of caution: do not skimp on the belt! A quality gun belt is essential for concealed carry and comfort.

Are you really discreet? Wear the holster properly adjusted. As a test, check fit and comfort with a triple-checked unloaded handgun. Carefully don your covering garment and check your profile in a full-length mirror. Look for printing. Printing is the outline of the handgun showing from beneath covering garments. Look carefully, turning around in front of the mirror. Bend over at the waist. Does the gun's butt show? Perhaps it would be a good idea to stoop or bend at the knees instead of bending in order not to give the pistol's position away. This is the first test. When carrying a concealed weapon, there is a certain acclimation period before you feel comfortable. It is like breaking in a pair of shoes. After a time you will no longer be a person with a gun attached but a complete unit that moves smoothly – and that is the mark of a professional gun person.

Concealment Vests

Concealed Carry Outfitters offers concealment vests that offer an option for carrying several important items such as a gun, knife and spare ammunition. Some of these vest-holsters are designed for summer and others for winter use. The summer winter and light duty vests are interesting. They are innocuous enough in appearance and they offer discreet carry. I find that few outside the concealed carry community

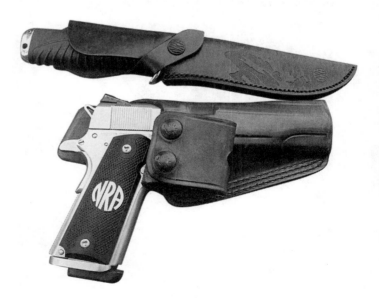

This is a first-class concealment holster from Null Holsters. Note the double stitching and strong spine. This holster is crafted in shell horsehide, the premier holster material.

recognize them as concealment vests. Some folks look natural when wearing a concealment vest and they offer discreet carry for these individuals. For some, the fanny pack is not an option. But the vest may take some of the load off of the belt and offers various pockets suitable for a handgun, spare gun loads, a knife and even a day planner. Some practice is required to acclimate and remember where each item is nestled. A tell tale thump on the chair when you seat yourself should be avoided. Overall I like the vest concept very much, and it isn't just for old guys. The Concealed Carry Outfitters vest is well-designed and well-executed.

I also have on hand a Royal Robbins vest that I use often. I also have a heavy Concealed Carry Outfitters vest for winter use and a Royal Robbins for summer carry and IDPA. The Royal Robbins breathes well, keeping me cool in warm weather. The vest is well-designed, with good closures on the pockets and an ideal drape for concealed carry. It doesn't scream "gun!" and is fashionable enough that I wear it often.

Magazines

A quality semi-automatic pistol needs spare magazines. A minimum of four is necessary. I usually keep one in the handgun, one as a spare gunload, one as a spare, and one resting. I keep duty magazines rotated on the high capacity types. I suppose

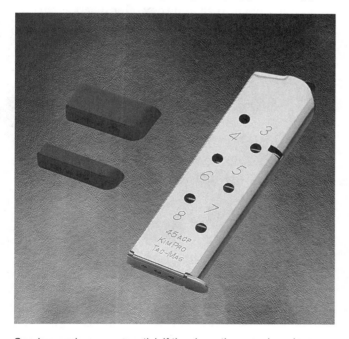

Good magazines are essential. If they have the same brand name as your gun, they are probably well suited to that handgun.

I have on hand well over forty for the 1911 and ten or so for the High Power. More would be better. I do not like the term "range magazine" for an inexpensive magazine as every magazine should be suitable for service use. The spare is the magazine worn on the belt. All others should be combat-worthy or discarded. Since shooters are continually looking for a deal on ammunition, leather and bargain basement magazines are offered. They must be avoided for personal defense. While some shooters like to have ten or twenty 1911 magazines for range use the service magazines must be of first quality. It is not worth the savings to mix the good with the bad. And by the same token if you suffer a malfunction on the range, how will you know whether it was gun-related or magazine-related if you are using gun show magazines?

In all non-1911 types including the Beretta, H&K, Glock and SIG, the magazines should be factory original with the same name on the magazine as on the gun. Nothing else is acceptable. In the case of the 1911, quality aftermarket magazines are available. One of the best bets currently available for all 1911 pistols is the Kimber magazine, offered as an aftermarket accessory.

GI magazines and especially Colt magazines were once a high mark of reliability as long as hardball ammunition was used. These magazines were well made of good quality material. The bullet nose of military ammunition was bounced off the feed ramp into the chamber. Obviously, hollowpoint ammunition is potentially troublesome with these magazines. The Wilson Combat magazine neatly solved these problems and raised the bar considerably in reliability. This magazine uses a stainless steel body and a synthetic follower. The magazine uses a floor plate that allows a .1-inch longer magazine body, eleven magazine coils, and an eight-round capacity in comparison to the seven rounds of the GI magazine. The follower presents the bullet nose into the chamber rather than onto the feed ramp, resulting in excellent feed reliability. The Wilson Combat magazine is a first-class feed device that is proven in hard use and competition.

There are other 1911 magazines with merit. The Tripp Engineering Cobra magazine has given good service in my test programs. This magazine features thirteen magazine coils and a slightly longer body than the Wilson Combat magazine. I have evaluated a limited number but the company produces no junk and they seem to be a genuine improvement in 1911 magazines. This magazine has operated flawlessly in any number of 1911 pistols. As for the author's arsenal, the majority of my service magazines are from Metalform. These magazines are of a more traditional design in appearance but the internal parts are modern including an advanced feed reliable follower. They also offer good quality GI type magazines, .22-caliber conversion magazines, and Officer's Model length magazines. I have used Metalform extensively for years in my first line 1911 pistols with excellent results. In particular I have experienced good service with Metalform magazines in .38 Super and 9mm caliber. If Metalform did not produce magazines in these calibers, my 1911s in .38 Super and 10mm would be underutilized to say the least.

If you like to use exotic bullet styles, attention to detail in choosing magazines is much more important. Metalform magazines have given the author excellent results in blue, stainless and ten-round configurations.

Revolver Speedloaders

I have tested a number of revolver speed loaders over the years with varying results. Buffer Technologies once offered a variant that I found viable for personal defense use. I have it on hand after a decade of use. Overall, for efficient use and longevity the HKS speedloader cannot be faulted. I have used these speedloaders in five- and six-shot variations for Charter Arms, Colt, Ruger, Smith and Wesson, and Ruger revolvers with excellent results. They are well worth their modest price.

Combat Lights

Combat lights are small but powerful and durable handheld flashlights with above-average performance. Some are designed solely for illumination; others are durable enough to be used as impact weapons. Some are just neat little lights. I have tested lights from Browning, Inova, Pila and SureFire during the past few months. Some are less expensive and will not represent a hardship if lost or broken. The Inova is pretty neat, a slim light little light that I find comforting when wearing light clothing. If you really need a combat light – and most of us need to train with the light – the Surefire models are ideal.

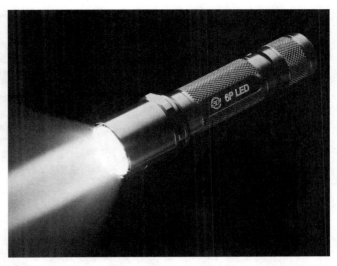

They have the backing of a company with vast experience in the field and they are rugged, built-to-last units. Much research has gone into these lights. All that remains is for the operator to study their proper use.

When it comes to holsters and other accessories, practical experience must carry the day. I have collected a good deal of information from friends who have been in bad situations. Many have had to fire on more than one occasion to save their lives or to protect the public. One thing is for sure: the presence of a handgun is often a lifesaver whether the pistol is fired or not. You have to have a good holster that has good retention to keep the handgun in place and also to allow a good sharp draw. You must maximize your capabilities. Proficiency and surprise are a one-two punch with undeniable effectiveness.

Discreet carry sometimes brings to mind the vision of a gambler with his derringer pointed at an adversary under the table. By the time an assailant realizes you are armed, it may be too late for him to murder you. It is not always about a fast draw. We have to remember surprise is a two-way street and sometimes the bad guy is surprised. Discreet carry should also mean discreet access. Practice carefully placing your hand on your handgun and not actually drawing but standing ready. Get comfortable with the handgun and with the draw.

When it comes to other accessories such as magazines and combat lights, bite the bullet and purchase quality. There may be some concessions and you may end up with the relatively inexpensive Pila, which works just fine. But obtain the best you are able to afford. You won't be sorry and in the end the life you save may be your own.

For all-around use and transportation, the London Bridge Trading Company drag bag is excellent protection for your rifle and gear.

Rifle Accessories

Among the most important accessories is extra magazines. I have enjoyed good luck with the AR-15 magazines from Bravo Company. While they function as designed, they are affordable. A pack of a dozen is good insurance. A recognized standard of excellence is the Heckler & Koch magazine for the AR-15 rifle. They are pricey but they certainly do the business.

Sights are not really an accessory but some rifles are delivered without sights. The flat-top AR-15 is practically universal and a good red dot scope is demanded. There is a place for iron sights and I strongly prefer them for personal defense, but then I am getting to be long in the tooth as far as this game goes. The Bushnell Holosight is one option and the Meprolight reflex sight another. A good set of backup sights is a wise investment. While there are several good options, the Wilson Combat backup

sight works well for me. I have used this sight on several flat top rifles and also on the rail of the FN Herstal SLP automatic shotgun. The Wilson Combat sight is high quality and built to last. Those who figure predators into their list of concerns may use a standard scope. One of my Bushmaster rifles features an ATN illuminated reticule scope with a ranging adjustment for 100, 200, and 300 yards. I have fitted this scope to a standard rifle with the rail with the help of a mount from Brownells. I am able to use the iron sights while the ATN scope gives excellent utility.

A good addition to the AR-15's sights comes from KNS, available from Dillon Precision. This is a front sight fitted with a round post with internal crosshairs. I appreciate this sight very much and have fitted it to my son's personal AR-15. KNS also makes a quality rear sight for AR-15 rifles. Dillon Precision offers these sights as well as the GRSC snap sling.

Handgun Ammunition

It is possible that we spend more time studying and evaluating ammunition than we should. But most of us enjoy shooting for its own sake and like to use accurate ammunition. As long as the ammunition goes bang every time we press the trigger, marksmanship is the most important component of "stopping power." Loads I use on the range may not necessarily be what I would carry in my personal defense firearm for critical use. I carefully produce my own handloads for practice and I also hunt with these loads, but I leave the ammunition in my carry gun to the major makers.

I use generic ball and the occasional find in surplus ammunition as burner ammunition on the range to supplement handloads. When it comes to personal defense ammunition, I am very demanding.

The Fiocchi brand is an exception to the rule in foreign produced ammunition. However, many of their loads are produced in the USA in Ozark, Missouri, in a modern plant.

A cartridge case, powder primer and bullet make up a loaded cartridge.

My interest in handguns has ignited an insatiable appetite for ammunition testing. I have fired a great deal of ammunition under controlled conditions. Sometimes the handgun was tested for reliability and other times for accuracy. Just as often I used a proven firearm to test ammunition. I am far more interested in firing my handguns than simply owning them. Once I became a rider, the train was going full steam!

Early on I discovered that some of the claims made concerning ammunition were simply not true. Many of these claims were made by writers. Ammunition that would "expand viciously" in flesh would actually expand only if it hit a brick wall. I tested well-known loads and even carried some of them in my service handguns with perfect trust. Along the way I discovered that a once highly recommended load has a rather short shelf life. I once ordered specialty 9mm loads from Germany at a dollar a pop. (Pretty pricey for 1981!) When restricted to the 9mm, we felt that this was the way to go and the "anti-terror" loads looked good. As time went by, Cor-Bon and others offered readily available +P loads and the need for the expensive import was less apparent. Eventually I was authorized to carry the .45 and seldom used the 9mm. I discovered the Berdan-primed

When it comes to inexpensive practice, Wolf ammunition is a price leader and a resource the author makes the most of.

German loads did not always fire after a relatively short storage of two years in a dry environment. I believe the hard primers were intended for use in submachineguns with a very hard firing pin fall.

Foreign-produced ammunition most often has two problems. The major problem is quality control and the second is poorly designed bullets with little research and evaluation. (There are exceptions. Fiocchi ammunition produced in Italy is high quality and the commercial loadings produced in their Ozark, Missouri, plant, using the XTP bullet, are also of good quality.) There have been numerous soft-point pistol bullets that produced indifferent results. There loads aware designed more for political correctness than for effect on felons. Over time, factory ammunition has improved measurably but we still should conduct our own test program. I have done so and frankly some of the exotic loads do not make it in my test program. A number of utilitarian loads that do not get a lot of attention in the popular press are head-and-shoulders superior. Why? Because they go bang when I pull the trigger!

The single most important factor to consider is cartridge integrity. Will the cartridge fire every time? Does the load have good primer and case mouth seal? When I am traveling or hiking in country that may

Winchester USA personal defense ammunition is affordable but offers Winchester's high quality. This is the 125-grain .38 Special JHP.

harbor large, angry animals, I load my .44 Magnum Taurus double-action revolver with the Black Hills 300-grain load. Often I load my 1911s with Black Hills 230-grain JHP. Each is proven in a personal test program. My hideout .38 is often loaded with Winchester's 158-grain lead SWC HP +P, not what is on sale at Wal-Mart.

Some time ago I undertook a simple test in which I soaked a number of cartridges overnight

This is a comparison of Boxer, above, and Berdan priming, below. Clean, fresh, boxer-primed cartridges are preferred. The economical aluminum-cased Blazer ammunition is berdan-primed and that is just fine for a practice load.

This is one of our more proven personal defense bullets. The Speer Gold Dot offers good expansion but also a balance of penetration and expansion, important in a personal defense handgun.

in water, solvent, and oil, respectively. It was surprising how many cartridges failed. But most loads from the major American makers did not fail. The little red splash of primer seal on Winchester ammunition works! If ammunition will not pass this simple test, it is burner ammunition only, no matter how advanced the projectile.

I have also cycled a number of rounds in the action of a semi-automatic pistol several times. In other words I cycle the same cartridge a half dozen or more times, working the slide, jacking the round out, then reloading the round in the magazine and starting over. Sometimes the bullet will be set back in the case after the second or third cycle. This breaks the case mouth break seal, allowing moisture or oil into the case. If the bullet is sufficiently pressed into the case, pressure may rise to dangerous levels. This is another mark against a loading. Premium loadings from Black Hills, Cor-Bon, Federal, Hornady, Pro Load, Remington, Speer and Winchester are most often reliable as ammunition can be. It is best to choose ammunition with a good reputation for quality control. Then prove the quality control for yourself and be certain the ammunition feeds, chambers, fires and ejects in your personal handgun. Quality handguns are omnivorous, feeding most ammunition – but just the same a grueling check of at least four hundred rounds should be conducted with the chosen defense cartridge. Fire the handgun when it is a little dirty and fire it with the weak hand. This is a sure test of the handgun and ammunition. No malfunctions are allowable.

Since my first choice in a defense handgun is the .45 ACP, I have studied the loads available and I have several comparable choices. The Winchester 230-grain SXT is the choice of the LAPD SWAT team, a highly acclaimed unit. The Black Hills 230-grain JHP is a bit faster than most 230-grain JHP loads and very accurate. The Speer Gold Dot performs well in most conditions and offers good accuracy. For older handguns that may not feed hollowpoints or for the man or woman who does not trust holllowpoints, the Hornady 230-grain flat point is a good choice. The .45 does not demand expansion for effectiveness. If the .45 doesn't feed hollowpoints, a reasonable counterpoint is the Cor-Bon PowRBall, a jacketed hollowpoint with a polymer ball in the nose that both insures good feeding and promotes expansion.

As for caliber, we won't beat a dead horse. The bigger bullets present more frontal diameter and produce a larger wound. Larger wounds let more blood out and allow more air in. If you cannot depend on bullet expansion, then the big bore is the only choice. In the real world the .45 is about twice as effective as a 9mm when each is loaded with jacketed non-expanding bullet ammunition. With expanding bullets the 9mm has given acceptable results with certain select loadings.

When expanding bullets are used, a balance of expansion and penetration is needed. The bullet must reach the vital organs to do its job. Today, figures are published by the major companies outlining penetration and expansion in ballistic gelatin. Often, these figures are very accurate. They may not take into account short-barrel ballistics and every situa-

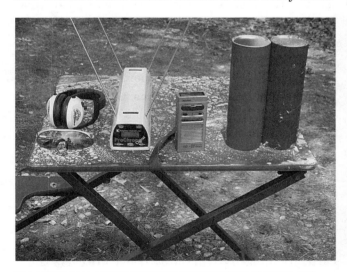

The author uses several resources in testing both shooters and ammunition, including a chronograph, various timers, and the Bullet Test Tube.

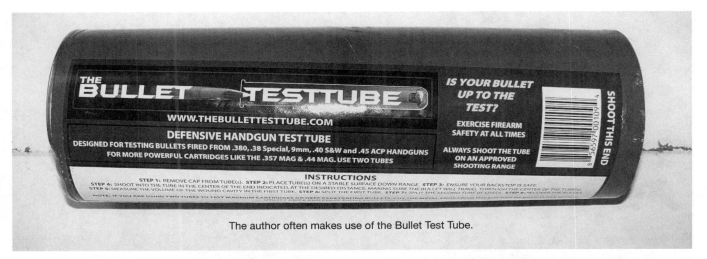

The author often makes use of the Bullet Test Tube.

First, you fire into the Bullet Test Tube.

Then you cut the wax-like substance apart and check the wound channel. Then the whole thing can be melted and used again.

tion but they are a good approximation of handgun performance. The bullet should penetrate a minimum of twelve inches of gelatin in order to reach the vital organs and to handle interference from clothing to heavy bones. The Winchester SXT, Federal HST, Speer Gold Dot and Hornady XTP are ideal examples of effective handgun bullets.

The difference in the total damage done by larger calibers is simple to calculate. If the wound channel is twelve inches long, the difference in wound volume between a .355-inch bullet and a .451-inch projectile is considerable over this length. We also must respect the historical record of the big-bore cartridges. If you do chose a small bore, load selection is more important. Expansion and penetration results for a number of calibers and loadings are listed in

this chapter. Choose a serviceable loading that is resistant to water and solvent and that feeds flawlessly in your handgun. Differences in shot placement are far more important than a perceived difference in effect by expansion.

The Federal Bureau of Investigation has conducted handgun ammunition test programs that would be difficult for an individual or a smaller agency to duplicate. The FBI protocol includes firing into various common materials and then checking the penetration and expansion of the bullet after it penetrates this material and lands in ballistic gelatin. The tests are conducted against bare gelatin, heavy clothed gelatin, sheet metal, wallboard, and vehicle glass. The test program is repeated at several distances. The tests against bare gelatin and clothed

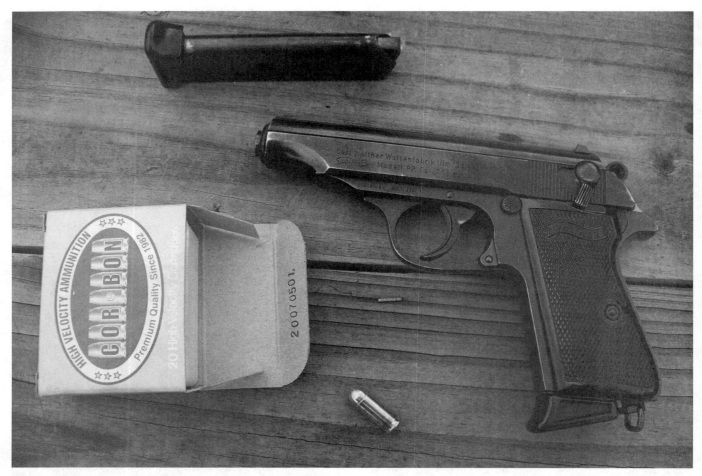

gelatin are most important for civilian shooters. The FBI also measures accuracy, powder flash and unburned powder with a degree of accuracy not possible for even a well-heeled enthusiast.

As for the effectiveness of handgun calibers and ammunition, it is vital to separate fact from fiction. Over the previous twenty-five years I have seen outrageous claims disproved and writers forced to backtrack on past statements. As the same time some of these pundits have assailed the writings of Elmer Keith, Skeeter Skelton and Jeff Cooper as sea stories or war stories. Some have even questioned the record of Sergeant Alvin York, although none would have done so to his face. Keith and the others were men of considerable experience and they were good observers. They hunted game extensively with handguns. The considerable experience of these soldiers, lawmen and hunters is often minimized while the scribes flaunt their own intellectual achievements with the typewriter. There is no room for secret sources or unverifiable results in choosing personal defense ammunition. The true test of science is that it be repeatable. Only laboratory results are repeatable.

If for some reason you must use a small bore, then bullet selection is even more critical. The Cor-Bon .32 ACP makes the most of the caliber.

Too many of us spend the majority of our time concerned with terminal ballistics. We see photographs of perfectly expanded bullets with stellate or starfish-like extensions. Experiments are interesting but there are other criteria that are more important. We mentioned cartridge integrity in the face of repeated chambering and exposure to solvent. But there are other considerations that are equally important.

Feed Reliability

The bullet must properly feed in the feed ramp and into the chamber. If the bullet nose catches on the feed ramp or a sharp edge of the chamber, it is not suited to that handgun. I have tested a high performance load produced in Mexico that worked just fine for the first box of ammunition but the second would not feed and allow the slide to close. As it turned out the crimp was improperly applied. I was able to fire the second box after nursing it through my RCBS .45 ACP crimping die. It might be a good idea to drop a cartridge or two from each box of service ammunition into our chambers, just in case. Rely upon premium sources or rely on hardball! When you consider the likelihood of injury or death if your handgun malfunctions, testing the ammunition for feed and function is not a difficult program.

Cycle Reliability

This is why you must actually live fire your ammunition to check for reliability! A round may show good feed reliability when hand cycled but fail in a firing test. If the load is too heavy for the pistol or too light or too fast, the slide may short cycle and fail to feed or properly function. The load is not hot enough or it is too hot. Slide velocity may be increased by a hot load to the point that slide velocity outstrips the ability of the magazine to feed. In short an automatic

pistol needs a load that falls within a certain parameter to function properly. With many pistols, these parameters are by no means narrow but just the same, the proper combination of momentum must be respected. Many handguns do not function well with subsonic ammunition and others are prone to malfunction with +P or +P+ loadings. Begin with standard pressure ammunition and consider +P loads only if special circumstances warrant.

Bullet Types

Since there is some confusion concerning bullet types and their proper use I have included a description of the popular types. Among the most common is the round nose lead bullet used in revolvers and the round nose jacketed bullet used in automatic pistols. The FMJ (full metal jacket) is commonly used to

When practicing, good quality ammunition that will not misfire or tie the pistol up is demanded. Anything else is frustrating.

promote feed reliability in automatic pistols and the RNL (round nose lead) is used in revolvers because it is inexpensive. When a RNL bullet strikes flesh, the part struck is simply pressed away. Often the wound is less than caliber diameter. The RNL bullet will bounce off bone rather than break resilient bones in some instances, especially in the case of the minor calibers.

RNL bullets of all types are prone to ricochet. The RNL and FMJ are fine for practice but not suited to personal defense. They are not necessarily cheap or inaccurate bullets. As an example the Cor-Bon Performance Match load uses FMJ bullets. They are fine for accuracy but poor for effect on target. (.45 ACP hardball is an exception.) In personal defense the main application of FMJ bullets is in the small-bore calibers that lack sufficient penetration to properly utilize a JHP bullet.

Flat Point Bullets

These are simply the RN with a flattened nose or meplat. The flat meplat has greater wound potential as flesh may be excised cleanly instead of being pushed away. The Hornady flat point (FP) in 9mm and .45 was seriously considered as a service load by our armed forces. The 124-grain FP 9mm and the 230-grain .45 FP remain good choices if for some reason a JHP is prohibited, either by legislation or by feed reliability problems. Perhaps the most effective FP ever offered is the 255-grain FP load in .45 Colt caliber. This heavy revolver has earned a tremendous and enduring reputation.

Wadcutter

The wadcutter or cookie cutter is a cylindrical bullet with a flat nose. It is intended for target use. The bullet cuts paper neatly and makes scoring easier. I have used the .32 caliber Fiocchi load with excellent results. A .38 Special revolver loaded with the 148-grain wadcutter is accurate and very easy to control. This load has often been recommended as a defense load for the recoil shy. There are worse choices available.

Semi-Wadcutter

The semi-wadcutter (SWC) remains an excellent choice for personal defense. The SWC features a full-caliber driving band, sharp shoulder, long nose and a considerable flat point. A true SWC features a flat point and sharp shoulder in order to cut rather than push flesh away. The flat nose will seldom bounce off bone. Factory swaged SWC bullets are of-

ten very soft and the sharp edges are more rounded, fine for target work but not ideal for defense use. The SWC bullet seats further out in the case than a RN bullet of comparable weight. This allows greater case capacity and velocity for roughly the same pressure in a given loading. The SWC remains a good choice for personal defense in heavy revolvers, with Grizzly Cartridge among those offering good full power loadings in both .357 Magnum and .44 Special. The 200-grain Hensley and Gibbs SWC design for the .45 ACP has proven among the most accurate of handgun bullets.

Bullet velocity makes a considerable difference. Look at a paper target shot with an RNL bullet, a SWC and a hollowpoint. The SWC hole will be more even, cleanly cut, and often larger. If a JHP fails to expand, the SWC is the superior choice. At present the Black Hills .45 Auto Rim load is a recommended load in that caliber with a hard cast 255-grain SWC at about 800 fps. The .44 Special 255-grain load is another standout from Black Hills. An even better choice, hedging the bet, is the SWC-HP. The semi-wadcutter hollowpoint bullet is often cast softer than a standard SWC bullet and is intended for personal defense, not hunting. These bullets were once in the province of the handloader but now are available from the factory. The Winchester .38 Special +P 158-grain SWCHP is a fine load and so is the Federal 200-grain SWCHP in .44 Special.

Jacketed Hollow Point

Jacketed hollowpoint (JHP) bullets are often misunderstood and properties are given them in legend that do not exist. A well-designed expanding bullet adds to the wound potential of the cartridge. The JHP is a soft lead core with a hollow tip placed in a copper gilding metal jacket. The copper jacket allows the bullet to be driven at higher than normal velocity without the danger of leading the barrel. The jacketed nose of a JHP designed for semi-automatic pistol use allows good feeding in the slam bang automatic action. Naturally, more leeway is present in the design of a revolver bullet. Just the same, semi-automatic pistols have seen the most development in personal defense ammunition. There are conventional JHP bullets such as the Sierra that Cor-Bon uses in most of their offerings. Then there is the Winchester USA JHP and the Federal Classic line. Two very popular types are the bonded core Speer Gold Dot bullet and the Hornady XTP. (In bonded core designs

The author often uses the proven Hornady XTP bullet in both personal hand loads and defense loads. This is an accurate, capable bullet.

the core will not separate from the jacket, resulting in a bullet with a high degree of weight retention and mushroom retention as well as the possibility for deep penetration.)

Then there is the all copper Barnes bullet as loaded in the Cor-Bon DPX. I feel that the best loads in each caliber use the standard bullet weights: 158 grains in the .38, 115 to 124 grains in the 9mm, and 230 grains in the .45. When you go to a light bullet, penetration is sacrificed and bullet pull as well. When the bullet is light, bullet pull is not ideal and we often have erratic ignition, a high standard deviation of velocity between shots, and uneven powder burn.

Exceptions to light bullet rules occur with the Barnes X bullet. The 185-grain DPX bullet is as long as a 230-grain .45 due to its solid copper construction. As a result this load has a high ballistic coefficient. Even the .38 caliber load penetrates to 15 inches and expands to 60 caliber while the .45 caliber load penetrates just short of fourteen inches and expands to .80 caliber. At this time I have not shot any game with these loads but bullets recovered from ballistic media look promising.

We will look at the difference in some of the main competitors. JHP bullets range from moderate expansion to fragmentation. In fragmentation, the bullet and jacket separate and the bullet nose is blown off. While the bullet may expand at some

point, a good wound channel is best created by a bullet that expands and holds that expansion by maintaining a mushroomed nose that does not blow off during penetration. The question is at what depth of penetration does expansion occur? Is expansion in the first few inches of contact with the target or later? The question has been debated but I have a simple answer. How the bullet performs is dependent on the target. A hit in the soft stomach muscles may not produce expansion. The idea is to combine a good balance of expansion and penetration.

I am aware of cases in which bullets failed to adequately penetrate oir overpenetrated. I am aware of an incident in which a 147-grain 9mm JHP fully penetrated a target with little effect and nearly struck another officer who was outside a window of the home in which the shooting took place. In another case thirteen 9mm 147-grain bullets failed to expand and nearly resulted in the death of a child that was being attacked by a pit bull. I personally experienced a dramatic underpenetration by a .45 caliber 200-grain JHP (the load praised in the popular firearms press). Rather than enhancing the caliber, the hollow point in question seemed to have robbed the caliber of effectiveness.

Many changes were made after the famous Miami Massacre in 1986 in which well-trained FBI agents were killed going up against well armed and motivated felons. The gunfight is beyond the scope of this book but many of the nuances of the battle have never been fully explored. As an example, Matix and Platt, the shooters, were not the archetypical wild eyed psycho gunmen. Each had respectable military service behind him. Each had suffered personal tragedy. Both had marketable skills in reputable business. Neither appeared to be addicted to drugs or alcohol but each had committed murder during robberies. When cornered by the FBI it took a lot of shooting to put them down, with one taking a dozen hits. After this shooting intense discussion and much experimentation took place. Small-bore handguns were soon abandoned by the FBI. The .45 was adopted for special team use and the 10mm for general duty.

The .40 Smith & Wesson is now the standard issue caliber of the FBI. The FBI ammunition test program was the most thorough ever undertaken and at the time among a few comprehensive projectile tests ever attempted. Just as importantly, for the first time law enforcement told manufacturers what type of bullet they wanted, gave them a goal, and encouraged competition on that basis rather than the low bid. Practically all of the information we have today on handgun ammunition performance sprang from the FBI test program. So-called studies with secret sources and secret animal testing belong in the category of paranormal activity and fortune telling. Their validity is comparable. They have no credibility in the professional community. An abstract by the author has been published by the Armed M, a gun related branch of the American Mensa Society. (I am not a member myself.) In this report I discussed flawed methods among stopping power theories. One correspondent compared the author to the Amazing Randi, a magician who debunks hoaxers. I appreciate the comparison and enjoy the Amazing Randi. At the same time I do not appreciate those who offer speculation and wild theory as fact in the personal defense field.

An offshoot of some of these "studies" is criticism of the FBI test program as focusing too much on penetration. I do not agree. Half of the felons the FBI faces each year are behind some type of cover including vehicles. Penetration is vital as the above mentioned incidents demonstrate. The FBI has millions of dollars to spend, qualified individuals, and advanced testing facilities. There are enthusiasts in the FBI who enjoy handguns as much as anyone and have considerably more experience and education

than the average gun writer. I believe the FBI test criteria is excellent and it should stand. The conclusion as to what makes a good handgun load makes sense to me, and we would be wise to adopt this program.

As a result of its study, the FBI concluded that a handgun bullet should expand to 1.5 times its original diameter while penetrating a minimum of twelve inches of ballistic gelatin. That is .60 caliber for the .40 caliber and .68 in .45 caliber, .53 caliber for the 9mm and .38. We have ammunition that does this in tissue simulations and some are proven in the field. As for penetration, it is best to err on the side of caution. If you live in a state that offers a true four-season climate, consider the archetypical six-foot-tall 190-lb. man wearing a heavy jacket. What if he is a little heavier and wearing several layers of clothing? What if there is an intermediate barrier such as a truck door between you and him?

Let's look at some of the more promising types of hollowpoint bullets. Remember, exact performance depends on the barrel length for velocity and the material that is used in testing.

The Winchester Silvertip and the Winchester SXT

Winchester's Silvertip remains popular for personal defense for several reasons. The original crease-fold hollowpoint offers reliable expansion. The special bullets used in the .38 Super and .357 Magnum are particularly impressive. The .41 Magnum Silvertip is among the most capable personal defense loads ever offered, in my opinion. The Magnum revolver loads are what may be termed seventy-five percent loads. They are not loaded to full power but are still formidable. The 215-grain .44 Magnum enjoys an excellent reputation and is quite accurate. The 9mm and .45 caliber Silvertip do not offer as much penetration as some loads but have given good results overall. Either usually stays in the body whether or not it expands dramatically. This is a product of lightweight bullet meeting resistance. The .357 Magnum Silvertip is my first choice for personal defense in that caliber. The 155-grain .40 caliber Silvertip is easily one of my top two choices in that caliber.

The SXT builds upon the proven crease-fold reverse taper design but offers a better balance of expansion and penetration. The SXT features an eight-point segmented hollow cavity that has given good results in testing and in police use. This is a modern hollowpoint with an ideal balance of expansion and penetration. The bullet also gives excellent feed reliability. I have carried this load professionally and would do so again. A particularly effective load is a +P version of the 230-grain SXT in .45 ACP.

Remington Golden Saber

This is the Big Green's entry into the police market. I have tested custom-loaded .460 Rowland ammunition using the 230-grain Golden Saber with excellent results. The bullet was jolted to a velocity well past its design parameters but just the same the Golden Saber performed well. Remington has long had a reputation for feed reliability and this follows with the Golden Saber. The jacket of the Golden Saber is of stiff cartridge brass with a driving band to increase accuracy potential. The jacket that wraps around the bullet nose is cut into a spiral pattern. The Golden Saber is available in the popular handgun calibers but the standout is the 230-grain .45 adopted by the Federal Bureau of Investigation. The 165-grain .40 Smith & Wesson load is also a standout that has been used with good results in law enforcement and corrections use.

Speer Gold Dot

The Gold Dot is Speer's answer to the FBI's handgun load criteria. At this point the Gold Dot has become among the most popular police service loads with good reason. The Gold Dot is a bonded core bullet. This means the core and the bullet cannot separate because they are bonded together. A star-shaped press imparts the class Gold Dot configuration to the lead core. When the bullet expands as designed, the trademark Gold Dot, actually the base of the jacket, is visible. I have tested the Gold

Careful selection is necessary in small bore cartridges The 135-grain Gold Dot in .38 Special +P looks good.

Dot in many loads from several makers (Speer sells the bullet to other ammunition companies such as Black Hills, Buffalo Bore, Pro Load, and others) and the Gold Dot always gives reliable expansion. Whether the bullet exits the body or not, more damage is done by an expanding bullet and even if an expanded bullet exits the body, it will not fly very straight and will have limited penetration. The Gold Dot offers a good balance of expansion and penetration.

Makers often release figures for expansion from service handguns. I have the results of a test program that used a short-barreled handgun, specifically the Glock Model 30. Such a short barrel may lose up to eighty feet per second of projectile velocity compared to a full-length service pistol. Just the same, results were more than acceptable. In the test, the bullets were fired first into bare gelatin and then the gelatin was placed behind barriers.

Speer Gold Dot 230 grain .45 ACP test program. Fired from Glock Model 30.

Average velocity 752-770 fps.
All tests showed a one hundred percent weight retention with the Gold Dot bullet.

Material	Expansion (inches)	Penetration
Bare gelatin	.73	14.5 inches
Heavy clothing	.752	14.5 inches
4 layers of denim	.73	14.5 inches
After penetrating steel	.51	15.8 inches
After penetrating plywood	.451	

The XTP

The Hornady XTP was among the first bullets designed in response to the FBI test program. The Hornady bullet is among the most accurate handgun bullets ever designed and always gives match grade accurate results in quality handguns. The XTP expands less than some designs, with the emphasis on penetration. Expansion is reliable simply not as pronounced as others. My favorite 9mm XTP is the 124-grain loading. This one delivered good results in feed reliability and accuracy and does not compromise penetration while offering more expansion than the 147-grain load.

The 155 grain 10mm at 1350 fps is in a class by itself with good power, accuracy and penetration and expansion. Horandy offers a personal defense line that expands more than the conventional XTP line and a Hornady Tactical Application Police (TAP) line for police duty. The TAP line features bullets with greater penetration that are based on the XTP. The 9x18 Makarov loading is often noted as the one load that makes the caliber suitable for defense. The Hornady load maximizes the caliber but I prefer something heavier. Overall the XTP has been a success story and one that meets the needs of those who favor greater penetration.

Federal EFMJ

If you think feed reliability problems with jacketed hollowpoint bullets are solved, guess again. There are still handguns that are problematic with JHP bullets. One hundred per cent reliability seems elusive. This is especially true when agencies wish to use the same bullet in the pistol and in a carbine or submachinegun. Then there are the jurisdictions both foreign and domestic that prohibit hollowpoint ammunition even for police use.

For years Speer and Federal have sold jacketed softpoint ammunition to Europe, as one example, but JSP loads have dubious value at best when it comes to expansion. Federal has some up with an ingenious design, the EFMJ (Expanding Full Metal Jacket). Not a warmed-over hollowpoint with a cap over the cavity or a rule-beating JSP with a dip in the nose, this is a new design from the inside out. In outward appearance the expanding full metal jacket bullet is a FMJ bullet. But the jacket has been heavily scored internally. The base is lead and a rubber plug is inserted into the jacket above the lead core. On impact, the nose collapses and flattens the rubber plug creating a unique form of bullet expansion. Accuracy is often good and the famous Federal quality control is present.

Federal HST and Hydra Shock

The Hydra Shock was once accused of being a gimmick. The jacketed bullet with the post in the center is far from a gimmick, however. For hundreds of law officers the Hydra Shock has been a lifesaver. I authorized the Federal Hydra Shock in 124-grain +P+ for agency-issued SIG 9mm pistols. We had two cases in which a single shot was instantly effective. In another case an officer was forced to destroy a large deer that had been struck and crippled in its rear legs. A single shot in the neck immediately put the creature down. Compare these incidents with the poor results reported by game officers attempting to put down deer-sized animals with the 147-grain 9mm and you see that the +P+ loading and the Hydra Shock bullet are a good combination.

The .45 Hydra Shock is among the most proven defense loads in this caliber. A relatively overlooked powerhouse is the 185-grain +P Hydra Shock in .45 ACP. This is a load that gives the .45 ACP shooting a flat-shooting and hard hitting load. (This load should not be used in the Glock or HK USP, per my personal experience. Flattened primers were evident, a sure sign of excess pressure.)

The Hydra Shock would seem a practically ideal personal defense load. While some police agencies have gone to bullets with greater penetration, the Hydra Shock should never be discounted. The HST is a new loading that offers good expansion but meets the penetration demands of police agencies. Both have worked well per my testing but the Hydra Shock is proven – and once again both have Federal's quality control.

Cor-Bon PowRBall

Cor-Bon has demonstrated good performance and excellent cartridge integrity in my personal test programs. While Cor-Bon ships over a million rounds of ammunition a year I still regard their quality as custom level. The PowRBall load is a standout and an answer to the feed reliability problem experienced with various handguns. It has proven popular and the concept has been expanded to revolver loads, strangely enough.

The PowRBall is a hollowpoint bullet that features a huge nose cavity plugged by a polymer insert. This results in a round nose profile and perfect feed reliability. Any handgun that will feed a RN or FMJ bullet will feed PowRBall. The polymer ball is driven into the bullet nose on impact, instigating expansion. From my five-inch barrel Kimber, the 165-grain PowRBall in .45 ACP breaks 1225 fps. From a Wilson Combat modified RIA .38 Super, the 100-grain PowRBall breaks just over 1500 fps. From a four-inch .357 Magnum the 100 grain PowRBall breaks 1350 fps and well over 1200 fps from the two-inch-barreled Taurus. Due to the light bullet, recoil is also light, even though these two revolvers are considered difficult to control with full power ammunition. Accuracy is good and the bullet usually expands well. Expansion is limited but adequate solving problems of over-penetration as well as feed reliability. The PowRBall revolver loads feed very well from speed loaders.

DPX

Cor-Bon offers high velocity loadings that for the most part use the Sierra jacketed hollowpoint bullet. This is an accurate and reliable bullet with many good attributes. Expansion is rapid and the bullet often fragments. Realizing that, while these loads are effective in many scenarios, there is a need for a deeper-penetrating bullet for other scenarios, Cor-Bon has introduced the DPX line. The Barnes X bullet is a solid copper bullet with good expansion and penetration capability. I have tested these bullets extensively in my personal handloads and the Cor-Bon line with good results. There is no more accurate bullet anywhere. The long bearing surface allows good accuracy while retaining the light weight needed for high velocity. The highest velocity possible with the bullet weight may not be realized as the heavy bullet is long and limits case capacity, but velocity is adequate for expansion.

The DPX is a special bullet and standard rules do not quite apply to it. There are several loads available including a special 160-grain DPX bullet for short-barreled .45s. You have to put the thinking cap on and look hard at a bullet that outperforms other lightweights by a considerable margin. Recently I was able to test several of the DPX loads in popular calibers. I think the results speak for themselves.

Glaser Safety Slug

The Glaser Safety Slug has a reputation of almost legendary proportions. I do not recommend the Glaser as a service round for all-around use due to its low predicted penetration, sometimes indifferent accuracy, and its expense. But in certain scenarios the lack of penetration is a good thing. The Safety Slug also is the least prone of all bullets by design to ricochet.

The Glaser was first offered as a virtually hand-made cartridge in the 1970s. A copper jacket was filled with #12 shot and sealed with a flat cap, later changed to a round cap. In some semi-automatic pistols, feed and cycle reliability were poor. This is expensive ammunition to test fire for feed reliability! Today the Glaser design is produced by parent company Cor-Bon. Cycle and feed reliability are good, largely due to improved powder technology and rigorous testing. Just the same, you must prove reliability in your personal handgun.

My test results in all semi-automatic pistols with the modern version of the Glaser have been good. I have tested calibers from .380 ACP to .357 SIG and the .45 ACP. While function could not have been better, always prove the load in your personal handgun. While now mass-produced, the Glaser remains an exotic loading that might not function well in all pistols, the H&K P7 being one example.

The construction of the bullet is the cause of inaccuracy. Although the Glaser now uses a compressed core rather than the original loose shot, accuracy simply is not going to be comparable to ball ammunition. Just the same, accuracy has improved considerably under Cor-Bon's production. I remember 1980s-vintage .45 Glasers that barely stayed on a man sized target at 25 yards. A ten-inch group was average to good at that range! Today a six-inch group or less at 25 yards may be expected but still this is short range ammunition. (And some pistols do much better accuracy-wise.)

The Glaser is prefragmented. It does not expand; it is already in pieces. When the bullet strikes flesh the nose is blown off or inwards and the shot

DPX results		
Handgun and load velocity	**Expansion (inches)**	**Penetration**
Browning High Power 9mm 115 gr./1260 fps	.65	14.5 inches
CZ75 Compact .40 caliber 140 grain/1135 fps	.69	16 inches
SW1911 PD .45 ACP 185 grain/1070 fps	.80	14 inches

emerges from the jacket, traveling in clumps and shredding tissue. At least this is what occurs ideally. In laboratory testing and in my own limited testing on pests the Glaser has preformed as advertised. The wound will be shallow but complex and difficult to repair. I have tested the Glaser (very carefully) against metal and safety glass to qualify the claimed lack of ricochet. The safety factor is indeed there. The Glaser simply does not and perhaps will not ricochet. Part of the term "safety slug" applies to the ability to quickly put down attackers but the lack of dangerous ricochet and overpenetration is also important. I have fired at a vehicle fender at an extreme angle to test the Glaser and all that was apparent was a lead smear. This is a true "Safety Slug."

A consideration is that the Glaser often strikes low in relation to the point of aim as the bullets are very light. This varies from handgun to handgun and some, such as a .38 snubbie, are just about on the money while others may strike several inches low. You must test this tendency to strike low in your personal handgun.

The Glaser is practically ideal for use in revolvers for home defense and for use in urban areas as an anti-mugger load. A .357 Magnum loaded with Glaser Safety Slugs is spitting out a bullet at 1700 fps, something to be reckoned with.

Extreme Shock

The Extreme Shock round is interesting because the bullets are of conventional weight. While a Glaser Safety Slug in 9mm may weigh only eighty grains, the Extreme Shock is full weight in most cases. This means the load should have good cycle reliability and strike to the same point of aim as standard weight ammunition.

I have tested several hundred rounds of this expensive ammunition in a dozen .45 semi-automatics without a single failure to feed, chamber fire or eject. This is the first step. By all criteria the Extreme Shock loads are of high quality and accuracy is above average for an exotic load. There have been enthusiastic claims concerning the ammunition and imaginative advertising connected with these loads. I cannot refute the ads but neither can I confirm the information. My personal testing has shown good results. The Extreme Shock seems to fit most of the necessary parameters for hostage rescue and special team use including accuracy, shock and a lack of ricochet.

The load dumps maximum energy in an expanding cone of destruction, the advertising claims. This is accomplished by the use of a Tungsten NyTrillium composite core. The load fragments on impact with concrete and other building material. I have shot the usual water-filled milk jugs and water balloons with impressive results. I have enjoyed using the Extreme Shock and I have learned something about frangible ammunition. Based on my experience, feed reliability, ignition reliability, and accuracy are good. I want to see shooting results and autopsy photographs but at present the Extreme Shock offers an alternative to conventional jacketed hollowpoint ammunition for special use.

Black Hills Ammunition

I probably use more Black Hills defense loads than any other. Their philosophy, bullet choices and quality control are most often in line with my personal preferences. The tables show the results of my personal test with Black Hills ammunition. I think that these loads offer a good balance of expansion and penetration, and quality control is excellent.

Black Hills Ammunition Test Results				
Handgun Used	Caliber and Load	Velocity	Penetration (inches)	Expansion (inches)
Browning Practical 9mm	9mm 115 gr. EXP	1288 fps	10.8	.69
Browning Practical 9mm	9mm 115 gr. +P	1334 fps	13.5	.68
Browning Practical 9mm	9mm 124 gr.	1209 fps	13.6	.58
Browning Practical 9mm	9mm 147 gr.	1001 fps	15.0	.43
Baby Desert Eagle .40	.40 155 gr. JHP	1090 fps	14.5	.50
Baby Desert Eagle .40	.40 165 gr. EXP	1101 fps	15.0	.64
Baby Desert Eagle .40	.40 180 gr. JHP	954 fps	16.0	.59
Smith and Wesson M65, 3"	.357 Magnum 125 gr. JHP	1240 fps	13.0	.56
Kimber Custom II	.45 ACP 185 gr. JHP	990 fps	12.0	.68
Kimber Custom II	.45 ACP 230 gr. JHP	880 fps	13.5	.72
Kimber Custom II	45 ACP 230 gr. JHP +P	940 fps	16.0	.68

Non-Hollowpoints

Some calibers do not have sufficient penetration to allow the use of hollowpoint ammunition. The .22, .25 and the .32 ACP are not the best performers, often exhibiting underpenetration. Even with deeper penetrating FMJ ammunition these loads are problematical at best. In the .380, the Black Hills JHP, the Hornady XTP and the Winchester SXT look OK but I am leery. Without penetration we have nothing.

If your pistol is not perfectly feed-reliable, do not use hollowpoints. Another reason not to use hollowpoints is when velocity is so low that a JHP will probably not expand. As an example, in my personal .44 Special and .45 Colt revolvers I prefer loads with 250-grain bullets at about 800 to 850 fps. The Black Hills 255-grain SWC is ideal in .44 Special. It is an accurate load, not difficult to control, and certainly this load has adequate penetration. JHP ammunition is good but use common sense in application.

Remanufactured Loads

Remanufactured loads are high-quality commercial reloads. The single most expensive part of the cartridge is the brass cartridge case. By reusing the brass we are able to realize great savings. Some of us load our own but commercial reloaders are a boon to those who do not reload – and even to reloaders who are too busy! Using remanufactured loads for practice makes good economic sense. Done correctly, remanufactured loads are as reliable as any other factory product. Black Hills blue box is among the popular choices. I have enjoyed good results with Conley Precision and Weber, among others.

Weber in particular has carried me through over twenty handgun tests with good results. Recently I ordered a case of .45 ACP from Mastercast bullets. These loads have proven accurate, with a clean powder burn. These loads are a resource that should never be overlooked. You pay your money and your make your choice but unless you have a Brinks truck full of money following you around, remanufactured loads are a fine training resource.

Shotgun Shells

Due to the construction of shotgun ammunition it is termed a shell rather than a cartridge. This relates to artillery shell and the shotgun shell is a po-

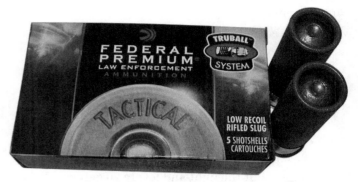

These Federal slugs give a 12 gauge shotgun another tier of effectiveness.

tent concoction in its most powerful loadings. There are three types we need to be concerned with in personal defense. There are buckshot, slugs, and other shot.

A buckshot load is a shell loaded with the largest size shot. The smallest buckshot that should be considered in the 12 gauge is the .33-caliber balls in #00 buck. It is true that there are twenty-seven .24 inch buckshot pellets in a 2-3/4-inch 12-ga load of #4 buck, but the larger diameter buckshot has proven more effective.

Slugs are simply shotgun shells with a single projectile. These slugs vary in design, and some of the more modern examples are in fact highly developed projectiles similar to rifle bullets. But the traditional slug used in personal defense is a single large lead projectile of .72 inch or so diameter in the 12 gauge shotgun.

Shot loads are the traditional shotgun hunting load, used for hunting small game such as rabbit and squirrel and for birds such as dove and quail. Canada geese are also taken with highly developed long range shotgun loads. Except for practice, shot loads using birdshot and the like are not well suited to personal defense. For the most part penetration is inadequate.

The term "gauge" is an antiquated but still-used term that denotes the inner diameter of a shotgun's barrel. It refers to the number of lead balls of that diameter that would equal one pound of weight. The larger the number, the smaller the bore. Twelve lead balls would make one pound in 12 gauge, twenty in 20 gauge, etc.. Of course there is the lonely .410, an exception. Though commonly and mistakenly referred to as the ".410 gauge" or ".410 bore," the .410 is neither. It's a .410-caliber shotgun, meaning that the guns it is fired in have an inner barrel diameter that is approximately .410".

When considering a shotgun gauge, the 12 gauge is the most suitable choice. However, the 20 gauge has much to recommend it. The 20 gauge has about three quarters of the payload of the 12 gauge by most estimates, while recoil is about half that of the 12 gauge. To a jaded shotgunner used to recoil, the difference may not be that great but when it comes to beginners the 20 gauge is a good option. I will take the 12 gauge but the light and lovely 20 gauge will do the business in home defense situations.

The best choice for home defense is the 12 gauge reduced recoil load. These loads are available to civilians as the Winlite from Winchester. The Federal version is a favorite at gun shows and often available. These shells retain a high degree of effectiveness while offering an alternative to hard-kicking full-power loads.

As for reduced power slugs, they are certainly controllable but as I have mentioned their effect at long range is not as pronounced as that of the full power slug. Full power slugs have expanded and proven instantly effective in a number of critical in-cidents. Reduced velocity slugs present a .72-caliber profile and should prove effective, but the full power slugs are superior per my personal testing. As for penetration, the bottom line is that the 12 gauge slug has plenty of penetration and should be used only when the need for penetration is great. For example, the full power 12 gauge slug will penetration a typical wall, complete with wallboard, sheet rock and insulation, and continue to penetration 26 to 29 inches of ballistic gelatin. Interestingly the slug will most often mushroom during this test. Shotgun slugs are not elephant rifles but they are the most powerful shoulder-fired firearm in our defensive arsenal.

Rifle Ammunition

For practice ammunition, much the same criteria as we recommended for handgun ammunition applies to rifle ammunition as well. Black Hills offers high-quality blue box loads that are excellent for practice. Winchester offers their White Box line and a number of regional loaders offer this ammunition in bulk. The Russian Wolf line is a price leader that gives us an affordable choice for high volume shooting. Practice ammunition is in some ways less of a

These are the primary rifle calibers to be concerned with in personal defense: the .223 Remington (the small cartridge) and the Russian 7.62x39mm.

The author has found that Black Hills produces excellent .223 ammunition. The Army Marksmanship unit agrees and so do the Marines.

problem for rifles. I suppose we tend to fire more ammunition from our high-capacity rifles and the major companies realize this.

When it comes to rifle information, if I do not cover your choice some interpolation is necessary. AR-15 type rifles are available in other fast centerfire cartridges but frankly the 5.56mm/.223 is the only one that makes practical sense. The .204 Ruger is a fine varmint round but for personal defense, use the .223. For maximum effect, the .308 is still a solid choice, especially for rural officers and in the wide open western spaces. We will look at the major calibers and choices.

.223 Rifle

The .223 in general and the AR-15 in particular are my first choice for personal defense. My friend Paul tells me he needs to get the job done with one round and so he clings to his .30-30 Winchester Trapper. He is correct. Just the same, I like the AR-15 and have come to appreciate the .223 cartridge.

Over the years there have been a number of barrel twist rates offered in .223 caliber. Some of these are most appropriate for heavy bullets at long range. The rule is, the more modern twists will stabilize both light and heavy bullets but the 1 in 14-inch turn is not well suited to heavier bullets. The following table will give you some idea of the possible application of bullet twists.

Barrel Twists Appropriate For Given Bullet Weights

Twist	Bullet Weight in Grains
1 in 14	55 grains
1 in 12	up to 69 grains
1 in 9	69-77 grains
1 in 8	80 grains
1 in 5	90 grains

The 1 in 9 inch twist of my Bushmaster carbine seems ideal, giving good accuracy with every load I have fired in this 16-inch-barreled carbine. I have been reluctant to use or recommend any bullet weight below 52 grains because of poor results with many of the early loads in .223/40-grain versions. Feed and function were sometimes sluggish and any loss in function cannot be tolerated. I prefer the 60 gr. JSP for service use but there are certainly plenty of good 55-grain loads. The 77-grain Open Tip offered by Black Hills is a fine load that has proven especially accurate and lethal in the war effort. I admit that Black Hills has produced credible loads in the 36- to 40-grain weight that seem to perform well and certainly offer an option for crowded environments or even for the apartment dweller whose only weapon may be a .223. Just the same, I recom-

mend nothing under the 52 gr. Match loading for personal defense use in the .223 rifle.

The .223 rifle has proven instantly effective in any number of police shootings. In military use it has been noted that the lethality of the cartridge falls off rapidly after 100 yards. This is to be expected as military bullets are FMJ bullets that generally break at the cannelure and produce a more severe wound. When velocity has fallen to the point that the bullet does not fragment, it is to be expected that the effectiveness of the cartridge falls off.

For civilian and police personal defense shooters the .223 remains effective inside the range of any reasonable threat. The .223 often produces a severe wound and leaves a void in tissue. An important question is, how much penetration does the .223 have? We have mentioned that test programs show that the .223 will penetrate body armor. Even from a short-barreled rifle, the 55-grain load maintains some 3,000 to 3,100 fps. In wallboard tests, the average penetration of four wallboards in line is three for 55-grain JSP bullets, with fragments often striking the fourth wallboard.

With the adoption of the .223 as a police caliber, there has been widespread research on the penetration ability of the .223 cartridge. Much of this research was conducted by peace officers in an effort to convince the administration that the cartridge is not more offensive than a typical pistol cartridge when it comes to penetration. They have succeeded. While the fast light bullet has good penetration against body armor, by the same token it meets flesh and blood or a gelatin substitute, the soft lead expanding bullet performs as designed and expands. The typical result is a penetration of eight to nine and one half inches in gelatin and bullet fragmentation. Typically the bullet will be in two pieces with several pieces of shaved lead. Interestingly after penetrating a construct representing a typical interior wall in the home, the .223 has fragmented and penetrates less than six inches in gelatin after penetrating this wall. This compared to a typical penetration of as much as twenty inches from typical 180-grain .40 and 147-grain 9mm handgun ammunition after penetrating a simulated wall. We could produce different results by using high velocity light bullet handgun loads but the basic relationship would remain the same. The .223 rifle is less likely to overpenetrate and produce offensive penetration than typical handgun ammunition. This is a solid advantage of the cartridge and the rifle.

Coupled with the ability to deliver a fight stopping hit with precision, the .223 combination is unequaled among defensive calibers. There is simply no concern for overpenetration compared to common handgun calibers. Due to the high velocity of the .223 cartridge, the bullet almost always expands as designed even after impacting and penetrating common dwelling material.

Performance of .223 Black Hills Ammunition	
Bullet weight in Grains	Velocity
36 gr.	3750 fps
40 gr. V Max	3600 fps
50 gr. V Max	3300 fps
52 gr. HP	3250 fps
55 gr. JSP	3200 fps
60 gr. JSP	3100 fps
69 gr. JSP	2950 fps
77 gr. Open Tip	2750 fps

29 Protection on the Cheap

When choosing a personal defense firearm, we should never let price be our only guide. There are a number of expensive firearms I do not care for, but most high-end makers produce reliable wares.

By the same token some inexpensive handguns are not suitable for personal defense and no amount of gunsmithing will help. For example, one of my weaknesses is a small collection of Spanish revolvers, some purchased for thirty dollars and none costing more than $125. Most are .32-20 caliber and another is a 8mm Lebel. I admit a fighting heart and determination may make up for a deficit in equipment, but these revolvers should never be considered for personal defense. They were prone to breakage when new and are not very smooth. I like to collect them because of the many mechanical innovations such as a Ruger-like disassembly out the bottom of the frame in one example and a Dan Wesson-type crane cylinder release on a revolver introduced prior to 1920. But do not be seduced by cheap firearms or someone who tells you you are only "paying for the name" in the case of more expensive firearms. Often as not, that name is worth the extra money. I would be perfectly happy to rearrange family finances in order to afford a quality handgun. In long guns, the seemingly never-ending supply of SKS rifles is problematical. Some of the well worn examples are not reliable.

That being said, young people just starting out in a household, those with considerable financial obligations and elderly people on a fixed income should not be denied a home defense handgun, rifle or shotgun. I can tell you that schoolbooks, music lessons, tutors and the dentist have had a higher priority in my life than firearms until very recently. Tithes and the retirement account should come before collecting – but a good defensive firearm is a pretty important piece of equipment. Often as not, more than one firearm is desirable. Even those on a budget may wish to purchase more than one home defense handgun: one for the husband and one for the wife or perhaps a house gun and a truck gun. A shotgun is a necessity.

One thousand dollars or more for a pair of good defense handguns is a considerable chunk out of a home budget. There are inexpensive handguns that are poorly made, unreliable, and unsuited for personal defense. There are others that are inexpensive and reliable but not really ideal home defense handguns. I see various H&R .22 caliber revolvers for sale at modest prices that generally give good service – but a .22 is not enough. Then, there is the Heritage Rough Rider, a superb recreational handgun sold for a song. But it is a single action .22 not well suited to personal defense. I suppose if push came to shove, the Heritage revolver with its .22 Magnum cylinder in place would give me some peace of mind until I were able to purchase a more powerful handgun.

Bargain Handguns

There are outstanding deals found on used handguns from time to time but these handguns are not a steady resource. Used handguns are sometimes well-worn and exhibit various problems, and the novice might not easily spot these problems without extensive training. The handguns we should concern ourselves with are those available from retail outlets. These handguns should have a track record we can verify. They may not be the most powerful or accurate handguns around. We can accept that. But if they are not reliable they are not worth owning.

Reliability and longevity are two separate issues. A handgun may be reliable out of the box for a few hundred rounds but will not endure much shooting. A quality handgun such as the Smith and Wesson SW1911 may take twenty thousand rounds of standard ammunition before it shows eccentric wear or begins to malfunction. We are more concerned with a handgun that will withstand moderate use. Kept under the cash register in your store or by the bedstead, the handgun should come up shooting.

The handgun must be reliable, but as you may suspect some have poor finishes and indifferent trigger actions. I will not quote suggested retail pricing as this varies, but as a general rule inexpensive handguns are often found at a deep discount from the list price. I considered the bottom line and remember, this is being written in 2007 in case the prices seem too low or outdated. I consider $400 to be the high end of inexpensive handguns. Some decent handguns list in the $300 range. There are a few regularly found for even less. This is a narrow field indeed, and there are numerous problems with the least expensive handguns. Those who own a quality handgun may consider some of the handguns as second or "truck" guns, but the majority will be considered by those on a strict budget needing a good defensive handgun.

I have extensively fired most of the inexpensive handguns on the market. Some were a waste of good ammunition but I hope the reader is saved time trouble and heartache by the author's test program. My profession demands that I test all types of handguns, good or bad, but just the same I am happier when I find a good product. I will not knock the poor examples of handguns that did not function properly. I simply have not included them in this work. I found a number of bargains in the mix that are far better handguns than their modest price would indicate.

As a rule, an inexpensive revolver is more likely to be completely reliable than an inexpensive semi-automatic, but some of the inexpensive semi-automatics are rule-beaters. I would counsel the reader to avoid surplus handguns. Like many of you I enjoy firing the Tokarev, CZ-52, and a few other surplus handguns. I have a small collection of Star pistols and a Ballester Molina .45 I enjoy very much. I sometimes use them for practice as they are each very much like my 1911 carry guns. But occasionally my Star 9mm Largo will drop a magazine during a firing string. The latch is worn out. I own a Walther PP .32 ACP that does the same thing although it is not as old. I find it interesting as it is an ex-German police

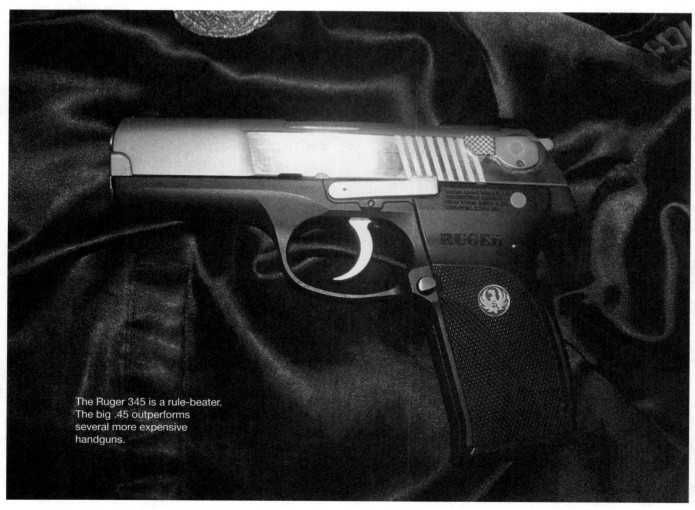

The Ruger 345 is a rule-beater. The big .45 outperforms several more expensive handguns.

pistol. The others are well past their prime and deserve an early retirement. They are fun guns and interesting historically. If such an example is all you have, keep it clean and lubricated and prove it on the range. And hope for the best.

On another note, just because you can purchase an inexpensive gun doesn't mean you should if you can afford better. Your life may be on the line. In the following pages we will look at some of the best buys and just how they perform. Remember: "quality remains after the price is forgotten. And perhaps "buy cheap, buy twice" might apply.

Semi-autos

Ruger

At present most Ruger centerfire handguns are priced just under or just over $400. Many shooters purchase a Ruger semi-automatic pistol because they are familiar with the long gun line and trust the brand. This trust is well-placed. Ruger pistols are inexpensive compared to handguns that give similar performance as far as reliability goes. The Ruger P90 is practically unknown in the gunsmith's shop. The polymer frame P95 has passed stringent military trials and is in use on a limited basis with the United States Army.

The Ruger pistols are always reliable. I do not believe I have seen one malfunction or give serious trouble. While not match grade accurate in most versions, they are accurate enough for personal defense. The new Ruger 345 is possibly the most accurate Ruger I have fired while the P94 .40-caliber pistol handles well and has a modern look many shooters find attractive.

The drawback in Ruger automatics is handling. The Ruger is often large for the caliber, clunky, and with a high bore axis that limits recoil recovery. The new 345 addresses most of these concerns. An acquaintance of mine owns both the SIG P220 and the Ruger 345 and finds the Ruger more accurate. I have fired both and the SIG is more accurate in my hands while the Ruger has less felt recoil. Both have about the same muzzle flip. Either is quite reliable.

In short, Ruger pistols are often good choices. If you are primarily a rifleman and wish to own a handgun for personal defense the Ruger is attractive if you own Ruger rifles and shotguns. They operate well but human engineering may stretch the average hand size. Just the same, these are good handguns..

Daewoo DH 51 9mm Luger

The Daewoo is available intermittently and at this time Century International Arms seems to have a steady supply. Since the DH 51 is the standard military issue pistol of South Korea the type has met strict military requirements. This handgun resembles the Smith & Wesson Third Generation pistols in some regards, but the external trigger bar is Walther like. The fit and finish are good. My example is nearing 2,500 trouble-free rounds. I find the pistol good enough to keep as a spare house gun and occasional training tool. Trigger action is heavier than comparable semi-autos but usable. Accuracy is on a par with early Smith & Wesson types.

The DH 51 features a double-action first shot followed by single-action fire but does not use a decocker. The pistol features a frame-mounted safety. This is much faster into action than any slide-mounted safety, and allows the pistol to be placed on safety without decocking the pistol during tactical movement. The pistol can be carried cocked and locked if you desire.

What sets this pistol apart from others is the Fast Action trigger mode. With the pistol cocked, hammer to the rear, the hammer can be pressed forward to decock the piece. The double-action trigger moves forward but is not in the double-action mode; the hammer is prepped against the sear for a very light trigger press. The Fast Action trigger breaks at perhaps four lbs. This allows very quick, accurate shooting. This is an advantage for those preferring the double-action trigger and who cannot tolerate cocked-and-locked carry.

My Daewoo has fired a considerable number of +P rounds and a few +P+ loads with no problems.

I am enthusiastic about this handgun. Loaded with +P loads such as Black Hills 115-grain 1,300 fps load this is a formidable defensive pistol. Recoil is light and pistol performs as well as most double action 9mms in combat drills. With the fast action trigger set, the pistol cleans the clocks in good order. Overall, a good buy.

FM High Power

There are three inexpensive handguns I am very enthusiastic about. These are the Argentine FM pistols, the Rock Island Armory 1911s and the Kel-Tec pistols. The FM High Power is a single-action variant based upon the Browning High Power. The FM is a solid performer, as covered in the section on the Browning High Power. I consider a FM Detective among my front-line defensive handguns. I am sometimes surprised how well this pistol performs. After extensive firing of several examples spanning over thirty years of service, I can give the FM High Power a clean bill of health. The only limiting factor with this handgun is the operator. I have stated that this is one of the few clones I actually find a little better

The Kel-Tec PF9 is a good shooter in trained hands and will not break the bank.

than the original, but the FM's lacquer finish is not as attractive as the blue finish applied to a top of the line High Power. Overall the FM is a fine choice.

Rock Island Armory 1911 .45

These handguns are closer to the $400 mark than they were a few years ago but remain an excellent buy. The High Standard GI pistol is basically a RIA pistol with better finish. All rules applying to the 1911 remain: keep the piece lubricated and use ammunition that feeds well. My RIA pistols have performed beyond expectation. I have had three customized and carried a stock 3.5-inch-barrel version on a daily basis until replaced by a Colt Defender. I replaced the sights on both of my personal .45 caliber RIA guns and also a custom .38 Super I built some time ago. The Yost Bonitz Old School sight is practically ideal for this pistol. I have also had a RIA .38 Super customized by Wilson Combat and another RIA is .45 caliber has been custom built by Rocky Mountain Arms. With quality ammunition I have had no problems and the pistol is simply all 1911 in performance. I would prefer better sights in a combat gun but at this price, we can afford to fit better sights. The only example I have had problems with was a .38 Super that came from the factory in need to both extractor and ejector tuning.

It is possible to pay more money and get more features but the Rock Island pistols are a good buy. You do get a better gun for more money but on the other hand the pistols that are less expensive than the Rock Island .45 are often much less reliable.

Kel-Tec Pistols

There are a number of Kel-Tec pistols but all share the same basic design. They are double-action-only semi-automatics with the action embedded in a polymer frame. The small-frame .32 and .380 pistols are hideout or backup pistols. The larger 9mm pistols are compact for the caliber. There are two Kel-Tec pistols well worth a hard look. These are the 9mm high-capacity and the 9mm PF9. An interesting point is that the P11 9mm uses Smith & Wesson magazines. The short ten-round magazine supplied with the pistol can be backed up with a fifteen-round magazine of the type used in the Smith & Wesson Model 5906.

The Kel-Tec has been criticized on some counts in the past and I have found these criticisms to be unfounded. First, the pistols have proven reliable but three things must be taken into account. The shooter must hold the pistol in a good firm grip. This is also true of the Glock and other polymer frame handguns. Some but not all Kel-Tec pistols require a break-in period. There are a dozen or more in my circle of friends in constant use and three or four needed this break in. Finally, the pistol must be cleaned and lubricated properly.

I am very careful in choosing personal defense handguns and the PF9 slimline 9mm is my favorite light automatic. At only 14.5 oz., this pistol makes the heavier Walther PPK, SIG P230 and other similar .380 ACP pistols obsolete. The PF9 requires good technique and proper control but in return it gives the shooter excellent protection in a small package. I had held my hand too high on the pistol during an initial evaluation and caused a misfeed until I worked the problem out: it was shooter error. I returned to the range with plenty of Winchester ammunition and worked my problems out. I fired the ammunition as quickly as I could load the two magazines I had on hand. I used the proper grip and carefully stroked the trigger. There was no room for error; I fired quickly and grooved in and pushed myself to the limit. After two hundred rounds of "light-kicking" 9mm my hand was branded with the alligator grip profile and for the first time in many years my hands trembled from the exertion of holding a pistol on target. But there were no malfunctions of any type and the target suffered.

The PF9 is an excellent defense pistol that is priced right. It compares to a number of pistols that cost twice as much. And the pricey pistols are heavier!

Firestorm 1911 .45

The Firestorm pistols are among the least expensive 1911 types that actually work and seem reliable. I ran an example of the older Firestorm pistols, a Spanish import, to about 1,300 rounds would good results. The front sight wore off, but it worked. Today, the importer relies upon Metro Firearms, a Philippine based company, for their 1911 pistols. The improvement is considerable. These handguns feature good blue finish, checkered wood grips and Novak like sights. The pistol feeds hollowpoints and seems quite accurate, considering its modest price. Cleaned, lubricated and kept at ready, it should last a long time and give good protection. I would not recommend this pistol as a recreational shooter to be

fired thousands of rounds a year, but for the person who understands how to use the 1911, this is a .45 that gives the person on a strict budget a fighting chance.

The maker is the sole remaining Spanish handgun manufacturer, the government having morphed together Astra Star and Llama in hopes of preserving the industry. The Firestorm looks like a late production Llama but I sincerely hope it is a better pistol.

Cobra's Patriot .45

The more I use this light .45 the more it grows on me. Not necessarily in terms of all-around performance but in terms of the specialized niche it fills so well. That is the niche reserved for a no-nonsense short-range defense pistol. The pistol is a double action only type, which simplifies things considerably. This is not a target gun but a pistol designed for defensive use at moderate range. The polymer frame makes the pistol light enough and it has proven reliable in limited testing, about five hundred rounds so far. The company recommends ball ammunition only

but my example feeds Winchester 230-grain SXT just fine. Ammunition loaded to less than full power will not function. Interestingly, five rounds of the Glaser Safety Slug worked just fine.

The Patriot uses a specially modified six-shot 1911 type magazine. Some will work with standard 1911 magazines but some may not. I used Metalform seven-round magazines in my personal Patriot with good results. The Patriot is far more powerful and effective than any light 9mm or .38 but little larger and no heavier. The heavier trigger makes it safer to carry than a Glock, and I sometimes carry mine simply thrust in the waistband. The Patriot is a true double- action-only. The trigger both cocks and fires the striker. The striker is not prepped by the slide. The pistol is difficult to use well compared to a compact Glock or 1911 but on the other hand it has the same power as a 1911. If fairly compared to a snubnosed .38 hideout, the Patriot comes out in a better light. I was able to strike man-sized targets at fifteen yards without great difficulty. I simply staged the trigger almost to the break and took a good sight picture, then finished the job.

I see the Patriot as a home defense or anti-mugger pistol for close-range action. It is inexpensive, with a minimum of moving parts, and is light and compact. Recoil is there, as it is with any lightweight .45. The Patriot may be a minimal defense handgun to some but it is not minimal in power. I like this handgun and respect its limitations.

Makarov 9 x 18

This is a handgun that is more reliable and powerful than the Walther PPK but sells for half

The humble Makarov is a great light handgun; its caliber is the only drawback.

the price. The Makarov is reliable above all else and the trigger action is usually smooth. It's accurate enough, sometimes surprisingly accurate. I am not overly thrilled with small bore pistols but the 9 x 18 is a more powerful cartridge than the .380 and good hollowpoint ammunition is available from Hornady. The Makarov may be a large pistol for the caliber but it is easy to use well.

The Makarov is a handgun with no flies on it; it works and works well. The safety and decocker are atypical of double-action pistols as they work in the correct manner. Up is on and a natural thumb motion downward moves the safety off. My sole concern is the caliber.

The Makarov is light enough and carries well. Good accessories are available at Makarov.com. I have seen several Chinese examples lately that are rattling wrecks. The Russian and Bulgarian examples are better choices.

Bersa .380 and Bersa Thunder

The Bersa is lighter than the Makarov and usually smoother in trigger action. This is not only the best buy in a .380 double-action pistol, it is possibly the best of the small .380s regardless of price. Accuracy and reliability are spotless. The Bersa is more accurate than we would think and it is very friendly to use. I don't really like slide-mounted safeties, but we can simply ignore the safety and use it to decock the piece only. The pistol feeds every hollowpoint you care to try including the hot Cor-Bon JHP. The trigger action is smooth and light in every example I have evaluated. Sometimes the action is so smooth and so light you may think it will not be durable but I am aware of several examples in constant use for over a decade, including both the .380- and the .22-caliber versions. This is a friendly pistol that offers a basis for protection for many homes in America. I am not enthusiastic about the .380 cartridge but here is a wonderfully reliable and well-made handgun available for a pittance.

Bersa 9mm or Thunder 9

Since this pistol is used by the Argentine equivalent of our own FBI, the pistol must be reliable. But leaving nothing to chance, I have tested the Thunder 9 extensively and found it a reliable handgun with all types of 9mm ammunition. The fit and finish may not be world-class but reliability seems to be excellent. This is a handgun that can be counted on, at least in my limited experience. I have used two with good results. I have seen perhaps twenty of the Bersa .380s in action with fine results. At this point I believe I would have heard comments or personally experienced a problem if the Thunder 9 had glaring faults. It is a reasonable size for its capacity and overall a good performer.

Taurus 24/7

The Taurus sneaks into this price range by the skin of its teeth with a price of $398 being the average in most shops in my home town. The Taurus is a double-action-only polymer frame pistol. That much is clear from inspection. But the action and performance of the pistol are another matter. The double-action-only trigger offers a second strike capability. If the pistol does not fire, press the trigger again. In my experience a cartridge that does not fire on the first strike will not fire on the second, but Taurus offers that option. I do have to admit that I recently tried a .45 GAP pistol that gave me a fit. The hand-loaded ammunition was slightly off in the crimp and often misfired – but a second hit always fired the ammunition. With the 24/7 I would not have had to constantly retract the slide to prep the trigger as I did with the Glock.

The Taurus features a well-designed rubber-covered grip that fits most hands well. The piece features Heinie custom sights, a big plus. The slide is attractively designed and the trigger action is smooth. When comparing the 24/7 to the Glock, it was a draw on most features, with the 24/7 giving comparable results. But the 24/7 grip is more comfortable and has a great advantage over the Glock in one particular regard. The 24/7 features a positive frame-mounted safety. This is a great asset for a service pistol. The safety works correctly: down is off safe, and the safety falls readily under the thumb. I am one of those who believe that a semi-automatic pistol without a safety abrogates many of the advantages of the type. The Taurus 24/7 is superior to most polymer frame pistols in this regard.

As this is written the Philippine national police have adopted the double-action first shot Taurus PT92 and several police agencies have approved the Taurus 24/7 for duty. The author has used a long slide (LS) pistol with good results and excellent accuracy with the Cor-Bon DPX load. Overall, the 24/7 is a pistol sure to make its mark in the near future.

Hi-Point Semi-Automatic Pistols

The humble Hi-Point has been the subject of derision in some circles. The fact is that the pistol is inexpensively made. There is no sugar-coating that one. But the sales behind the pistol are too big to ignore.

I have tested several. At present there are no centerfire revolvers of comparable price. I have seen Hi-Point 9mms recently at just over $130. The low price is achieved by use of non-critical material. The action is a straight blowback, the simplest of actions. Blowback is usually suitable only for small caliber weapons unless the slide is very large and heavy, and the Hi-Point's slide is indeed large and heavy for the caliber. While the 9mm could conceivably be concealed, the .45 would be very difficult to conceal. These are really shop and home defense weapons.

At this point I recommend the Hi-Point be kept at ready chamber empty, a limiting factor in personal defense. But the Hi-Point performs as designed. When loaded with ball ammunition, I have confirmed

that both the 9mm and the .45 will go 200 rounds or more with no failures to feed, chamber fire or eject. Accuracy is sufficient to strike a man-sized target at fifteen yards or more. The Hi-Point is a minimal defense handgun but for persons of limited means it could be a lifesaver. I hope none of you would mock another's modest clothing, and the Hi-Point is a modest handgun. The Hi-Point does not compare well to other pistols in range drills as the slide is heavy and the pistol not well balanced. But the handle does accommodate most hand sizes.

A friend who owns numerous first class handguns keeps a Hi-Point in the dash of his Ford as a "car gun." He feels that if the pistol is stolen, he hasn't lost much. But he also says, "have you ever seen a High Point that didn't work?" The answer is no, they work well for limited firing. At this point I will not damn the piece with faint praise. The Hi-Point does what it was designed to do.

Arcus 9mm

This is a larger and slightly heavier version of the Browning High Power. The piece uses High Power magazines and most of the internal parts seem to be High Power equivalent. The slide and frame are beefed up sufficiently that the pistol just may prove out to be tougher than the Browning, but by the same token the dimensions differ so that the High Power .22 caliber conversions will not work with the Arcus. Tightly fitted holsters designed for the High Power do not quite fit the Arcus. Grips and magazines are interchangeable with the Browning.

I have fired two examples of the Arcus. The pistols are very easy to use well and fed, chambered, fired and ejected everything fed them. Even with the powerful Cor-Bon +P load reliability and control were excellent. This seems to be a superior handgun to most of the High Power clones and I have heard nothing but good things concerning the Arcus.

This Taurus concealed hammer .38 snubbie is among the best choices for deep concealment. It is snag free and its characteristic humpback offers good recoil reduction.

Taurus revolvers give a lot of value for the money and respond well to a trained shooter.

Revolvers

Rossi and Taurus

A few years ago these two revolver companies were separate entities but now are combined under the Taurus umbrella. Both were makers of clones of the Smith & Wesson revolver in the early days but they now offer original designs. Traditionally Rossi revolvers were the rougher of the two with Taurus having a lead in quality. The Rossi five-shot two-inch-barreled snubnosed revolver was regarded as useable but little else. I have handled 1970s production that was pretty rough.

Let's put these revolvers in perspective. My grandfather once purchased a new Rossi for $35. A new Smith & Wesson was $98 at the time, and the Rossi was purchased in order to provide my great-grandfather with a pocket gun. For point-blank protection, the Rossi was OK. Today a good Rossi may cost less than half to two thirds the price of a new Smith & Wesson. Quality has considerably improved. Early revolvers sometimes spit lead and the action was rough. I have covered the six shot .357 Rossi earlier. While included in the previous chapter, I will mention it again because it is a good revolver and a good buy well worth a second look! This is not a true clone of anything Smith & Wesson has produced but rather an interesting adaptation of revolver geometry. The Taurus Tracker and the various Taurus centerfire revolvers are also good buys. Taurus revolver quality has progressed to the point they are comparable to anything available. The snubnosed .38s are especially attractive but the mid-frame .357s are also quite usable.

Charter Arms Revolvers

Charter Arms revolvers are among the most interesting mechanically of the 1960s era. When first introduced, they were unique. The steel frame is alloyed with aluminum parts for a very light revolver that maintains a steel frame. The transfer bar ignition was a first for centerfire US-made revolvers. The Ruger and Dan Wesson revolvers that were introduced soon afterward used this type of construction. If you purchase a Charter revolver I recommend only the very latest production as marketed by MKS Supply. These are the best revolvers ever offered under the Charter Arms banner. In the past certain runs were roughly made. Charter revolvers offer a good buy and usually give acceptable service. They may not be as smooth as some of the other types but with the steadily increasingly price of quality revolvers, they are a good buy.

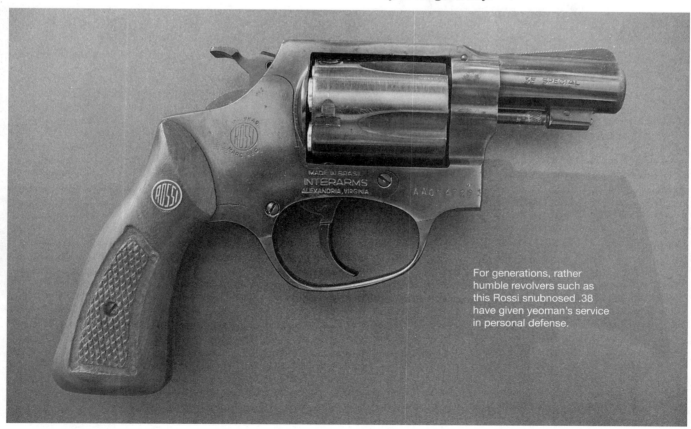

For generations, rather humble revolvers such as this Rossi snubnosed .38 have given yeoman's service in personal defense.

Ruger SP101 small-framed double action
revolvers offer strength and simplicity and
ease of maintenance at a reasonable price.

Charter Arms revolvers are well made of good material and often give excellent results on the range.

A Final Word

There are guns to avoid! Some were once acceptable but their service lives are over. I enjoy collecting Spanish steel but unless you find a Star PD or a late model Firestar in excellent condition, the days of Star as a defensive sidearm are over. Considering the PD saved my hide more than once, that is a hard pill to swallow but these pistols are long out of print. Spare parts and even spare magazines are problematical. Ex-military guns such as the Star Super and the Argentine FMAP Modello 1927 were good pistols when new but unless completely rebuilt their use is not recommended. I have rebuilt a couple of Modelo 1927 1911 pistols but with the availability of the Rock Island pistols there is little point in looking for an Argentine 1927.

When it comes to inexpensive handguns, let caution be your guide. Some have worked splendidly for years but when it comes to handguns purchase all of the quality you can afford.

Inexpensive Rifles and Shotguns

We have covered the Hi-Point carbine previously. The Hi-Point carbine has much to recommend as a defensive firearm. They are light, handy, and usually reliable even with good hollowpoint ammunition. A more advanced carbine that cost a bit more is available from Kel-Tec. The Kel-Tec carbine has proven reliable and very easy to use well. As a bonus, both of these carbines are a barrel of fun as recreational shoots and that means they will be used heavily for practice. That is a good point in their favor. The Hi-Point uses a single column magazine and the aftermarket high capacity magazines are not recommended. The Kel-Tec uses Glock magazines.

Among shotguns there are a goodly number of inexpensive choices. The Rossi single shot shotgun offers a transfer bar action, making it among a very few hammer-fired shotguns that is safe to keep fully loaded – providing you have a good gunrack or follow diligent safety precautions. The Rossi is not only affordable, but there are accessory barrels available for a song.

The Maverick pump action shotgun is basically a cut-down Mossberg. When the price is cut, some features are as well and the Maverick does not have the dual slide action bars we find so smooth with the Mossberg. I wonder if the difference in price is really worthwhile but those on a tight budget may find the Maverick line attractive.

Used firearms are always a good resource as long as they are quality firearms. Inspect all such firearms carefully. Gouges in the stock, names cut into the stock or metal, and signs of haphazard handling will show that a moron owned the firearm. Such firearms are to be avoided. With care and intelligence selection in the firearms process, you might find a good firearm on the bargain aisle, but you have to know what you are looking for.

This light and handy Rossi single shot is available in a Trifecta version with barrels in .22, .243 and 20 gauge. The shotgun is well suited to personal defense.

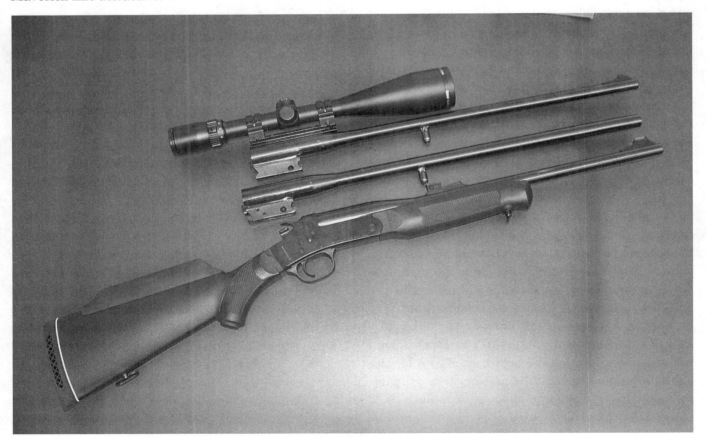

When I first became interested in hand-guns, the revolver ruled the world. Most civilian shooters clung to the double action Smith & Wesson or Colt revolver. A few die-hards might look to the 1911 semi-automatic pistol but the oddball 9mm caliber foreign pistols were suspect. Almost all revolvers were double-action although a few shooters liked the old single-actions.

How the world has changed! Today we have double-action and double-action-only semi-automatic pistols and a few such as the Glock and the Heckler & Koch P7 that defy description. We have enough to either confuse or satisfy every shooter. It is important to have a choice of both caliber and frame size as well as action type.

I am often asked questions that revolve around commonality of arms. Should a police agency issue only one handgun or allow a reasonable substitute? Often I receive calls from young people just starting out. They wonder if perhaps both partners should deploy the same handgun. Peace officers wonder if the backup should be the same type as their duty pistol.

There are advantages and disadvantages to be weighed. My backup handgun is seldom the same as my holster gun. The backup is most often of a simpler action type than the holster gun. My backup is often another revolver in hammerless DAO fashion or a DAO semi-automatic. Should an officer carrying a double-action first shot pistol carry a DA backup? My answer is the backup should be the same or simpler. If you carry a double-action semi-automatic or a cocked and locked 1911 or a revolver, for that matter, as a primary weapon, then a draw-and-shoot backup such as a DA or DAO revolver or a DAO semi-automatic is

Good home defense guns for a family? They are use the same action type and handle the same. The old .38 with the thin grips is a good hideout, the revolver with the heavier grips is easier to use well, and the big .44 Special hits hard.

Standardization makes the most sense with military and semi-military organizations. The LAPD SIS has adopted this rather nice Kimder SIS pistol. It works for them.

just fine. Press the trigger to fire; remove your finger to make the piece safe.

Let's look at commonality among the family. A shooter who wishes his or her uninterested spouse to learn to use a defensive handgun must be willing to accept the lowest common denominator. If the spouse is only willing to visit the range once a month or less, then the revolver is recommended. Both partners may end up with a mid-frame .38 and speedloaders. A concession to the more interested person might be a .357 Magnum. Nothing wrong with a pair of good .38s, but if one spouse heads to the range solo on a weekly basis, the more interested spouse may become bored. What if one progresses to a semi-automatic or, for an extreme example, decides the H&K P7 or Springfield Loaded Model is his or her love interest in handguns?

Whether the common handgun becomes standard equipment in your household or not, it is wor-

thy of some debate. Naturally if you are able to afford only one home defense handgun, the lowest common denominator must rule. Are two High Points better to have on hand than one SIGMA? Probably. But are two .38 revolvers better than the Taurus 24/7? Two armed citizens don't double your chances of success; with a backup your chances go up exponentially. One thing is certain: your other half should be familiar with your handgun in case the dreaded worst-case scenario occurs.

My other half likes revolvers. Her choice is the Taurus M44 .44 Magnum in stainless steel with a four-inch barrel. This revolver is usually loaded with Speer Gold Dot .44 Special loads. She doesn't fire a fifty-round group on the range very often but believes that a fast and hard hit is what counts. I enjoy shooting more than she does, so I use the .45 semi-automatic. It is more comfortable to fire for extended periods. We are each conversant with the other's handgun. (She feels that the semi-automatic is the better "recreational handgun.")

Don't kid yourself – the revolver requires practice. If a single handgun is accessible to family members, it should be a revolver. It should always be loaded and always in the same place. Our choice in a hideaway house gun is a Rossi/Taurus two-inch-barreled .357 Magnum, loaded with Glaser Safety Slugs. While there are other choices, this is ours. I would think that using pistols that are compatible in action but different in some incompatible manner could lead to trouble. For example, the CZ 75 Compact is one of my personal favorites. But I realize the SIG P229 is tactically equal. The same might be said of the Glock 17 and Taurus 24/7. There are fierce supporters of either type — but tactically they are equal.

Many of us purchase what we can afford. That may mean a Ruger P-89 this month and Taurus PT-92 somewhere down the line. But why have two similar handguns of the same caliber that do not take the same magazines or that have a slight difference in safety procedure. The P-89 may be a decocker; the Taurus has a frame-mounted safety. Are both spouses able to keep the difference straight? Neither pistol will give a dedicated shooter an advantage over the other. The magazines look similar but will not interchange.

When inspecting police handguns, I once found 9mm bullets in a .40-caliber magazine and a .40 in a 9mm magazine. Try it – they fit. A Glock 17 magazine will fit in a Glock 22. Even worse would be one shooter with the Glock 21 .45 and another with the Glock 37 .45 GAP. Anyone who owns more than one handgun has gone to the range and occasionally inserted the wrong magazine in a pistol. If we are going to have commonality, then let's live it.

On the other hand, a Glock magazine would never be confused with that of a 1911. A Taurus

This is a mismatched battery but quite common among interested handgunnners. A .45, a .40 and a 9mm and all operate differently. Perhaps "to each his own" works better in the scheme of things.

Here is another good compromise: a full-size and a compact Taurus, both using the same magazine.

stellar moon clip will not be confused with a HKS speed loader for the .38. Each shooter must proceed at his or her own pace. One may be more involved in training while the other will stop at their own comfort level. There are differences in ability and discretionary income. Seldom do shooters mature at the same level at the same pace.

After taking a hard look at commonality, the bottom line seems to be if you have similar tastes you should deploy identical weapons. If not, you must be familiar with the other's handgun. What is really important is common sense. Be certain you can trust your partner. The bottom line is determination.

I worked with a Chief for years who accompanied me often on building searches. He watched my back with a cocked and locked .45. When we flushed out screaming cats he did not budge and when we caught felons I knew my six o'clock was covered. Trust is what counts. Attitude and tactics are more important than commonality of the handgun.

Below: This setup might work well for those on a budget. The Browning Practical is a first-class 9mm. On the right is the FM, a less expensive High Power variant that performs well. The author is leery of the FEG in the middle. All are 9mm caliber and all use the same magazine.

31 The Orthopedic Handgun

I have lost count of the number of my friends who have recounted war stories that ended with, "Of course, I was a hell of a man in those days." Most of us are at our height in our thirties. While we are able to keep our physical fitness well into our later years, it stands to reason that at some point there will be the inevitable decline. Over the years I have suffered temporary injuries that limited my ability to use the more powerful handguns. At present I have several friends in their early eighties who still enjoy firing handguns but have alloyed their choices with good common sense. Another older shooter I know well occasionally suffers severe pain in his hand from arthritis. At this point I have suffered in my knees and ankles for the most part. Despite firing what must be well over a quarter of a million rounds of ammunition in my lifetime, my wrists and hands are fine.

I am not bragging or overstating the case. Figure this – two hundred rounds a week for forty years. That is over three hundred and eighty thousand rounds. Sometimes I fired five hundred rounds a week. I really don't know the figure, but it is probably short of a half million rounds. Then there is the time spent manually operating the loading machine. I am very thankful my hands have held out better than my legs. Today I enjoy three trips to the range on average during the week. Usually they are work-relaterd, but at least once a month I simply make brass, firing my cowboy guns, the old military pieces or a .22.

My friends with arthritis tell me the .45 is practically impossible but a full-size steel-frame 9mm is bearable. In an emergency, perhaps, but for practice they are not able to fire the heavy pistol well. They wish to be armed with something acceptable outside of a .22 or a .25. There are options. First, the manipulation of the handgun must be considered. For those with limited hand strength or pain in the joints, a pistol with a heavy recoil spring that is difficult to

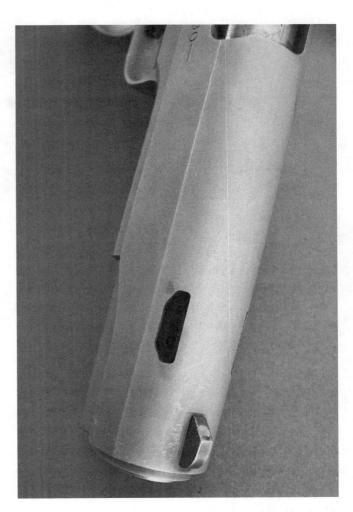

The author has his old service Colt Magna-Ported a few years ago. This is a good means of lessening felt recoil and increasing control.

rack is not a consideration. Neither is a pistol that requires a heavy trigger press.

There are physiological limitations that must be considered, too. With these considerations in mind, we move to the .32 caliber handguns. There are other choices I value more, but let's move to the worse case scenario. Remember: when evaluating a pistol for an elderly or disabled friend, student, or relative, your insight is limited. The person must make his or her own decision as to the ability to rack a slide or handle

The author's favorite 9mm. The Armalite AR-24 features a light trigger action in the single-action mode, a handy safety, and a well-shaped grip. If the author could not use a .45 this would be the piece he carried.

a certain trigger action. Some have use of only one limb and have limited strength in this limb. Tactically disabled persons are often at other disadvantages. They have distractions such as their own illness or injury and financial problems and often make easy prey. But quite a few disabled persons have obtained concealed carry permits and make themselves tactically aware. Remember, they cannot flee as easily as we can and they must consider a quite different world tactically. We should assist them in any way possible.

I have fired quite a few Walther PPK and SIG P230 pistols. They are usually accurate and reliable, although I would have to give the SIG the edge in this regard. The SIG is usually smoother as well. While most of these pistols are found in .380 ACP, there are .32 ACP versions as well. I am not certain there is an appreciable difference in the .32 and .380 in effectiveness, but the .32 pistols have lighter trigger actions. The hammer spring requires less force to override. The reason is that the hammer spring is partially responsible for keeping the slide locked in recoil. The hammer keeps the slide closed until recoil pressure has abated. The .32's spring is lighter. This results in a lighter trigger action. Loaded with the Con-Bon JHP load, either of the pistols is a reliable but weak choice for personal defense but certainly a choice worth consideration. If the person can handle a .380 automatic, the Bersa pistol is a great choice.

These double-action revolvers and double-action-only automatic are small enough for fit any hand and the trigger action is not difficult to use well. The only problem is recoil. The .38s may be loaded with lighter loads to address that problem.

While not ideal, a quality .22 caliber revolver like this Taurus may work for those with limited hand strength.

The reduction of tendonitis and strain on the muscles indicates a lighter caliber. Perhaps we will shoot more accurately and gain an edge. In revolvers, the .32 H&R Magnum offers a choice. The Black Hills 85-grain JHP is a good loading. I am not enthusiastic about any .32 but the bottom line is this: if you cannot use and fire at least a .38 Special revolver, the .32 H&R Magnum represents a step up from the .22. On the other hand, there are experienced shooters who favor the .22 Magnum over all others in the small bores. The .22 Magnum may exhibit well over 1,100 fps from a pistol barrel and the jacketed bullet used in these loads usually has enough penetration to reach the boiler room. In the end when personal experience and the expense of ammunition is considered in revolver cartridges, I believe the .22 Magnum is as viable a choice as the .32 H&R Magnum.

Other Choices

Before considering the .32 H&R Magnum, perhaps another revolver would be a better choice. A three-inch-barreled Smith and Wesson K frame revolver with a round butt is a great-handling revolver well suited to practically any hand size. Load this revolver with the . 38 Special 148-grain target wad-

cutter. Sure, this is a 700 fps load but the frontal diameter and mass are superior to that of the .32 H&R Magnum. And, at least to this jaded shooter, the .38 with Wadcutters is as comfortable as any .32 Magnum.

In the larger handguns, if you need just a little help MagnaPort can change your handgun. The difference is most noticeable with heavy loads but certainly helps at all levels. One of my Colt .45s features the MagnaPort and I have also fitted Herett's Oval grips as an experiment. These grips do not have sharp checkering but they have a slight palmswell to aid in grasping the handgun. I fitted a lighter recoil spring courtesy of WC Wolff Inc. (gunsprings.

There are shooters who love the 1911 but can no longer handle the recoil of the .45 ACP cartridge. This Wilson Combat modified 1911 takes the sting out firing with a credible, powerful cartridge. The .38 Super caliber is an excellent alternative to the .45.

If the shooter's hands are large enough, this is an easy revolver to use well, heavy in weight and light-kicking with .38 Special ammunition

com). I loaded a 185-grain SWC from Midsouth Supply over enough Titegroup to produce 800 fps. To the author the sensation is similar to firing a light .380 automatic. This is a 40-oz. pistol, remember. While a 800 fps 185-grain .45 is not something I would prefer over a 230-grain .45 ACP JHP at 870 fps, anyone is well advised to get out of its way.

It is a standing joke among shooters that our sights have become fuzzy as they have languished in the gun safe. Many older shooters have problems with visual acuity. The XS sight illustrated is a godsend to such citizens. The big front dot helps immensely. For those who need a little help, the Novak fiber optic front sight is a first-class choice. Superior sights certainly make for better shooters. TruGlo offers sight pain that really helps in acquiring the front sight quickly. My son's personal Novak Gunshop-modified .45 semi-automatic features a gold bead front sight. While he is young and sharp, this is also a good in-vestment for those who are visually challenged. For example, if you need reading glasses but do not wear glasses as a matter of course, the gold bead front is a classy addition with much merit.

There are two voices on frame material. The first states that steel is heavier and soaks up recoil. This is true as verified by the Colt experiment. Other shooters feel that polymer frames are ideal because they are lighter and soak up a portion of the recoil when the piece is fired as they demonstrate a little "give." They also point to the fact that the Heckler & Koch USP is an easy pistol to manipulate. Clearly, a balance between light and heavy frames is sought. Personally if at some point I have to leave behind the aluminum frame 1911 .45 for a steel frame Browning High Power, I doubt I will bemoan my fate. My end plan is to reach my majority intact but to leave this worldly body completely worn out. I intend to make use of this body until nothing worth using is left. With that in mind I am certain there will be good choices for my aging hands.

Postscript

Remember: those with an at-risk disability are not excused from the legal requirements of personal defense – but just the same, the leap from verbal warnings to deadly force will be quicker than with those of us who are younger and in good condition. But aging takes bone and muscle mass, and we must respect this process. Despicable as it is, felons often target the disabled, weak, and even the blind. We are able to find any number of articles in the popular press with warnings concerning financial crimes perpetrated against our elderly, but none concerning personal defense. Some have chosen to be armed at a late date in life while others simply have adjusted their armed lifestyle habits as they age. The right to personal defense is an important right for these citizens.

Trigger shoes were once widely recommended for those with weak trigger fingers. They are controversial and were the culprit in a number of accidental discharges as they rubbed the holster when the handgun was sheathed. But sometimes they do work for certain shooters.

About the Author

Robert Campbell served for over 23 years as a law enforcement officer and holds a degree in criminal justice. Today he serves as a professional in the private security sector and writes in the firearms, police and outdoor fields with over 600 articles to his credit. In addition, his credentials include 40 years of handgun/personal protection research. Robert and his family live in South Carolina.

THE BEST OFFENSE IS
AN EFFECTIVE DEFENSE

The Gun Digest® Book of Combat Handgunnery
6th Edition
by Massad Ayoob
Discover practical, life-saving instruction for handgun self defense from the nation's most recognized expert in the subject.
Softcover • 8-1/4 x 10-7/8 • 256 pages
500 b&w photos
Item# Z0880 • $24.99

Tactical Pistol Shooting
Your Guide to Tactics that Work
by Erik Lawrence
Presents basic and advanced instruction on defense mindsets, pistol terms, shooting fundamentals and shooting positions, with emphasis on important safety precautions and lawful personal defense. 250 detailed, step-by-step photos clearly illustrate the techniques.
Softcover • 6 x 9 • 216 pages
250 b&w photos
Item# TPS • $19.99

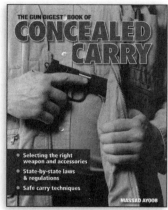

The Gun Digest® Book of Concealed Carry
by Massad Ayoob
Learn the legalities of concealed carry, how to select a gun, safe training and handling procedures and how to protect your family in this indispensable guide.
Softcover • 8-1/4 x 10-7/8 • 256 pages
350 color photos
Item# Z1782 • $24.99

The Complete Gun Owner
Your Guide to Selection, Use, Safety and Laws
by James M. Ayres
The only comprehensive guide to owning a firearm, this thorough reference take you through selecting ammunition, understanding the legal issues, where to buy a gun, how to shoot one safely, and properly clean and store a firearm.
Softcover • 8-1/4 x 10-7/8 • 272 pages
400 color photos
Item# Z2614 • $24.99

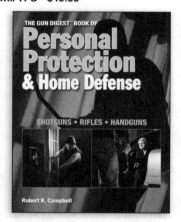

The Gun Digest® Book of Personal Protection & Home Defense
by Robert K. Campbell
Readers gain expert insight about the social and legal ramifications of personal defense, how to select the appropriate arms for protection, and practice drills to help build competence and confidence.
Softcover • 8-/1/4 x 10-7/8 • 256 pages
300 b&w photos
Item# Z3653 • $24.99

The Gun Digest® Book of Guns for Personal Defense
Arms & Accessories for Self-Defense
Edited by Kevin Michalowski
Covers uses of firearms, ammunition, holsters, firearms training options, buying a used gun, and includes a catalog of available personal defense firearms with pricing.
Softcover • 8-½ x 11 • 160 pages
200 b&w photos
Item# GDBPD • $14.99

Order directly from the publisher at www.gundigestbooks.com

Krause Publications, Offer GNB9
P.O. Box 5009
Iola, WI 54945-5009
www.gundigestbooks.com

Call 800-258-0929 M-F 8 a.m. - 6 p.m. to order direct from the publisher, or from booksellers nationwide or firearms dealers and outdoors outfitters
Please reference offer GNB9 with all direct-to-publisher orders

Get the latest gun news at www.gundigestmagazine.com